Spiritual Remedies

Spiritual Remedies

FAITH, PRAYER & HEALING

EDITORS OF GUIDEPOSTS

Guideposts

New York

Published by Guideposts Books & Inspirational Media
110 William Street
New York, New York 10038
Guideposts.org

This book is intended to be a spiritual reference volume only, not a medical manual. The presented information is meant to help you make informed decisions about your physical, emotional, and spiritual health. It is not intended to be a substitute for any treatment prescribed by your doctor. If you are experiencing symptoms or suspect that you have a medical problem, please seek medical help.

Acknowledgments

Every attempt has been made to credit the sources of copyrighted material used in this book. If any such acknowledgment has been inadvertently omitted or miscredited, receipt of such information would be appreciated.

Scripture quotations marked (AMP) are taken from *The Amplified Bible, Old Testament*. Copyright © 1965, 1987 by The Zondervan Corporation. *The Amplified New Testament*. Copyright © 1954, 1958, 1987 by The Lockman Foundation. Used by permission.

Scripture quotations marked (CEB) are taken from the *Common English Bible*. Copyright © 2011 by Common English Bible.

Scripture quotations marked (CJB) are taken from the *Complete Jewish Bible*. Copyright © 1998 by David H. Stern. All rights reserved.

Scripture quotations marked (ERV) are taken from the *Easy-to-Read Version*. Copyright © 2006 by Bible League International.

Scripture quotations marked (ESV) are taken from the *Holy Bible, English Standard Version*. Copyright © 2001 by Crossway Bibles, a division of Good News Publishers. Used by permission. All rights reserved.

Scripture quotations marked (ISV) are taken from the *International Standard Version of the Bible*. Copyright © 1995-2014 by ISV Foundation. All rights reserved internationally. Used by permission of Davidson Press, Inc.

Scripture quotations marked (KJV) are taken from *The King James Version of The Holy Bible*.

Scripture quotations marked (MEV) are taken from the *Modern English Version of The Holy Bible*. Copyright © 2014 by Military Bible Association. Used by permission. All rights reserved.

Scripture quotations marked (NAS) are taken from the *New American Standard Bible*. Copyright © 1960, 1962, 1963, 1968, 1971, 1972, 1973, 1975, 1977, 1995 by The Lockman Foundation. Used by permission. www.Lockman.org

Scripture quotations marked (NIV) are taken from the *New International Version of The Holy Bible*. Copyright © 1973, 1978, 1984, 2011 by Biblica. Used by permission of Zondervan. All rights reserved worldwide. www.zondervan.com

Scripture quotations marked (NKJV) are taken from the *New King James Version of The Holy Bible*. Copyright © 1979, 1980, 1982, 1983, 1985, 1990, 1997 by Thomas Nelson, Inc. Used by permission. All rights reserved.

Scripture quotations marked (NLT) are taken from *The Holy Bible, New Living Translation*. Copyright © 1996. Used by permission of Tyndale House Publishers, Inc., Wheaton, Illinois 60189. All rights reserved.

Scripture quotations marked (NRSV) are taken from the *New Revised Standard Version Bible*. Copyright © 1989 by the Division of Christian Education of the National Council of the Churches of Christ in the U.S.A. Used by permission. All rights reserved.

Scripture quotations marked (RSV) are taken from the *Revised Standard Version of the Bible*. Copyright © 1946, 1952, 1971 by the Division of Christian Education of the National Council of the Churches of Christ in the U.S.A. Used by permission. All rights reserved.

Scripture quotations marked (TLB) are taken from *The Living Bible*. Copyright © 1971 by Tyndale House Foundation. Used by permission of Tyndale House Publishers, Inc., Carol Stream, Illinois 60188. All rights reserved.

Cover design by W Design Studio
Cover photograph from iStockphoto
Interior design by Müllerhaus
Interior photos from iStockphoto
Typeset by Aptara, Inc.
Indexed by Indexing Research, Rochester, New York

Printed and bound in the United States of America
10 9 8 7 6 5 4 3 2 1

*Faith is the most powerful of all forces operating in humanity
and when you have it in depth nothing can get you down.*
—Norman Vincent Peale

Guideposts

New York

Inspiring the world to believe anything is possible
with hope, faith, and prayer.

· TABLE OF CONTENTS ·

INTRODUCTION

by Rev. Dr. Pablo R. Diaz

TRUST IN THE LORD with all your heart and lean not on your own understanding; in all your ways submit to him, and he will make your paths straight. —Proverbs 3:5-6

I have been a person of faith since my teens and involved in ministry for over forty years. That hasn't kept me from encountering my share of difficulties. I know firsthand what it is to fail, to have marital problems, to suffer setbacks. My faith and prayer life have helped me come through these hard times with grace and hope.

As a pastor, I have seen people overcome addiction and depression, restore broken relationships, and experience physical and emotional healing. Through it all, I have observed how God empowers and comforts people in their time of need. There is no mountain too high or valley too low for God. We can always turn to our faith for spiritual power and emotional strength.

Social worker and author, Virginia Satir, wrote, "Life is not the way it's supposed to be. It's the way it is. The way you cope with it is what makes the difference." In the midst of our struggles, worries, fears, anxieties, and loneliness, we are not alone. God is always with us. In our darkest and most vulnerable moments, we can face the present with hope and the future with faith.

The Audacity of Faith—Embracing Faith—Faith in Action

Several years ago, while shopping with my wife, I came across a framed picture with a caption that caught my attention. **FAITH** appeared in large bold letters. Below that were the words: *"Hope is the ability to hear the music of the future; faith is the courage to dance to* *it today.*" Faith and hope are essential, nourishment for the soul and the heartbeat of the human spirit, as fundamental as food and water are to our physical bodies.

Faith is the force that keeps us in the game when the odds are against us. When my colleague's mother, Pat, was sixty-five years old, she was diagnosed with bone cancer and given six months to live. Though devastated by this news, she did not let it defeat her. Pat faced her battle against cancer with faith and hope—and won. Ten years later, she was diagnosed with breast cancer. Once again, believing in the power of prayer, she received God's healing. Pat lived to be ninety-six years old.

Prayer helps us find our voice in difficult times. It's the voice that expresses our deepest emotions—pain, doubt, fear, anger, resentment, and loss. Through prayer we expose ourselves, as we surrender our deepest weaknesses and our greatest shame to the divine...God.

Having faith doesn't mean we will get all of the things we pray for or that our situation will improve overnight. However, it gives us the courage to bear challenges, weather the unexpected, and embrace change. When our human strength is depleted, faith connects us to the source of power. English Anglo-Catholic writer, Evelyn Underhill, wrote, "God's power is brought into action just where our power fails."

Admiral James Stockdale endured eight years of captivity in Vietnam. After his release, a reporter asked, "How in the world did you survive eight years in a prisoner-of-war camp? He answered, "I never lost faith in the end of the story. I never doubted not only that I would get out, but also that I would prevail in the end and turn the experience into the defining event of my life, which, in retrospect, I would not trade." The book of Hebrews states, "Faith is the assurance of things hoped for, the conviction of things not seen."

Let This Spiritual Reference Book Guide Your Way

In *Spiritual Remedies: Faith, Prayer & Healing*, you will discover valuable insight and clear strategies for dealing with spiritual, physical, and emotional issues. Whether you are coping with anger, addiction, pain, marital problems, illness, grief, stress, or countless other problems, you will find scriptures that align with the issue at hand, prayers, stories of hope, and more.

This is a spiritual reference book created to help you make informed decisions regarding your well-being. There are no quick fixes. But there are steps you can take that, with grace, time, and persistence, can change the way you think, feel, and live.

When you apply the tested principles in this book to your situation, it will make a significant difference. I suggest you pay close attention to the details found under each topic. These spiritual messages will help you develop and grow into the person you want to and can be. No one is perfect or free of pain. We are all in need of spiritual remedies. Read this book and its wisdom will guide you to believe that all things are possible with faith, hope, and prayer.

PART 1

Why Faith Heals

The Twelve Faith Factors

Believers know it. Solid medical studies show it. But why does faith help prevent and heal health problems? A growing number of medical experts believe they've traced the answer to a unique collection of spiritual factors that are as powerful and as vital to our emotional and physical health as certain foods, nutrients, and exercise.

In fact, research shows that no fewer than twelve aspects of faith may help deliver healing benefits—a package of all-natural health boosters that complements the medicine chest of prescription drugs, says psychiatrist and prayer researcher Dale A. Matthews, M.D., board-certified specialist in general internal medicine caring for adult patients with Executive Healthcare Services in Reston, Virginia, and author of *The Faith Factor*. Among the faith factors that Dr. Matthews and others have identified are:

1. **Social support.** From friends bringing over meals when we've lost a loved one to strangers who pray for us when they hear that we're in the hospital, it's hard to match the social support Christian community provides. "People who have a strong religious commitment are more connected to each other," says Dr. Matthews. "The Bible tells us to love our neighbors as ourselves. And we can't really do that if we aren't involved in other people's lives."

2. **Temperance.** In the interest of spiritual well-being, Scripture prohibits certain behaviors that lead to illness or poor health. The Bible mentions sexual immorality, drinking too much, laziness or lack of physical activity, and even overeating as activities to avoid. In addition, these are all documented risk factors for disease. The Apostle Paul encourages us to treat our bodies as a "temple of the Holy Spirit" (1 Corinthians 6:19 NKJV), even suggesting that "physical training is of some value" (1 Timothy 4:8 NIV).

3. **Peace.** Relationships falter. Jobs are lost. Health wanes. And as the pace of life quickens, we scramble to keep up. Such events subject us to high levels of stress and cause us to lose our peace. Yet studies by Herbert Benson, M.D., founder and director emeritus of the Benson-Henry Institute and mind body medicine professor of medicine at Harvard Medical School, have found that forms of meditation, including prayer, create a relaxation response, dramatically reducing the damaging effects of stress. While Dr. Benson believes we can meditate on just about any single word or phrase to reap the benefits of this peaceful activity, believers can also find peace in promises from the Bible. A wonderful place to start is with Hebrews 13:5: "I will never leave you nor forsake you" (NKJV). Or with Matthew 11:28: "Come to Me, all *you* who labor and are heavy laden, and I will give you rest" (NKJV). For longer passages of Scripture, many people find the book of Psalms soothing and comforting.

"Love and peace of mind do protect us," says Bernie Siegel, M.D., who wrote *Love, Medicine and Miracles*. "They allow us to overcome the problems that life hands us. They teach us to survive…to live now…"

4. **Appreciation of beauty.** A full moon on a warm, cloudless night. Soaring snowcapped vistas. Nearly everyone revels in nature's beauty, and the faithful are reminded to look up and enjoy the view: "The heavens declare the glory of God; And the firmament shows His handiwork" (Psalm 19:1 NKJV). What's more, worship services, though ultimately designed to give glory to God, provide a feast for the senses. Dr. Matthews has found that profound, uplifting hymns, stained glass, and candlelight services all help revive our spirits.

5. **Worship.** Through song, dance, uplifted hands, silent prayer, or hearing the words of Scripture read aloud, worship bathes us in a variety of healing faith factors: ritual, social support, and beauty. Also, as we come to worship God alone, the stress of striving for things like money, social or professional position, influence, and power begins to wane.

6. **Confession and starting over.** Faith can drive us to turn feelings of guilt into positive thoughts and actions. Christian faith, for example, encourages

us to confess our sins—no matter how bad we think they are—to a holy and loving God Who is eager to forgive. The promise is that once we confess our sins, He'll forgive us (1 John 1:9 NKJV), remove them "as far as the east is from the west" (Psalm 103:12 NKJV), and restore our fellowship with Him.

When we know God has forgiven us, we can more easily forgive ourselves. "Confession and forgiveness allow us to learn from our mistakes and sins and move on, rather than becoming unhealthily preoccupied with our shortcomings," says Dr. Matthews.

7. **The power of ritual.** Research shows that religious rituals in and of themselves have health benefits. Whether we're taking communion, saying the rosary, or repeating a familiar favorite prayer, such repetition provides comfort. "Ritual can give us a sense of security, assuring us that we have reached a safe harbor in a stormy world," observes Dr. Matthews.

8. **Hope.** Those with deep faith believe that God has their best interests at heart regardless of their circumstances and that "all things God works for the good of those who love him, who have been called according to his purpose"

(Romans 8:28 NIV). Psalm 147:11 says, "The LORD takes pleasure in those who fear Him, In those who hope in His mercy" (NKJV), and 1 Peter 1:3–4 offers these encouraging words: "Praise be to the God and Father of our Lord Jesus Christ! In his great mercy he has given us new birth into a living hope through the resurrection of Jesus Christ from the dead, and into an inheritance that can never perish, spoil or fade" (NIV). People of faith in God put their trust in the most powerful being in the universe, a God Who is living and active in their everyday lives and Who rewards their hope.

9. **Unity.** In recent years, the idea of community has become quite popular. People enjoy connecting with those who share their values, likes and dislikes, hopes, and dreams. They know that support and encouragement are rooted in togetherness, not in being alone. The same qualities make faith a healing activity. We long to be with people like ourselves, people who believe as we believe. But faith provides at least one other benefit that most clubs and hobbies probably don't: we hold each other accountable. "If my faith flags momentarily, my spiritual

brothers and sisters will remind me of God's promises and point me back to the tenets that we hold in common," observes Dr. Matthews.

10. **Meaning.** Imagine two cancer patients in a hospital: One hasn't moved from the chair next to his bed the entire weekend. He won't talk. He doesn't want to see the chaplain. The other is in for chemotherapy but is "just as happy and positive and bright and alive as anyone you've seen in your life. I mean, her eyes are glittering. Her skin is shining. A smile busting out all over," says Dana E. King, M.D., of the Medical University of South Carolina and co-chair and founder of Spirituality and Health Interest Group. The difference? "She has Jesus in her heart. Her life has meaning," says Dr. King.

11. **Trust.** Find people of deep faith and you've found ones who know how to trust. These are people who do what they are able to do with the strength, ingenuity, and desire that God gave them and then trust Him for the results. Such people probably don't even know the meaning of the word *anxiety* and, as a result, enjoy a sense of peace that is positively health-preserving, according to Dr. King.

12. **Love.** The awesome, healing power of love is probably best illustrated by what happens when we lose it, like a woman whose partner of fifty years passes away. "I've seen it far too many times," says Dr. King. "She literally dies of a broken heart. No real physical causes." Faith doesn't make us immune to the pain of such loss. But it does provide a sweet assurance to our souls and it helps us through the trauma because we know that God is near and His love will never fail.

HEALING FAITH

Clearly, certain aspects of faith can help heal us, but enjoying the full benefits of the twelve faith factors calls for more than regular church attendance. It also requires that our faith be active, vibrant, and growing. "Mother Teresa was not religious because her greatest desire was to achieve better health," says Dr. Matthews. "Her greatest desire was to worship and serve God. The people who seek to serve God, even though they are not looking specifically for better health, get the interesting by-product of better health." As Jesus says, "Seek first his kingdom and his righteousness, and all these things will be given to you as well" (Matthew 6:33 NIV).

· PART 2 ·

Coping with Illness and Physical Challenges

ADDICTION

Recovery from addiction is a process, not an isolated event. For seven years I worked at it. After a lifetime of deceit, I faced up to the truth and found the courage, for example, to tell my in-laws the real reason for my business failures. I began making amends to those from whom I stole time and love, especially my wife and children. But the most important moment for me came when a couple of people I respect deeply helped me realize that working at a problem is only part of the story. Prayer asks God to do the rest. —STEPHEN YURKO

The Road to Recovery

WITH A HEART ATTACK and a nasty recurring case of bronchitis to show for fifty years of smoking, Marge Waterbury knew she had to quit her two-pack-a-day habit. The question was how. The best she'd ever done over the years was stop for a few days—then start right back again.

So she turned to God, and sometimes through tears, she prayed: "I don't have the strength to do this on my own, Lord. I need Your help."

Then one morning, after eight months of fervent prayer, her craving, amazingly, was gone. Her prayer had been answered. "When I realized what had happened, I just started thanking God," said Waterbury, after more than seven years without cigarettes.

With God's help, Waterbury kicked her habit, but millions more still struggle to overcome addictions. Consider these statistics: Approximately twenty-eight million children in the United States have parents or a parent who is an alcoholic. The Centers for Disease Control website notes that in 2015, 15.1 percent of Americans who were eighteen years of age and older were smokers, an estimated 36.5 million adults. In 2014, there were approximately one million heroin users in the United States. According to a March 29, 2017 article on theguardian.com and based on a study of almost eighty thousand people, "Heroin use among American adults has increased almost fivefold in the last decade." Whether it's tobacco, alcohol, gambling, marijuana, prescription drugs, street drugs, pornography, or even things like sugar, caffeine, or an addiction to social media or video games, addictions are rampant in our culture.

HOW ADDICTION HAPPENS

How do we become addicted to something in the first place? It usually starts as an attempt to "self-medicate" a severe emotional problem or trauma with alcohol, drugs, or other substances, says author and addictions counselor David Stoop, Ph.D., founder and director of the Center for Family Therapy in Newport Beach, California, adjunct professor at Fuller Theological Seminary in Pasadena,

California, and member of the executive board of the American Association of Christian Counselors. For example, a child who feels unloved or unwanted might begin to smoke marijuana as a teenager in an effort to rebel against his or her family or to get attention. Or a child who grew up watching one parent seek solace in too many glasses of wine or mixed drinks after fighting with the other may come to believe that drinking is a way to cope with pain and conflict. Of course, some people also move toward substance abuse or other addictive behaviors after the death of a spouse or a divorce in order to distract themselves from their pain or grief.

Addiction involves other factors as well. People with a deep-seated fear of rejection have been known to turn to sexual addiction to fill their emotional voids, while people who abuse food may overeat in a desperate attempt to control at least part of their lives, says Dr. Stoop.

While any number of emotional problems can make us vulnerable to addiction, emotions are only half of the story. The other part is how the powerful chemicals in tobacco, alcohol, drugs, sugar, and other substances actually do make us feel better. These chemicals find their way to receptors in our brains, often generating a feeling of euphoria that temporarily relieves stress and generally improves the way we feel.

In fact, some drugs create such good feelings and cravings that even highly disciplined people would struggle to resist if exposed to them. "If someone shoots you up with heroin, there is a 99 percent probability that you will become addicted to it," says Dr. Stoop. "The same thing with crack cocaine." Often, the addiction begins with the first smoke. The drugs are that powerful.

What's the key to knowing if we're truly addicted to something? If our desire for it becomes unmanageable. If we say, "I want to stop a certain activity or using a substance but I haven't been able to," we're addicted, says Mark Laaser, Ph.D., M.Div., founder of Faithful & True, a Christian-based counseling center in Minneapolis, Minnesota.

As our addictions grow stronger, we develop another problem: our bodies develop a tolerance to what we're abusing, which means that we need more and more of it to make us feel "good," says Dr. Stoop.

Before long our lives begin to reflect the consequences of such behavior. Depending on what we're abusing, we may gain weight, lose our jobs, steal from our friends, wreck our cars or marriages, or worse. But true addicts are so enslaved physically and psychologically that they often just keep using in spite of the negative consequences, says Dr. Laaser. "We're talking about all kinds of social, legal, financial, and physical ramifications. Whatever controls them is what they worship. The drug addict, the sex addict, the food addict, nothing matters but the fulfillment of the addiction. They will do anything they have to in order to maintain it," says Dr. Stoop.

Remedies
FINDING THE WAY BACK

"THERE'S A SAYING THAT goes something like this: 'If you always do what you did, you always get what you got,'" says Dr. Charles Zeiders, Psy.D., psychotherapist, adjunct instructor at East University in St. David's, Pennsylvania, lecturer, public speaker, seminar leader, and peer supervisor. "If you keep hanging out in the bar, you're going to see yourself as kind of a pathetic addicted person who hangs out in the bar all the time."

Instead, try these suggestions for breaking the stranglehold of addiction.

See a doctor. One of the most dangerous times for people addicted to alcohol or drugs is just after they have stopped abusing substances, says Dr. Stoop. "The process of detoxification is so hard on the body that it's a good idea to go to a detoxification center or have the assistance of an M.D.," he says. "They have medications not just to make the withdrawal easier but also to alleviate some of the physical danger."

Seek professional help from a therapist or counselor. Addictions start because of underlying emotional needs. A professional therapist or counselor can help us uncover and understand the roots of addiction and work through them in healthy ways, guiding us to meet those needs in healthy, rather than unhealthy, ways.

Hand it over to God. Until they hit the wall, addicts say, "I can control this. I can manage this." But Scripture clearly communicates that the only One Who can manage our lives is God, and we must turn the control of our lives over to Him. "That's the basic message of salvation. That's the

message of the Gospel. And it's the message of recovery as well," says Dr. Stoop.

Change the scenery. One subtle factor that can keep us trapped in addiction is the social acceptance of addicted friends. This can take the place of the real love and care we truly need. "If you get a group of people together who haven't come to grips with their problems, anything goes. It's a pity party with drugs or alcohol," says Dr. Stoop. The solution is to seek friends who truly care about our welfare.

Make amends. We can write down the names of everyone our addictive behavior has hurt or wronged. Then we need to look for ways to right the wrongs we have committed against them. That means that people who have borrowed money need to pay it back. People who caused damage to someone's personal property need to pay for it. Those who have hurt, offended, or insulted others need to apologize. "This is where people get stuck," says Dr. Stoop. But we have to try to redeem ourselves, as painful as it might be. "If this is overlooked, it can short-circuit the whole recovery process."

Develop humility. Making amends goes a long way in helping us develop humility. "Not shame, but humility," says Dr. Stoop. "And that means God is the

A Mother's Love
SOMETIMES IT'S THE ONLY THING
ON EARTH THAT CAN SAVE US
BY EDWARD GRINNAN

Lynne Nichols's story began with a desperate late-night phone call from her drug-addicted son, Ben, who had just been expelled from a sober-recovery house for using drugs again. He had no money, nowhere to go, and little hope left for himself. In fact, the large quantity of drugs he ingested was no accident, as Lynne soon learned. Lynne wrestled with the dilemma of whether coming to her son's rescue yet again would be an act of love or just a continuation of her enabling. It is a quandary many mothers—many parents—face these days as drug addiction, especially opioid dependence, maintains its hold on our country.

Many years ago, I was Ben. I made a similar call. The walk to the phone was as difficult a journey as I had ever made. I fought it every unsteady step. But like with Ben, my options had reached a vanishing point. I was penniless, foodless, homeless; weakened by drugs and drink, dehydration, and hunger; broken in spirit, mind, and body. And yet I resisted. I didn't want to make that call. A dozen times I paused, wanting to turn around and disappear into the night, disappear forever.

I made the call, collect. And when the voice answered on the other end I sagged with relief. All I could say was "Mom?" Not "help" or "hello." Just "Mom." That one word was the beginning of my way back.

A mother's love is often our last refuge. I sympathize with Lynne's worry that she was enabling her son. In a narrow sense perhaps she was. But a mother's love is so much more than that. Sometimes it is the only thing on earth that can save us. I know mine saved me.

One who is powerful here. I'm powerless. And I need to do what He tells me to do on an ongoing basis."

Tell others. Dr. Stoop observes that the people who truly overcome addiction are those who view recovery as an ongoing process, who continue to share the message of recovery with others, and who help others who are struggling. He says, "They never get to a place where they say, 'I have arrived; I don't need this anymore.' They say, 'I'm going to stay here because it continues to help me.'"

Pray for healing. Although Marge Waterbury didn't have documentation that God removed her desire for cigarettes, she was convinced He did. And some experts say her miracle isn't uncommon. One study that looked at twenty northern California Alcoholics Anonymous (AA) groups, for example, found that prayer helped drive out the use of alcohol. Those AA members who practiced the eleventh step in AA's Twelve Steps—seeking "through prayer and meditation to improve our conscious contact with God...praying only for knowledge of His will for us and the power to carry that out"—reported being sober longer and felt like they had more purpose in life.

"I have talked to several people who were in the advanced stages of alcohol addiction who sought out Christian prayer for being delivered from alcohol. And I am convinced from my interviews with these people that the phenomenon does occur," says Dr. Zeiders.

Have a vision. "Many people who are addicted have trouble understanding that God has a special calling for them, or they don't know how to pursue it," says Dr. Zeiders. "So if we give them a vision of who they really are and the things they can do if they enter into their calling, they're going to be more likely to disengage from the activity that keeps them from it."

Connect with a community. A solid church, a strong twelve-step program, or going to a counselor all offer positive, chemical-free alternatives to the addictive life. "If you get people connected with a really healthy, vital church community where they are understanding themselves as children of God rather than guys at a bar, where they are participating in things like outreach or volunteer services, where they are having a meaningful impact on society and they are playing a direct role—all of these things are tangible, practical ways to incarnate the vision and work against the addiction," says Dr. Zeiders.

Discover true love. Since addicts fundamentally don't believe they're loved, many find freedom when they discover that God loves and cares about them. "Providing those insights, helping the person own it and grasp it intellectually and feel it within his spirit, is going to be part of the healing," says Dr. Zeiders.

A Prayer to Break Free from Addiction

God, I know You can help me overcome this addiction, and I'm so thankful, because I want to be free. Every time I come to You, I win another battle. Help me remember what Your Word says: You will never leave me or forsake me, and You love me no matter what. Thank You, Lord, for showing me who I am in You. Amen.

—JOYCE MEYER

ALZHEIMER'S DISEASE

As a medical doctor, I had seen the relentless mental destruction that Alzheimer's inevitably brings. I thought my medical training might make it easier for me to handle the experience when its symptoms became evident in my wife, Maria. I was wrong. The deterioration of this once vital and capable woman, without whom none of my life's dreams would have been realized, was harder to bear than I could ever have imagined.

Following the example Maria had set for years, I turned to prayer. Opening our Bible to the lines that had seen us through so many trials, I began to read aloud from 1 Corinthians 13:4, 7, "Love is patient; love is kind... It bears all things, believes all things, hopes all things, endures all things" (NRSV).

How could I best show Maria my love when she needed it most? The answer came in a flood of memories—memories of all she'd done. I grabbed a pen and began to do some counting. Fifty years of marriage and six children meant something like fifty thousand meals cooked and served, nine hundred and twenty thousand dishes washed, two hundred and thirty thousand diapers changed. I wrote out number after number, listing all the tasks that Maria had cheerfully and uncomplainingly performed for our children and me over the years. The numbers were just guesswork, of course, but writing them down helped make concrete for me the scope of Maria's labor of love.

Lord, I prayed, I don't think I ever really understood the sacrifices Maria made. Let her illness be a chance for me to repay her in some way.

Since that day, that is just what I tried to do. Moment by moment, I learned to treat each small service I performed for Maria—from washing sheets to cleaning up a spill to remaining patient when she was having a bad day—as an active prayer of thanks. A chance for me to consciously give back to Maria something of what she had given me.

"Love bears all things, believes all things, hopes all things, endures all things." I know now that those words aren't mere sentiments, but truths that go to the very heart of what it means to share one's life with another person, in sickness and in health.

Maria reached the point where she had considerable trouble forming complete sentences, but there is one that she said when she was unable to say anything else. She would take my hand and give it a squeeze, and tell me, "I love you." In those three words, I saw the proof of something else that St. Paul says in 1 Corinthians. It follows the passage that concludes with love "endures all things," and it is, I feel, the truest statement of all. "Love never ends" (NRSV).
—WALLACE A. REED, M.D.

Surviving a Loved One's Illness

IT WAS ONE OF those mornings for Sharon Fish, M.S.N., R.N., teacher of nursing research, gerontology, and parish nursing and spirituality. She was trying to get her seventy-eight-year-old mother out of bed, but Pearle, typical of many people with late-stage Alzheimer's disease, didn't want to cooperate. As soon as Fish finally got her mother out of bed, Pearle decided to sit on the floor. To make matters worse, she began striking Fish's legs with her cane.

Although her mother didn't hit her hard, Fish lost her patience. She grabbed the cane and banged it on the floor, causing it to snap in two. Immediately, Fish was horrified and ashamed of what she had done. Putting her arms around her mother, who was now laughing beside her on the floor, Fish laughed until she cried, wondering all the time if her anger and frustration would ever cause her to treat her mother as she treated the cane.

Later, while Fish was reading her Bible, she turned to Isaiah and found a passage that she had never seen before. It said: "A bruised reed he will not break, and a smoldering wick he will not snuff out" (Isaiah 42:3 NIV). "That really spoke to me about my frustration," says Fish, "but also about God's gentleness with us."

After reading the verse, Fish knew she needed to strive even harder to reach that delicate balance between firmness and gentleness with her ailing, recalcitrant mom.

THE CHILD BECOMES THE PARENT

Such frustration is common among Alzheimer's caregivers. No wonder: while those who have the disease gradually experience memory loss and a worsening ability to think, understand, or make decisions, they also commonly exhibit agitation, aggression, and depression and are likely to wander as the disease progresses. Giving care under these circumstances can try one's patience and quickly become exhausting.

Fish, an R.N. and author of *Alzheimer's: Caring for Your Loved One, Caring for Yourself* says that the emotional stress of caring for her mother for the last ten years of her life was far more difficult than any of the physical work required. "The role change that took place was particularly difficult," she says. "I can remember the time when she first called me 'Mom.' And then I became 'Grandma' as her dementia became worse. She actually saw me as a different person, not as her daughter anymore. I became the parent. That created a profound sadness in me. It was very difficult."

Remedies
CARING FOR LILLIE

THE LATE REVEREND Herman Riffel, pastor, and lecturer and seminar leader about the voice of God and dreams in nearly fifty countries, had a similar experience. Although he still wrote and occasionally conducted religious seminars, the

Villanova, Pennsylvania resident's biggest job became helping care for Lillie, his beloved wife of fifty-five years. She was not formally diagnosed with Alzheimer's, but she had many of the symptoms, such as severe memory loss and confusion.

Instead of showing childlike aggression and agitated behavior, Lillie insisted on staying active. But that often meant she set the dining room table with the wrong items. Or she kept the house so tidy that things that should have been visible were no longer where they were supposed to be, and she couldn't remember where she put them. "She loved to do these things and tried to be helpful, but it's frustrating sometimes—no question about it," says Riffel.

Herman Riffel's deep faith and the support of his daughter often helped him avoid the symptoms of caregiver stress. These include anger, social withdrawal, anxiety, depression, exhaustion, sleeplessness, irritability, lack of concentration, and health problems.

"We didn't want to get into a situation where we were gritting our teeth about this," says Riffel. "For me, it was a matter of loving and recognizing that my wife was a wonderful person who had been very helpful to me. Once she had a disability,

I needed to show her my love and God's love."

Here are some other suggestions to keep our stress levels under control when caring for loved ones with Alzheimer's.

Find faith. In one study conducted by researchers at Indiana University School of Nursing, Alzheimer caregivers who said that their spiritual needs were being met and who attended worship services regularly reported greater levels of well-being and less stress than those whose spiritual needs were not addressed.

Sharon Fish also learned firsthand how big a difference faith can make. After her mother was diagnosed with Alzheimer's, she found herself angry at God, and the further she drifted from Him, the more miserable and angry she became. "It took a while, but thankfully, that wasn't a permanent condition for me," she says. "Eventually, I found a church that accepted my mom and really reached out to me. When I moved back into a church family, I reexperienced the love of God in a very special way. He was my strength in all of this."

Encourage family to pitch in. Not all of us are suited to or are good at primary Alzheimer's care. But from getting financial assistance to adding handrails and

Facing Alzheimer's Together

Caring for someone with Alzheimer's can be overwhelming. The Alzheimer's Association has made these important points about helping your loved one—and yourself:

- Provide Structure. Alzheimer's patients are easily disoriented, so it's important that their environment is stable and familiar, and their routines respected.

- Stay Calm. Easier said than done when a patient is agitated, but it is crucial that you maintain your cool. Always use a soothing tone of voice, keep eye contact, and offer repeated reassurance verbally as well as with a gentle touch.

- Play It Safe. Be sure to take precautions, such as keeping doors locked. Child-proof gates and door alarms are also useful.

- Don't Take It Personally. Some people with Alzheimer's can't help being belligerent or abusive on occasion. Don't argue with them or contradict what they say. Change the subject, or defuse the situation with humor. Distract, rather than react.

- Keep Talking. Studies show that even when your loved one can no longer fully comprehend what you are saying, the sound of your voice itself is comforting. When you run out of things to say or reminisce about, read aloud from a book or magazine.

- Treat Yourself With Compassion. Unless you take care of yourself, you won't be able to take care of anyone else. Eat right, get plenty of rest, and be aware that your own feelings of anger, guilt, inadequacy, and grief are natural.

- Reach Out for Help. Contact the Alzheimer's Association's 24/7 Helpline at 1-800-272-3900 or www.alz.org or the Family Caregiver Alliance at 1-800-445-8106 or www.caregiver.org.

lighting, making the bathroom wheelchair accessible, and arranging for help with meals or household chores, there's plenty to do, and it can make a big difference if all family members, including those out of town, help out, says Fish.

Lean on good friends. Fish wouldn't suggest we ask friends to provide extended care for a loved one with Alzheimer's. But friends can help in other ways. "I wasn't shy about letting them pick up groceries or run an errand," she says. And if we're the friends of someone caring for an Alzheimer's patient, we should understand that this is the best time to pitch in. According to Proverbs 27:10, "...better a neighbor nearby than a relative far away" (NIV).

Be patient. When his patience with his wife began to grow thin, Herman Riffel reminded himself of God's love for us. "He's very patient, very loving, and accepting of us in the midst of all of our foolish mistakes and all of our stubbornness," he said. "It's kind of hard to be tough on someone else when we recognize how much we ourselves fail."

Pray for solutions to specific problems. When Lillie wanted to get up and get dressed in the middle of the night, Herman Riffel discovered that she was following the directions of voices inside her head. Instead of trying to convince her to go back to sleep, Herman prayed with her that God would silence those voices, and in his experience God did.

Have fun together. It takes work, but we can find simple things to do with our loved one that bring joy and, as a result, make the journey a little easier. "As Mom's dementia progressed, her table manners regressed. But that didn't mean we had to stay home. I found a restaurant where I took Mom routinely for pancakes because she loved them," says Fish. "We had our own little booth and since we went at two or three in the afternoon, we had the place pretty much to ourselves."

Gain strength from the Psalms. In the Bible, "David struggled a lot with his emotions, but was very honest about those emotions in the Psalms," says Fish. Reading them, she says, "helped me identify my own emotions and be more honest about them with God. Through them and other passages in the Bible, I learned that He can take my frustrations and give me hope."

Talk it through. Another huge potential source of stress is the strain that caring for a parent who has Alzheimer's disease can place on a marriage. "There have to be discussions about what we're going to do about Mom or Dad," says Wilford Wooten, a licensed marriage, family, and child counselor and former director of the counseling department at Focus on the Family. According to him, we need to ask, "'Does she have the funds to place her somewhere? Can she live closer and be in her own apartment?' Whatever the situation, we have to talk."

Know where to go for help. Whether it's a community health nursing department or a local office on aging, we probably have caregiving resources literally in our own backyards, says Fish. "Sometimes even local nursing homes have support groups not only for those people with loved ones who stay at the nursing home but also for people in the community." Check the Internet for more information or visit the Alzheimer's Association website at www .alz.org.

Remember to take care of ourselves. "Eating right, exercising, and getting plenty of sleep helped me have the physical and emotional resources to assist my mom. I was much more patient when I was able to get out and have a life of my own rather than just staying in the house all day long," says Fish. "That can produce a lot of anxiety. Being able to maintain a life and relationships out of the home is very important."

Roll with the changes. Sometimes the decline in an Alzheimer's patient is gradual; other times, it's fast and steep. Though medical science has made significant progress in treating Alzheimer's symptoms in recent years, some type of decline is inevitable for people who have this disease. Fish says she found that the key was being prepared mentally and emotionally. In some cases, for example, a person could go from a moderate memory loss to asking the same questions over and over in just a few months.

"It can be very trying and frustrating for the person who might have to answer the same question fifteen times in an hour," says Fish. "But we have to realize that this is part of the disease process. Some of these are phases that they pass through; they won't necessarily become fixated on them forever."

Get real. We want to do all we can, and we should. But as sad as it seems, we may not be able to care for our loved ones in our homes for the duration of the disease. To determine when we need to find appropriate alternate living arrangements, Fish suggests that we ask ourselves two questions: Is my loved one safe at home? And is caring for the person harming my health? "When an older person is caring for a loved one, the one without Alzheimer's may give out quicker than the person with it. We need to be realistic about our limits and listen to others who may be more aware of our limits."

Remind them of our love. "I would tell Mom a lot that I loved her," says Fish.

"And often, I would be sitting doing something and out of the blue this little voice would say, 'I love you.' Until I came back to the Lord and began to see things from His perspective, I thought this was a burden. But after that, I felt it was a privilege, even though there were many difficult times."

· HEALING WORDS ·

Alzheimer's

O God, my Comforter, today I should visit my father in the nursing home, and I don't want to go. He has Alzheimer's disease, and he doesn't know me anymore. I'm a familiar face, that's all. But he does seem happy when I'm with him. It's hard for me to talk to him now, because it's a struggle for him to put his words in order, and when I can't understand him, he's embarrassed. I want to help him, yet I don't know how. All I can do is put my arms around him and tell him I love him. Perhaps, Lord, that is enough—to let him know that he makes me happy, too, just by being with me.
Be with my father and me today, Lord. And teach me how to say "I love you" without words.
—PHYLLIS HOBE

EATING DISORDERS

Prayer for Health

If ever a book was written to take off pounds, I read it. If ever a dessert was invented to put on pounds, I ate it.

But one day I asked myself, "How can I go on asking God to 'Bless this food to the use for which it was intended' when I know the extra food I consume is just abusing the body, the temple of the Holy Spirit?" And, as the mother of five children, I had an obligation to keep my body healthy.

I began to want to eat less, not only to get slim, but so as not to offend God. Before, when tempted by a candy bar, I'd indulge in a bit of self-deception and say, "What harm if I just indulge once?" But it's a great deal more difficult to do this when I ask myself, "What harm is done if I offend God just this once?"

As many times a day as I felt compelled to eat, just as many times did I compel myself to say a private grace, be it for a nibble or a feast.

Psychiatrists say some of us are compulsive eaters because of our emotions. I know only that a frustration or emotion is a "care" and the Bible says, "[Cast] all your care upon him; for he careth for you" (1 Peter 5:7 KJV). I know that prayer is the answer, and I, for one, am placing this whole wide girl in His hands.

—ROMAYNE ALLEN

Solving the Food Puzzle

JENA KELLER WAS A pigtailed ten-year-old when she simply stopped eating. Convinced she was suffering from some mysterious medical problem, her parents took her to countless doctors, searching for a cure. But as the weeks passed, her weight continued to drop—from seventy to forty-eight pounds—and their desperation grew more and more intense.

Finally, a doctor suggested they make an appointment with a psychologist. But instead of trying to figure out a new way to make their daughter eat, the psychologist told Ward and Kay Keller that one of the best things they could do for their daughter was to learn how to improve their troubled marriage.

The psychologist diagnosed Jena with anorexia nervosa. She was starving herself, and the psychologist believed her parents were at the center of the problem. Among other things, Ward was a demanding and controlling husband and father who drove his family relentlessly, while Kay's tendencies as a people pleaser prevented her from objecting to her husband's behavior even though she knew it was harmful.

"This counselor said to me, 'I believe you're the kind of man who thinks he doesn't need anybody in his life,'" says Ward Keller, "and my little daughter probably thought in her heart I viewed her that way: completely dispensable. Understanding that was like a knife going into my heart."

Ward Keller cried out to God to ask forgiveness. And then he told Jena that he needed her, just as the counselor suggested. The next morning, instead of rushing to school, Jena got up, popped a bagel into the toaster, and promptly ate.

"We were so stunned, we didn't know what to say," says Kay Keller. After two years of sometimes rocky family and individual counseling sessions, Jena was on her way to recovery.

As a result of this experience, Ward Keller left his businesses and, with Kay's help, opened Remuda Ranch, an inpatient eating-disorder clinic in Wickenberg, Arizona. Since that time, in 1990, the clinic has helped thousands of patients. When the ranch opened, Jena, equipped with a premed degree, went to work full-time at the facility. "We got professional help, and that was important. But the main thing for us was the way things changed at home," says Ward.

THE ROOT OF THE PROBLEM

According to nationaleatingdisorders.org, in the United States, approximately twenty million women and ten million men struggle with a significant eating disorder, including anorexia nervosa, bulimia, and others, over the course of their lifetimes. This website also reports that more than "one-half of teenage girls and one-third of teenage boys use unhealthy weight control behaviors such as skipping meals, fasting, smoking cigarettes, vomiting, and taking laxatives." This preoccupation with weight makes them vulnerable to eating disorders.

What causes these disorders? Research shows that some people may be genetically predisposed to them, says Jacqueline Abbott, Dr.P.H., former codirector of the Kartini Clinic, a treatment center for eating disorders in Portland, Oregon. But there are several other contributing factors, she says. "Feelings of low self-worth and sometimes trauma related to a history of sexual abuse may be involved."

Also, Dr. Abbott thinks society's emphasis on dieting is a major factor. Drastically restricting the total amount of food we eat can starve our bodies, in effect. And when our bodies don't get adequate nutrition, they overreact, she says, sometimes leading to binge-eating.

There's another factor, too: some of us are obsessed with obtaining our culture's standard of the perfect body. The average American woman today is five feet four inches tall and weighs 165 pounds, according to nationaleatingdisorders.org. The same website states that the "average Miss America winner is five feet seven inches tall and weighs 121 pounds." The idea that Miss America body types are most beautiful and desirable drives some people to want to be thin at the expense of their health.

When depressed women—and an increasing number of men—discover that they can find temporary solace in the comforts of their favorite foods, it's often the beginning of a vicious bulimic cycle. Several days of strict dieting give way to binges. The only interruptions are trips to the bathroom to purge.

It's remarkable that family members even discover that a loved one is suffering from bulimia. While many people with anorexia are pencil-thin, most people with bulimia are close to normal weight or a little bit above, making the disorder even more difficult to detect.

"We're talking about someone who eats, but before she throws up her food, her body might assimilate enough nutrition to keep her weight relatively normal," says Ward Keller. But if her weight isn't a clue to her behavior, there are other, not-so-pleasant physical symptoms of such binge-purge behavior. Vomiting several times a day eventually eats away at the sufferer's tooth enamel and damages the esophagus, intestines, and cardiac muscle. It can cause liver and kidney dysfunction as well. Frequent use of diuretics and laxatives to shed pounds also exacerbates many of these dangerous conditions.

Still, those with bulimia often manage to hide their behavior—for a while. "You wouldn't believe the number of cases that I've seen where a daughter or wife has been throwing up food for four to five years and no one ever knew it. They noticed that she went to the bathroom all the time right around dinner, but they never really put things together," says Ward Keller. This kind of behavior is why bulimia has been called "the hidden disease."

But this secretive behavior is also common among those who have anorexia, even though signs of weight loss are visible in them. Some people with eating disorders exercise frequently—biking miles and miles—but won't admit to exercising every day. Sometimes they put things in their pockets in an attempt to appear heavier at their check-ins with doctors and psychiatrists.

Remedies
THE HEALING EFFECT

WITH ALL THE DECEPTION and potentially serious health consequences involved, it may not seem that any good could ever come from having an eating disorder or having a daughter, son, or spouse with one. But some counselors say that properly treating this condition often has a healing effect not only on the one suffering from it but on the entire family. "Somebody once said that the person with an eating disorder is the match, but the logs have already been set up for a fire. Often, the person who comes in is merely the catalyst for the rest of the family's problems being addressed," says Dr. Abbott.

If we have an eating disorder, or if someone we love struggles with one, we should seek help immediately. "There is really no such thing as waiting until someone with an eating disorder 'hits bottom,'" says Dr. Abbott. "People can die from the consequences of eating disorders, even in their early phases."

When we look for help, Dr. Abbott recommends seeking a team that can address all the possible triggers for the disorder. First and foremost, a physician should provide treatment for any medical conditions. Then a nutritionist trained in treating eating disorders can help us or our loved one learn to eat properly again. An individual psychotherapist and often a family therapist should also be part of the team. Most important, all team members should be encouraged to communicate among themselves, with us, and with our families.

Beyond this, there are practical things we can do to try to prevent eating disorders in our families or end ones that already exist. Here's what experts suggest.

Eat dinner together. This creates a regular eating pattern and lets the family provide care and support in a loving way, says Dr. Abbott. Also, it encourages the person with the eating disorder to be accountable.

Fight the fix-it syndrome. We may be tempted to try to "fix" a loved one who has anorexia or bulimia. Big mistake. Talking too much about a person's eating habits or calling attention to them only makes the situation worse. Friends and family members need to see their role as supporting and loving the person struggling with the disorder and realize that trying to solve the problem is the responsibility of the treatment team.

Speak the truth in love. This biblical admonition from Ephesians 4:15 "means looking the person in the eye and saying, 'I'm very concerned for you. This is the behavior I see. This is what it appears that you are doing to yourself. Here is what I see in your life, and we need to get help for you,'" says Ward Keller.

Remember the Apostle Paul's words. When he found believers in Corinth giving in to the evils of that city, Paul reminded them that the Israelites did the same thing (the passage even refers to out-of-control eating and drinking), and it cost them their lives. To avoid the same consequences, he urged them to recognize God's power in their struggles, a concept we would do well to remember today. Said Paul, "No

Eating-Disorder Symptoms

According to Dr. Abbott, the following symptoms indicate a need to contact our family physician:

- The desire to be thinner than others
- Spending an inordinate amount of time thinking about weight or physical shape
- Checking weight more than once a week
- Believing that gaining weight signifies failure
- Believing that losing weight signifies success
- Experiencing menstrual periods ceasing or becoming irregular
- Using vomiting, laxatives, or diuretics as a means of weight control
- Eating all day whether hungry or not
- Being extremely afraid of gaining weight and looking fat
- Constantly starting new diets
- Becoming angry when people ask what we've eaten
- Bingeing on large amounts of food to the point of sickness
- Eating during periods of stress

For more information about eating disorders, contact the National Association of Anorexia Nervosa and Associated Disorders by visiting their website, anad.org, or at 750 E. Diehl Road, Suite 127, Naperville, IL 60563, or the National Eating Disorders Association, online at nationaleatingdisorders.org, or at 165 West Forty-sixth Street, Suite 402, New York, NY 10036.

temptation has overtaken you except such as is common to man; but God *is* faithful, who will not allow you to be tempted beyond what you are able, but with the temptation will also make the way of escape, that you may be able to bear *it*" (1 Corinthians 10:13 NKJV).

The point is that through Christ and our relationship with Him, we have the power to overcome our difficulties and change our lives for the better.

Change the inner messages. Eating disorders can act like recording devices that constantly play and replay shaming, self-defeating, and demoralizing messages in the mind, says Dr. Abbott.

One of the best ways to rid ourselves of these negative messages is to meditate on Scripture that describes how God sees us. Some verses that will encourage those who struggle to see themselves as God sees them are Psalm 139; Isaiah 49:16; Zephaniah 3:17, 2; 2 Corinthians 5:17; Ephesians 2:10; Philippians 1:6; and 1 Peter 5:6–7.

Stop dieting. Instead of eating fat-free and other "diet" foods, we need to enjoy a variety of "real" foods at regular times each day, suggests Dr. Abbott. We should view food as the medicine that can nourish and heal an exhausted body, spirit, and self-worth. Also, we should throw away the bathroom scale. "Don't let weight be the gauge of a self-worth level," she says.

Build the body. Although exercise is undoubtedly important for good physical and mental health, we're talking here about building the spiritual body. We can join Bible study groups or a church or simply get to know a new friend. This can help end the isolation and self-focus that anorexia and bulimia feed on. People with eating disorders "like to be alone," says Ward Keller, but they need to be with others.

Plan time for prayer. Prayer allows us to take our heavy mental and physical burdens off our backs and place them in the powerful hands of a loving, compassionate God. Wesley Duewel, a leader in world missions for seventy-five years, said, "God waits for you to communicate with Him. You have instant, direct access to God. God loves mankind so much, and in a very special sense His children, that He has made Himself available to you at all times."

"What? Do you not know that your body is the temple of the Holy Spirit, who is in you, whom you have received from God, and that you are not your own? You were bought with a price. Therefore glorify God in your body and in your spirit, which are God's" (1 CORINTHIANS 6:19–20 MEV).

PAIN

No Hopeless Cases

Even when a disease or an affliction seems hopeless and physical suffering tempts you to withdraw from the world around you, remember that help is always available—from others who have had similar experiences, from the latest news, from newly developed treatments, medical procedures, and surgery. Don't ever close yourself off and assume nothing can be done. Even if nothing can be done today, it doesn't mean there won't be something to be done tomorrow. In God's amazing world, there will always be ongoing research, medical breakthroughs, new therapies, and new information and understanding. More important, God also sends people to guide and encourage us, sometimes when we least expect it.

You may have to learn to live with pain, but there's one thing you never have to live without. Hope. —PHYLLIS HOBE

Finding Relief and Acceptance

AS A THIRTY-SOMETHING ACCOUNTANT in Indianapolis, Tim Doyle created the website suffering.net, which is devoted to the meaning and experience of suffering from a Christian perspective. This is a topic he knows quite a bit about, not through academic study but from firsthand experience. As Tim explains:

- His family consists of seven children, now all adults, and his parents.
- Growing up, they were a very athletic and loving Catholic family. However, during their high school years, Tim and three of the other children developed weaknesses that they now know are caused by muscular dystrophy.
- One of Tim's siblings who has muscular dystrophy and another one who doesn't have muscular dystrophy both have been diagnosed with multiple sclerosis.
- Today, four of the seven siblings, including Tim, use wheelchairs.

All this agony has left the Doyle family wondering, "Why us?" "Why this?" "Why now?" When it comes to pain, "Why?" is definitely the burning question. The experience of physical suffering seems so cruel and so unfairly distributed that it can turn even the most literal-minded among us into skeptical theologians. Does God wish us ill? If He doesn't wish us ill, why does He allow so much pain? If He does wish us ill, why?

Tim Doyle has struggled with these questions, too. And though he has found comfort in reading the Bible, he still asks, "Why, Lord?"

But as Tim notes, "The Bible is clear: We're never going to understand all of our suffering on this side of eternity. But it really helps me to see that, in His sovereignty, God chose suffering for His own Son. I feel that God is honoring me by saying, 'Tim, the path of pain that I chose for My Son is the same path that I'm using to bring you to Me.'"

Remedies
SOOTHING THE WOUNDED SPIRIT

PASTORAL COUNSELORS who work daily with people in pain will tell you that Tim Doyle's story is neither unique nor universal. Many people, at least initially, find their beliefs more a stumbling block than a blessing in coping with pain. "I see a lot of anger," says the Reverend Kent Richmond, S.T.D., chaplain, Coronary Intensive Care, Lutheran General Hospital, Park Ridge, Illinois, and author of *Preaching to Sufferers*. "A lot of people feel their faith should have protected them, should have made them special, if you will. The discovery that that doesn't happen is often difficult."

So difficult, Dr. Richmond adds, that many decide they want nothing to do with God anymore. That's a tragedy, because as difficult as it may be to reconcile suffering with belief, overwhelming evidence documents that faith and prayer can help people learn how to live with pain, if they have to, and in some cases, overcome it. Here are some suggestions for getting in touch with God when we're in pain.

Have faith in God's presence. Maybe we can't understand why God allows pain, but we can be certain that He is with us in our suffering. Far from being aloof and unmoved, God suffers with us. He actively participates in our pain. This shared suffering, says Dr. Richmond, is central to the meaning of Christ's journey to the cross, as prophesied in the Bible: "Surely he has borne our infirmities and carried our diseases..." (Isaiah 53:4 NRSV).

Find your own understanding. Believers throughout the ages have found different ways to view the problem of pain, and we need to search for answers that make sense in our hearts. Dr. Richmond, for example, doesn't necessarily share Tim Doyle's view that God wills suffering as a means of drawing sinners closer to Him. "I think that we live in an unfinished creation," he says. "God seeks our willingness to participate in the completion of that creation and the humanizing of it. Pain is part of that. God is not responsible for it, but God will give us strength to help us cope."

If our particular view of God is adding to our suffering rather than easing it, we may want to reexamine our beliefs, Dr. Richmond suggests.

Share sorrow. Naturally, pastoral counselors believe that sharing our pain with someone can help lighten the load. What's more surprising is that research scientists, who have found that communicating the experience of illness has definite therapeutic advantages, also support this view. "Telling our stories is a way of processing what's happening," says Frank Baker, Ph.D., consultant at Connecticut Department of Correction and former director of research at the Connecticut Department of Mental Health and Addiction Services. "It helps put life in order and gives meaning to suffering."

Many people find comfort in attending support groups where they can share what they're going through with others undergoing the same experience. Thousands of such groups exist, meeting in person and on the Internet, and they address a variety of conditions and situations, from cancer and miscarriage to Lyme disease and arthritis. Doctors, pastors, and social workers at

The Way I Am

By Barbara Alexander

My daughter, Jennifer, limped into the kitchen after track practice. Her left knee was so swollen she could barely bend it. Jennifer loved running cross-country for the University of Utah team, and an injury now would sideline her for an important meet.

"Mom, will you pray for me?" she asked, grimacing. "It really hurts."

I'm no stranger to pain. When I was a child, chasing around on the playground, sudden, sharp pangs in my leg often felled me. My worsening pain baffled my doctors. Medication and surgery didn't help. Slowly, I had to give up activities I loved—tennis, jogging, golf. Yet the mysterious pain stayed with me.

Gently, I rested my hands on my daughter's leg. "Lord, please help make Jennifer's knee better. Amen," I said. Jennifer thanked me, then gingerly made her way to her room.

The next day when I drove into the garage after work, Jennifer bounded out to greet me. "Mom," she exulted, "my knee feels great!"

Delighted by the swiftness of Jennifer's healing, I went inside. "Thank you, Lord, for helping my daughter," I prayed. But deep down I found myself wondering why there seemed to be no help from Him for my pain. For years I'd prayed, begging God for answers, a miracle. I felt guilty having these thoughts, yet I couldn't help but ask, Lord, why Jennifer and not me, too?

That night I told my husband what was troubling me.

"Barbara," he said, "maybe God is using your pain."

Could it really be? I thought. My experiences had helped in my job at the American Cancer Society. Friends frequently asked me to visit loved ones in the hospital. And so often I heard of wondrous answers to the prayers I'd offered for others.

Maybe I'd already gotten my miracle: I'd been able to do so much. I helped people in my job. I had a wonderful family. "Thanks," I said to my husband. Silently I added: and thank you, God, for everything you've done for me, just the way I am.

hospitals and local health departments can often provide lists of these groups. To find groups, search the Internet using key words describing the condition or circumstances in which you find yourself and "support groups" or "help with."

Dr. Justin Tull, D.Min., M.Th., S.T.M., ordained United Methodist minister, and author of *Why God Why? Sermons on the Problem of Pain*, recommends approaching these groups with some caution, initially. "Many support groups are tremendously helpful," he says. "But some groups tend to dwell on the problem rather than moving forward. Also, support groups may not be the right solution for every person at a particular time." Be prepared to attend several meetings before making up your mind.

Serve others. Research has shown that it's possible to ameliorate pain by distracting yourself from it, Dr. Baker says, and one of the most effective ways of doing that is to help others.

Dr. Tull cites the case of two members of his church: a woman who had just lost her husband and a young man who had a chronic illness. The young man sent the woman flowers and cards to let her know that he was thinking of her in her time of grief, and she did the same when he was in the hospital. "Here were two people in pain for different reasons," Dr. Tull says, "and the fact that they would take the time to think of each other had tremendous power."

For Tim Doyle, testifying to God's power in his life, both in person and through his website, has been a major factor in his coming to terms with his disease. "I've been a much more powerful witness for Him in this wheelchair than I ever could have been without it," he says. "I just thank God for choosing me to be in His service."

Cope with one day at a time. Suffering is easier to handle in small doses, says Dr. Tull. "Don't ask how you're going to endure this for the next twenty years," he says. "Just concentrate on how you're going to get through today."

Take the long view. Paradoxically, Tim Doyle finds he can get through difficult days by focusing on what he calls God's eternal perspective.

He cites Romans 8:18, "I consider that the sufferings of this present time are not worth comparing with the glory about to be revealed to us" (NRSV). Another key passage for Doyle: "For this slight momentary affliction is preparing us for an eternal weight of glory beyond all measure" (2 Corinthians 4:17 NRSV).

"I receive tremendous comfort in God's eternal promises, as they provide an endless source of strength to help me through the toughest days. As my body weakens, His strength, through His promises, increases," says Doyle.

Pray with others. Praying with those who care for you is a potent combination. "I can hardly think of anything more helpful than that," says the Reverend Steven Estes, senior pastor at Community Evangelical Free Church in Elverson, Pennsylvania and coauthor of *When God Weeps.*

SPIRITUAL HEALING

A lot of people think of prayer and faith as basically passive activities: we ask God for help and sit back and let it happen. Not so. As the New Testament says, faith without works is dead (James 2:17), and nowhere is that more true than with pain.

Some pain experts say attitude has everything to do with how well, or how poorly, people deal with pain. Happily, attitude is something that prayer and faith can rectify dramatically. Pastoral counselors see the evidence of this in their daily hospital rounds, and research studies on the health benefits of religion confirm it.

Often, the influence our attitudes have on our health is described in terms of the mind-body connection, meaning that what goes on between our ears has a dramatic impact on the entire body. That's fine, as far as it goes, but experts Dr. Dale A. Matthews and Dr. Kenneth A. Larsen, director of clinical pastoral education and counseling at the New England Baptist Hospital, have demonstrated that what's really involved is a "mind-body-spirit" connection. Each element of the triad influences the other.

The effects of the mind-body-spirit connection are especially clear when it comes to the relationship between pain and stress, according to Dr. Larsen. Pain causes stress, and stress unleashes a cascade of physiological responses, from the release of toxic hormones to the suppression of the immune system. All can exacerbate and prolong pain. Prayer and a faithful attitude of calm acceptance can help keep those processes from setting in. "The body

How to Persevere Through Permanent Pain

BY ANNE FITZPATRICK

What a relief it was to find, after years of tests, that the leg pain I suffer is fibromyalgia, an often-misdiagnosed form of muscular rheumatism. But it has no cure, and that was depressing news. I'd become a member of a not-so-exclusive club—one made up of millions of people who daily must cope with chronic pain.

Doctors had little to offer—mostly medication and therapy that provided only temporary relief. I began to have difficulty getting around to interview people in my work as a writer. Tennis was out of the question, and I missed the long walks my husband, Bill, and I used to take. The future looked dismal.

Then I spent an evening with Marianne, a young woman who had struggled with serious health problems for a long time. Now she faced surgery. I was surprised by her optimistic determination, but she had a ready reply: "I've got a lot of living to do yet!"

From Marianne and others I've learned how to manage chronic pain so it doesn't dominate my life. Some of these ideas may help you, too.

1. Learning. My husband came home one day with an armload of books on pain control. Though I found little about fibromyalgia, I did learn about various relaxation techniques useful for anyone who's hurting. One doctor suggests using your imagination to see yourself as healthy and vigorous. Eyes closed, I picture knotted-up muscles smoothing into bright, flowing silk ribbons.

2. Pacing. I've often found myself gritting my teeth to do one more bit of baking or to finish cleaning the kitchen, even though I know another half hour on my feet will leave me almost unable to walk for the rest of the day. At first I was

afraid that "pacing" meant giving in to pain. Instead, I've found that resting before reaching total exhaustion is a way of responding to my body's needs.

3. Laughing. Proverbs 17:22 says, "A merry heart does good, like medicine" (NKJV). Some researchers say laughter releases endorphins, natural painkillers in the brain. Once, in a glum mood, I found in the morning mail a postcard that made me laugh aloud; the sender's unique wit helped me forget pain for a few moments.

4. Rejoicing. When I have a good day, I'm tempted to catch up with the ironing, do the cleaning I've let slide, or pull some weeds. But before I know it the "eased" feeling has become sheer pain and fatigue. One friend showed me a better way. "When I feel good," she said, "that's my time to enjoy a good book, or take a short walk. I do something just for me when I'm feeling well enough to enjoy it."

5. Helping. Studies show that people who became involved in doing things for others reportedly forgot their own pain temporarily. The idea is to move the focus outward, toward others and away from pain.

6. Praying. Prayer is important to all areas of our lives. But one night my "Why me, Lord?" prayer was interrupted when I remembered I'd been asked to pray for a child who was to undergo heart surgery. That made me aware of the serious concerns and needs of others. Focusing on those needs in prayer keeps me from closing in on my hurting.

No one has all the answers to living with chronic pain, but by practicing these techniques, I can say, as does a friend I admire, "I've got this awful chronic pain, but it hasn't got me!"

has its own internal wisdom, which we can learn to facilitate," Dr. Larsen says. "By finding a place of peace and tranquility, we can touch our connection to God, and that can directly affect the pain process."

Here are some specific ways we can use the mind-body-spirit connection to relieve pain.

Breathe. Breathing peacefully is the starting point of learning how to relax, in

Dr. Larsen's view. The key is a technique he calls diaphragmatic breathing. Most of us focus our breathing on inhaling, using the muscles of the chest to pull air into our lungs. Diaphragmatic breathing reverses that. We use our abdominal muscles as a pump to push all the air out of our lungs.

To practice diaphragmatic breathing, we need to pull our abdominal muscles in sharply as we exhale. That forces our diaphragms upward, which forces air out of our lungs. The lungs are emptied far more efficiently, so we exchange more stale air with fresh air with every breath. That increased efficiency helps fight pain by enhancing the body's healing processes, and by helping us become more relaxed, says Dr. Matthews.

Deep breathing is an important element in almost any form of meditation. Dr. Larsen describes it as a form of "body prayer."

Relax. Progressive muscle relaxation takes us to the next level of serenity, says Dr. Larsen. The idea is to systematically guide ourselves mentally through each part of our bodies, concentrating on relaxing the muscles in each area. Some teachers recommend using what is called the clench-and-release approach to this exercise, meaning that we clench each muscle group tightly for a few

seconds before releasing it. This has the advantage of reminding our muscles the difference between tension and relaxation.

Here's how it's done, according to Dr. Larsen:

- We begin by closing our eyes and relaxing them
- Focus on relaxing the eyelids
- Focus on relaxing the face and the crown of the head
- Focus on relaxing the neck and shoulders; we need to concentrate our efforts here; this is the most critical area as far as stress is concerned
- Focus on relaxing the arms and hands
- Focus on relaxing the lower back
- Focus on relaxing the buttocks
- Focus on relaxing the pelvic area
- Focus on relaxing the thighs and the calves
- Focus on relaxing the feet

If we're in pain, Dr. Larsen recommends practicing progressive muscle relaxation for twenty minutes, two or three times a day. By coupling progressive muscle relaxation with diaphragmatic breathing, he says, eventually, we'll be able to initiate a state of physical, psychological, and spiritual repose almost automatically, any time we wish, with a single cleansing breath.

Meditate. Breathing and muscle relaxation exercises set the stage for meditation.

Research has shown that meditating has many physical and psychological benefits, from lowering blood pressure to lowering anxiety and depression. In addition, patients with chronic pain who meditate can lessen the severity of their pain, according to Dr. Larsen.

One of the leaders in meditation research is Herbert Benson, M.D., who first described the relaxation response. Over the years, Dr. Benson has observed that 80 percent of his patients use a religious focus for their meditations, and that faith enhances meditation's healing effects. Ultimately, he came to believe in an inherent, genetic connection between prayer and health. Human beings, Dr. Benson writes, are "wired for God."

Visualize. Another common pain-fighting tool is visualization—mentally picturing a peaceful, relaxing scene or some other image that helps distract us from our pain. In fact, Dr. Larsen has had patients who visualize Jesus walking or sitting beside them when they're in pain. One woman, a Catholic, pictured Jesus on the cross, so Dr. Larsen suggested that she try to place some of the pain she was suffering on Him so He could help her carry it. "I believe that these sorts of images have authority in the psyche and help

remove patients' anxiety by triggering specific chemical responses in the body," Dr. Larsen says.

Think positively. It's easy to get depressed and discouraged when we're in pain. We need to fight those negative feelings with positive, encouraging thoughts. Keeping a constructive mental attitude literally enhances the body's healing process, according to Dr. Larsen. "Motivation changes chemistry," he says.

One way to promote constructive mental attitudes is to set goals for ourselves, Dr. Larsen says. These should be simple, specific, achievable goals we can accomplish without having to depend on others. If pain is keeping us away from our jobs, for example, we might set a specific date to return to work. Or if we've been bedridden for a while, we might resolve to get back into shape by walking once around the block today and twice tomorrow.

Exercise. Physical exercise releases endorphins, hormones that act as natural opiates in the body, says James G. Garrick, M.D., founder of the Center for Sports Medicine in San Francisco. Endorphins are thought to directly improve our tolerance for pain. By promoting a sense of calm and well-being, endorphins may also enhance the body's self-healing process, he says.

Listen to music. Music is a delightful way to relax and distract yourself from pain. It can also heal. Research suggests that music can lower respiration, heart rate, and blood pressure and reduce muscle tension. Choose soothing music, though, because our heartbeats respond to rhythm. An aggressive, driving beat can make you more tense and less relaxed, says Stephen Halpern, Ph.D., who has studied the relationship between music and healing for more than twenty years. Dr. Halpern also recommends choosing music with simple melodies rather than scores that swell to giant crescendos.

· HEALING WORDS ·

Prayer for a Pain-Free Night

Help me, Lord, to sleep this night.
I don't know fully what tomorrow brings,
what further traumas, tests, or troubles
will be thrust upon me.
I do know that I hurt right now,
that I am worried,
that I'm "down."
Help me accept Your offer, Lord,
to share my burden,
to bear me up,
to give me peace.
Yes, Lord, I bring to You my cares.
Into Your outstretched hands
I place my illness, stress, and problems.
I thank You, Father.
I love You so!
And now to sleep.
—EILEEN M. BERGER

SURGERY

Solo Act

One year, I was scheduled to sing the Christmas portions of Handel's *Messiah* in a church concert. I wouldn't be singing any solos, but that was all right with me. I had enough on my mind. The next day I was going into the hospital for hip surgery.

As I drove to the concert, anxiety about the operation weighed on me. Had I made the right decision? Was this the best thing to do for the pain? Should I have waited? "Dear Lord," I prayed, "please be with me."

The orchestra was already tuning when I arrived at the church. During rehearsal the conductor led us through some of the trickier passages. It was a professional group, and the singers were well trained and confident. But where was the soprano soloist?

Finally, someone rushed off to call her and reported, "She's sick and can't make it."

"What?" the conductor bellowed. "The soloist is sick? What are we going to do?" Frantic, he scanned the soprano section, then pointed at me. "You know the solos! You will do it."

Sure, I'd heard them for years and had even practiced the arias a few times, but I'd never sung the long recitatives. Now I was being asked to sing them with an orchestra before an audience. Nervously I made my way to the front.

As people entered the church, I pleaded for the second time that day, "God, be with me." When my moment in the concert came I raised my score and sang, "'There were shepherds abiding in the field . . .'"

The music flowed from me, as though grace were carrying me along. At the end the conductor exclaimed, "I have never heard you sing so well!" My husband and son, who were sitting in the congregation, came up to congratulate me. "You didn't tell us you were singing the solos," my son said.

"I didn't know myself," I replied.

That night I slept easier. I was still anxious about my surgery, but I had no doubt about Who was in charge. "Fear not," I'd sung, the angel's words to the shepherds, words I'd needed to hear. They made me realize God had been orchestrating things in my favor all along. —JO ANN COHEN

Let Go, Let God

AS A STAFF CHAPLAIN at Memorial Sloan Kettering Cancer Center in New York City, Sister Elaine Goodell offers to pray with virtually every patient who goes into surgery there—some thirty-five or forty patients a day. Whatever their religious affiliations or beliefs, few of them refuse the offer, not even one seemingly tough guy named Bill.

He was in his late twenties or so, and when Sister Elaine went to his room, he was gulping down a beer. This was the afternoon prior to his surgery, and beer was not appropriate for someone about to undergo surgery. His wife, his brother, and his sister were waiting with him.

"I was shocked," Sister Elaine recalls, "but I acted as if we give beer to everybody, and I gave my usual introduction: 'Bill, I don't know if you have any belief system, but if you like, I could say a little prayer for you and your surgeon.'"

Bill's family members were audibly thrilled. "Oh, yes!" they cried in unison. But Bill lay silently, sipping his beer.

"What about you, Bill?" Sister Elaine asked.

Bill paused and looked at his family. "I suppose it wouldn't hurt," he finally said.

While Sister Elaine prayed, Bill drank his beer and fidgeted. It wasn't until she began praying for God to guide the hands of his surgeon that he bowed his head and listened.

"When I finished, no one said a word," Sister Elaine recalls. "All at once, Bill jumped off the bed, grabbed hold of me tightly—he wouldn't let me go—and said, 'Oh, thank you! Thank you! That was exactly what I needed!'"

HOW PRAYER CAN HELP

Not every surgery is as dramatic as those at Memorial Sloan Kettering, but when we undergo operations, they may be among the more significant events in our lives. Prayer and faith can help us get through them. In fact, research repeatedly shows that people of faith survive major surgery more often, with fewer problems, than people who are not religious. There are many reasons this is true.

For one, believers who pray before surgery often gain a sense of calm acceptance that helps prepare them psychologically and physiologically for the operation.

"Statistics show that surgery has a better outcome if the person goes in with a sense of tranquility," says Dr. Kenneth A. Larsen. Calm also helps the body heal itself effectively after surgery, he adds.

Another important advantage religious people often enjoy is social support—the loving presence of friends and family—which numerous studies have shown to be a major factor in recovering health after illness. These benefits add up to a good foundation for successful surgery, says Dr. Dale A. Matthews.

Dr. Matthews adds that there is one other benefit he believes may be the most fundamental of all: the training that religious people have in letting go. "In a sense, faith is like anesthesia," he says. "You're saying, 'I don't know what's going to happen, but I trust that everything is going to work out fine.' That's an important attitude to have when going into surgery. It's like getting on a plane; there's nothing you can do. It's all up to the pilot."

Best Seat in the House

By Bonnie Kidder

I almost didn't go to the class at church that night. With four children and a full-time teaching job, I had plenty to do. But my eleven-year-old son, Brady, was having surgery the next day. I hated to think of him alone in the operating room. I'd been praying for weeks, asking God to be with Brady and his doctors during surgery, but it didn't feel like enough.

Standing in the doorway of the church hall, I couldn't believe how many people showed up for this class. It looked like more than a hundred were seated at the tables scattered throughout the hall—but not a familiar face among them. No one I could ask to pray with me for Brady. I sat down at a table next to a dark-haired man, but the instructor immediately asked us to move. "Let's fill in all these vacant chairs up front," she said. The dark-haired man got up to look for another seat. I crossed the room to an empty chair. But just as I got there, someone else took it. I spotted another chair at the next table. The same thing happened again. And again. I did not come here for a game of musical chairs, I thought as I made a beeline for another chair. I flung myself into it and turned to see the same dark-haired man I'd seen earlier.

"We meet again," he said as the instructor stood to speak.

"Tonight I thought we'd talk about our lives outside of church," she said. "Everybody share with the people at your table how you work your faith into your daily life."

The dark-haired man said, "I'm an anesthesiologist. Before I put a patient under, I pray for him. I ask each patient if they'd like to pray, too. I used to be embarrassed about this."

"I think it's wonderful!" I interrupted. "My son is having surgery tomorrow. I'd feel so much better if his doctor could pray with him."

"Where is his surgery?" he asked.

I mentioned the hospital. "Dr. Duplechain is doing the operation."

"Then I can assure you that your son will be surrounded by prayer," he said, "because I'm the one scheduled to take him into the operating room."

In a room full of strangers, God had seated me—twice!—next to the one man who could pray with me tonight and with my son in the morning.

Remedies

PREPARING FOR THE BEST

WE DON'T HAVE TO have a lifetime of spiritual discipline behind us for prayer and faith to be helpful when preparing for surgery. To the contrary, doctors who spend lots of time in hospital wards say that surgery is an event that can summon a strong sense of spiritual connection for almost anyone, as the tough guy at Memorial Sloan Kettering found out.

"A lot of times, our spiritual lives remain mostly on an intellectual level," says Dr. Larsen. "It's only in times of suffering that we have this great opportunity to bring our intellectual understanding together with the reality of our physical and emotional lives."

Indeed, ministry professionals and doctors agree that surgery can be one of the greatest spiritual opportunities many of us will ever have. Here's how to weather surgery—major or minor—as peacefully and productively as possible.

Garner support. In addition to the prayers our friends and families offer on our behalf, we have a long list of prayer resources to draw on, says the Reverend Siang-Yang Tan, Ph.D., professor of psychology at Fuller Theological Seminary in Pasadena, California, and senior pastor of First Evangelical Church Glendale in Glendale, California. We can ask our pastors to visit us at home and in the hospital.

We can ask members of our churches to conduct small group prayer sessions, perhaps including praying for us while laying hands on us, as has been done since biblical times. We can take part in special healing services and prayer chains that can extend to a whole network of believers.

During Sunday services, many churches also offer individual prayer requests up before the entire congregation, Dr. Tan adds. If we're not concerned about privacy, we can have hundreds of people in our immediate community praying on our behalf.

We shouldn't let shyness prevent us from taking advantage of these resources. "Many patients feel they don't deserve this kind of attention," says the Reverend George Handzo, M.Div., B.C.C., vice president of health services research and quality at HealthCare Chaplaincy Network in New York, New York, and one of the world's foremost authorities on professional health-care chaplaincy, "but they do."

Call on church leaders. The New Testament describes a healing ceremony from the Book of James that Dr. Tan particularly recommends: "Are any among you sick? They should call for the elders of the church and have them pray over them, anointing them with oil in the name of the Lord. The prayer of faith will save the sick,

and the Lord will raise them up; and anyone who has committed sins will be forgiven" (James 5:14–15 NRSV). The "elders of the church" usually refers to church pastors and leaders who are spiritually mature Christians, says Dr. Tan, who feels the ceremony can appropriately take place either at a home or at church.

Call a counselor. We should also feel free to take advantage of the pastoral counseling services offered by the hospital when we get there, says Handzo. "It helps that someone cares enough to come pray with us," he says.

Sister Elaine's experience shows that we don't need to have a personal relationship with the person praying for us to get a tremendous boost from his or her prayer. Nor is it necessary for the prayers to be lengthy. Sister Elaine has received many letters about her prayers' profound impact on people's lives, all in the course of a hurried moment before the escorts took them to the operating room.

Pray for the surgeon. We should feel perfectly comfortable praying for our surgeons, for the attending doctors, the nurses, or for everyone on the hospital staff. Asking others to pray for them is a good idea, too. Sister Elaine makes a habit of doing this for the patients she prays with, and they seem to appreciate those prayers as much as, if not more than, the prayers that she says for the patients themselves. That's only logical, she says. Our primary need when we undergo surgery is for the person performing the procedure to do the job well.

Pray with your surgeon. Many patients want to go a step further and actually pray with their doctors. Not all doctors are comfortable with such requests. Many are, however. The growing body of research showing that prayer and faith can contribute to the success of surgery has made some doctors receptive to prayer, according to Dr. Tan. At the same time, we need to appreciate that our doctors may be hesitant to offer prayers because they don't want to force their beliefs on others. We can use our instincts to judge how our doctors are likely to respond, Dr. Tan says. Ultimately, it doesn't hurt to ask, and it could help—a lot.

Relax. We can enhance the sense of inner peace with which we enter the operating room by practicing deep breathing, meditation, and muscle-relaxation exercises, says Dr. Larsen. These will help speed recovery as well.

Dr. Larsen has a regimen of relaxation exercises he teaches to his patients who are experiencing chronic pain. These exercises, discussed in the chapter on Pain, are just as useful in preparing for surgery.

Relieve mental or emotional burdens. Unburdening ourselves of resentments toward others is a key element of preparing ourselves for surgery, Dr. Larsen believes. He also suggests trying to let go of regrets for losses we have suffered in the past.

The reason? The body remembers these losses and grudges as wounds, Dr. Larsen believes, and therefore is clenched defensively against new wounds, which can interfere with surgical healing.

We can't expect to solve years' worth of emotional problems in a few weeks or days, but we can take steps to temporarily put aside some of our baggage, Dr. Larsen says. He suggests that we off-load our problems onto someone we trust. This can consist in sharing burdens verbally or simply "assigning" the load symbolically and mentally to another person. "We need to let our hurts and resentments breathe by talking about them," he says. "It doesn't have to be in detail; just let off some of the steam." In this way, we can practice the forgiveness that the Bible encourages.

Pray for acceptance. It's important to understand that prayer will not make all our anxiety magically disappear. There's nothing wrong with our faith if we still feel somewhat nervous as the day of surgery nears, Dr. Tan says. Some nervousness in the face of surgery is perfectly normal and appropriate.

We can still pray for a sense of peace, he says. "We can be tense but, at the same time, have certain peace and hope and faith that will help us go through the surgery."

· HEALING WORDS ·

A Guiding Hand

Where can I go from your spirit? Or where can I flee from your presence?
If I ascend to heaven, you are there; if I make my bed in Sheol, you are there.
If I take the wings of the morning and settle at the farthest limits of the sea,
even there your hand shall lead me, and your right hand shall hold me fast.
If I say, "Surely the darkness shall cover me, and the light around me become night,"
even the darkness is not dark to you; the night is as bright as the day,
for darkness is as light to you."

—PSALM 139:7–12 NRSV

… The Lord is near. Do not worry about anything, but in everything by prayer
and supplication with thanksgiving let your requests be made known to God.

—PHILIPPIANS 4:5–6 NRSV

TERMINAL ILLNESS

This Thing Called Prayer

When our daughter Angelina turned seven, I wanted to encourage her to expand her prayer life — but how? All of a sudden I had an idea. "You know how you love to draw pictures?" I said. "Why don't you draw a picture in your mind to show God how you feel in your heart?"

It worked! When she wanted God to know how happy and thankful she was, Angelina told us she imagined her heart with wings, fluttering in our backyard like a butterfly. And when a close friend moved from the neighborhood, Angelina pictured herself on the playground, alone and sad. That was her way of asking for God's solace. Picture prayers have added a new and deeper dimension to Angelina's concept of what prayer really is.

But picture prayers aren't for children alone. While thinking about a friend who had a terminal illness, I did not know whether to ask God for healing or a peaceful passing for Susan. So I pictured her in my mind, imagining Jesus standing beside her bed with His hand on her shoulder to give her comfort. There were no words, yet I knew I had prayed. —KAREN BORAK

Fulfillment on the Final Journey

IF WE RECEIVE A terminal diagnosis or are told that a serious illness could lead to death, our emotions are understandably fragile and our feelings intense. Our outlooks will change dramatically, possibly many times, possibly from minute to minute.

Suddenly, life and all it entails will take on a different hue, an urgency, and possibly despair.

The disheartening diagnosis can come at any time. As Jesus' brother James wrote: "...you do not know what *will* happen tomorrow. For what *is* your life? It is even a vapor that appears for a little time and then vanishes away" (James 4:14 NKJV).

No, we do not know what will happen tomorrow. Neither do the doctors. Despite their best guesses, however, we can always hope.

HOLD ON TO HOPE

We are allowed to hope that somehow, miraculously, we will get better. Such miracles do happen. That's why it's important to try to hold on to hope. We also need to try to hold on to an appreciation for all that is beautiful and good in life, says Dr. James E. Miller, D. Min., president of Willowgreen

Inc., Fort Wayne, Indiana, clergyman, grief counselor, retreat and workshop facilitator, public speaker, and author of numerous books and resources used in hospices, hospitals, funeral homes, and counseling services.

We need to try hard because life-threatening illness and terminal disease may twist our perspectives and change our outlooks. If we have only a limited time to live—or there's a possibility we may not live long—should we spend it feeling sorry for ourselves, feeling miserable, concentrating on and cursing our illnesses? "A better approach is to do what we can to appreciate and find meaning in whatever time we have left," says Dr. Miller. "...I have set before you life and death," God says, "...therefore choose life" (Deuteronomy 30:19 NKJV).

That's not to say we won't feel sorry for ourselves, or that we won't feel angry at times and curse our fate. It's also not to say we won't feel excruciating pain or incredible waves of illness at times. But they need not be all we feel, says Dr. Miller.

We may also feel grateful that God gives us each new day. We may realize this could be our last chance in this life to experience the majesty of a sunrise or sunset;

or to experience the sensations of love, joy, awe, pleasure, and laughter; or to make a difference in someone else's life; or to let someone know how much they've meant to us. This may be the day we write the poem that will light up lives a hundred years from now. This may be a day in which we simply appreciate beauty in the world around us or hold a loved one's hand. This day is, to a great extent, what we make it.

Want to make a day better? Consider Philippians 4:8:

"…Whatever things are true, whatever things *are* noble, whatever things *are* just, whatever things *are* pure, whatever things *are* lovely, whatever things *are* of good report, if *there* is any virtue and if *there is* anything praiseworthy—meditate on these things" (NKJV).

We can do that despite our pain, despite our illnesses. We can do things we enjoy despite even disabling pain, says Margaret Caudill, M.D., Ph.D., author of *Managing Pain Before It Manages You.*

Yes, we should respect the stress of pain, says Dr. Caudill. But it's important to engage in pleasurable activities that can balance the stress, such as watching sunsets and sunrises, eating ice cream, enjoying our hobbies, and looking at the birds and flowers, she says.

"Move as much as possible, because that keeps the body from becoming weaker, which can increase dysfunction and increase the pain," Dr. Caudill says. Gentle stretching or yoga exercises might be just the right combination. And if we can't get out of bed, we can get a massage, listen to audio books, watch humorous or inspiring videos, and continue to live in the time we have.

FIND STRENGTH IN FAITH

Science proves that people with and without illnesses who attend church regularly live longer and fare better than those who do not, says Dr. Dale A. Matthews. He notes that well-researched studies show that seriously ill religious people require less pain medication and experience less death anxiety and depression than do the nonreligious.

The power of prayer itself seems evident in an unusual study in San Francisco, where approximately four hundred patients were divided into two groups. Roughly half the patients were prayed for by Christian prayer groups and half were not. Neither doctors nor patients knew which patients were being prayed for. Those praying only knew the patients' first names, diagnosis, and general condition. They were asked to pray daily specifically for rapid recovery and prevention of complications and death.

The prayer group required less medication, had fewer incidences of pneumonia, fewer cardiac arrests, and needed intravenous fluids or mechanical ventilation less frequently than those in the group that was not prayed for.

Of course, there was no way to control which patients also had friends and family praying for them, which is considered one of the inherent problems with the study. The results of the study have not been replicated to date; thus, its findings are not considered conclusively proven. But, says Dr. Matthews, how can it hurt to ask our churches and friends to pray for us?

For further proof that faith is good for us in times of trouble, Dr. Matthews says

· INSPIRING REFLECTIONS ·

May I Have This Dance?

BY NANCY ALBANESE

More than anything, Mom and Dad loved to slow-dance. When Mom was diagnosed with a terminal illness and moved into comfort care, it was hard to see her so far from his side. "I'll wait for him in heaven," she confided to me, "so we can dance through eternity together."

I loved to think of her back in Dad's arms, but I couldn't tell him what she'd said. I didn't want Dad to give up on his earthly life just yet. But Dad's health slipped after Mom died. Now he was in hospice care.

One evening, while my son, Kyle, and I visited, Dad started speaking to an empty corner of the room. "My, that's a nice outfit," he said.

"Who are you talking to, Granddad?" Kyle asked.

"Your grandmother," Dad said. He turned to Kyle. "Do I look nice?"

Kyle laughed. "You look great," he said. "Where are you going?"

"We're going dancing," Dad said. I'd never told him that was Mom's plan exactly. But now I know that they're back in each other's arms, dancing through eternity.

we can look at other studies that show that regular churchgoers and highly religious people are less likely to die following major surgeries, are less likely to develop debilitating diseases, and tend to live longer, in general.

Why do people of faith tend to face death with less fear and anxiety? "Most cultures, at most times, in most places in the world, believe and have believed that there is a life beyond this physical life," says Dr. Mel Lawrenz, minister-at-large at Elmbrook Church in Brookfield, Wisconsin, teaching in North America, Asia, Africa, and Latin America, and coauthor of six books, including *Life After Grief* and *Overcoming Grief and Trauma*. That belief, he says, gives believers hope. It tells them that "the end" is not "THE END," but rather a passage from this life to a more divine form of existence.

"If we believe that the only lives we have are the physical lives of our own bodies, then we will desperately cling to that," explains Dr. Lawrenz. The key here is to explore our faith, what it teaches us, and what we believe about life on "the other side." We will find comfort in that.

Remedies
HEALTHY WAYS TO APPROACH THE END OF LIFE

WHEN WE'RE TOLD we are dying, or that we may be, we can go through the process poorly or we can do it well. To do it as well as possible, consider these suggestions from Dr. Miller.

Insist upon dignity. We are more than our illnesses. But maybe it's all our doctors talk about. Sometimes even friends and relatives seem to want to discuss nothing else. "With some people, we feel completely depersonified," Dr. Miller says. We become simply a case, a disease, a patient, or another experiment. It's as though they have completely written off the rest of us. They see us only as sick bodies.

They're wrong, and they may need to be told so. After all, we have minds, hearts, and souls, besides bodies. Remember, we are and always have been someone. We do have personalities and interests and a uniqueness that has always set us apart from the rest of the world. This was true before we got sick. It is true now. We mustn't let anyone rob us of that.

Go ahead and feel. Our feelings will be many, unpredictable, and intense. We should feel whatever we feel. It's okay, says Dr. Miller. We have permission.

Expect sadness, pain, fear, confusion, shock, panic, anger, envy, emptiness, pressure, and more emotions during a time of terminal illness. Realize that we may also feel love, joy, and pride at times. We may have a jumble of feelings. They may arrive exactly when we wish they wouldn't. That's the way it is with feelings. So invite them in and let them be what they are. Don't pass judgment on them. They are neither good nor bad; they just are. They are proof that we are feeling people, that we care. We shouldn't let anyone tell us to subdue them or hide them, advises Dr. Miller.

Find a friend. We should look for someone we can really talk to, who won't judge us, correct us, or cut us off. Tell them of our confusion, of our emotions, of our fears and doubts, and so on. Or seek support groups or several friends with whom we feel comfortable venting. "There is not a firm rule of thumb about who those people should be or how many there should be," says Dr. Miller. "We're all different; we all seem to have different needs in that way. For some people, just having one other

person is all it takes. And others value having complete networks of people."

Let the tears flow. Tears provide powerful expressions. We should always feel free to cry or weep—as loud and long as we like. And if we feel like it, we might explore on paper what we are crying about, what we are feeling, and what we are remembering that is important to us, suggests Dr. Miller.

Make history. We could consider keeping a journal. Or "have someone help us write a journal," says Dr. Miller. "Sometimes people are too ill to do it themselves and it's a great help if someone else will write down what they tell them." What do we put in a journal? Record thoughts about life and death. Tell about things we've learned. Share our wisdom and wit. We can record stories about our families and their accomplishments, which others may have forgotten or may not know. We can talk about how our perspectives have changed now that we know we have reached the end of our lives. This can be a wonderful gift and memory for the family and friends we leave behind as well as a great spiritual exercise to experience.

Talk to God. Praying has always been considered an appropriate way to unburden and pour out our souls. We can always pray, or we can meditate or worship in whatever way we are comfortable. "As a mother comforts her child, so I will comfort you," promises God (Isaiah 66:13 NIV).

Create a list of wants and needs. Our lists can be continually developing because our needs and desires can change from day to day. But this way, when anyone says, "If you need anything, just let me know," we are prepared to respond with things that we really need. People feel better when they know their efforts are really helping and are needed and appreciated. People cannot know for certain everything we want and need until we tell them. Keeping a list is a great way to do this, says Dr. Miller.

Take care. We need to eat healthfully. We should take an active role in treatment decisions; that is, study, understand, and choose life-enhancing medications and therapies. We should get plenty of rest and do everything we reasonably can to give ourselves a fighting chance at survival and/or enjoying our final days, says Dr. Miller. We should pamper ourselves. Now. Because that's where we live.

Hope

Faith, hope, love—
Yes, love is greatest and always will be,
but without hope, how could I bear this day
when problems crowd around and illness rears its head?
—when death becomes the enemy to keep at bay?
—when financial burdens threaten to engulf?
—when life itself becomes a trying time?
But hope endures.
It comes and brings a smile upon my lips.
It brings assurance that this, too, shall pass—
this time that seems so long, so overwhelming,
so exhausting,
so constricting,
till most of what I see is only the Painful Now.
My hope is in You, Lord.
Your presence is within and around me,
in relatives and friends,
in nurses giving special care, beyond "duty,"
the doctor taking from his busy day the time to ask,
have I unanswered questions?
My pastor, others, praying with and for us.
I will not fear.
I do have hope.
Accepting all Your promises.
I am secure!
—Eileen M. Berger

WEIGHT MANAGEMENT

Weight Management the Old-Fashioned Way

I'd lost a hundred pounds in the past year. No pills, juice cleanses, or support groups. I'd done it on my own the old-fashioned way—dieting and exercise.

A year earlier my doctor had been shocked and dismayed at my blood work. "Gail, you're borderline diabetic and your cholesterol numbers are through the roof. You've got to lose weight and get in shape *now*."

"I don't have time," I said. "Dieting and exercise take planning, and I already have enough to plan with my daughter getting married next year."

"You'd better make time," she said. "It's not a matter of if, it's a matter of when you're going to have a heart attack." A heart attack? I was only fifty-five! Now I was shocked and dismayed. I had to live to see Erin walk down the aisle. To see my six-year-old granddaughter grow up.

I took a deep breath. "Okay. Just tell me what to do." My doctor recommended a fitness app that would count calories and track the food I ate and the exercise I did every day. I downloaded the app to my phone as soon as I got home. I entered my height, current weight, and goal weight, and it gave me the number of calories I could consume each day to meet my goal of losing a hundred pounds.

Its database had the nutritional information for all kinds of foods. There was even a pie chart (no pun intended!) breaking down the calories I ate by category—fat, protein, carbohydrates—so I could catch myself if I was overindulging.

I set about dieting the same way I'd furthered my career, with discipline and determination. I logged all my meals in the app. Keeping track made me aware of every single bite I took. I ate less and enjoyed it more. The weight came off.

Next, exercise. I'd joined the YMCA, but after three months I still hadn't gone. Then I got an e-mail from the Y offering five free sessions with a personal trainer. What did I have to lose, except some more weight? I met with a trainer named Jake. At first, our sessions were torture. My body hadn't moved like that in years. Every muscle ached.

Jake's positive attitude was like a magnet. I kept going back. And I began to see results. Eventually I hit my goal. As hard as losing the weight was, though, keeping it off was even harder. I found that I had to be even more determined and disciplined.

But taking charge of my body was worth it. My doctor was thrilled with my blood work. I could no longer be considered diabetic. My cholesterol was normal.

The day of my daughter's wedding came. For the first time in years, I wasn't self-conscious about getting my picture taken. It felt incredible to wear a sequined outfit in a regular size, not to have to suck my stomach in, to stand proudly beside my husband instead of behind him.

Then I took a fall and hurt my wrist on a rock, badly enough to warrant a visit to the emergency room. The doctor said not to put any pressure on the wrist for four to six weeks. No swimming, no biking, no machines at the gym. Angry and disappointed, I could think only about how I could keep off the weight I'd fought so hard to lose.

"Why aren't you looking out for me, Lord?" I asked. I gazed off across the river, waiting for a sign.

An enormous brown bird swooped into view. It reminded me of something. A verse we'd discussed recently in Bible study, Matthew 6:26: "Look at the birds of the air: they neither sow nor reap nor gather into barns, and yet your heavenly Father feeds them. Are you not of more value than they?"

If God saw to the needs of birds, surely I could trust him to take care of me, to provide what I needed when I needed it.

With a spring in my step, I headed for my car. That's when it hit me. I couldn't swim, bike, or lift weights, but I could walk.

And I did, every day until my wrist healed. In fact, two years later, walking is a key part of my workout regimen, and part of the reason I've been able to maintain my weight. So is realizing that I'm not doing it all on my own. —GAIL BINDEWALD

Ending Emotional Eating

WHEN SHE WAS THIRTY-FIVE, Carre Anderson of Westerville, Ohio, tried a new diet nearly every week. Most tried to change what she ate. Yet none forced her to confront her growing love affair with food. "I was constantly organizing, planning, and scheming to make sure I got enough to eat," said the stay-at-home mother of three.

Years of this behavior left Anderson frustrated and extremely overweight. Though only five feet five inches tall, Anderson tipped the scales at 217 pounds.

Finally, her failure to handle her eating drove her to her knees. "Lord," she prayed, "You know my needs, but I can't stand any more diets, and I want to lose weight." Soon after, her pastor's wife invited her to preview a video for a faith-based weight-loss study program the church was considering. The video said that weight loss was simply a matter of putting God first and using our internal controls over hunger and fullness to "rise above the magnetic pull of the refrigerator."

While watching the video, Anderson was transfixed. "The Bible verses convinced me that I was dealing with more than just an issue of controlling the food. I wanted the freedom only God could give me."

Anderson joined the church study group and adopted its principles. The result? In one year, she lost a hundred pounds. And not only did she keep the weight off; she went on to lead the church weight-loss group as well.

EATING FOR THE WRONG REASONS

At psychologytoday.com Lisa Firestone, Ph.D., writes: "Many of us eat for reasons other than to nourish our bodies or even to enjoy one of life's pleasures." She notes that

· PRACTICAL ADVICE ·

How to Help Someone You Love Lose Weight

Is someone you love trying to lose weight? Want to help? Here's how.

Encourage. Don't criticize. Be gentle. Anger, loneliness, and rejection can all be excuses to ditch a diet.

Pitch in. Take a salad or a tasty low-fat dessert to get-togethers so there's at least one healthy option on the table.

Out of sight, out of mind. Put away candy, cookies, and other tempting foods. Better yet, keep them out of the house.

Two's company. Next time you go for a jog or to the gym, invite a friend or loved one to join you.

Take off. Years ago only wealthy or famous people went to spas. These days spas are affordable. Look for camps, cruises, and getaways with nutritious meal choices (not all-you-can-eat buffets) and fun ways to stay fit (such as yoga, rock climbing, and dancing).

Celebrate. Ask everyone in the family to drop a dollar in a jar for each pound your loved one loses. Use the money for something special when he or she reaches a weight goal.

if we want to know why we eat too much, snack too often, eat unhealthy foods, or binge, we need to understand the emotions behind our eating behavior. Are we eating because we are angry, sad, confused, or frustrated? Are we eating because we feel rejected or abandoned? Or perhaps we are eating the way we do because our parents and families modeled unhealthy food habits for us for years, says Firestone, and we have not developed healthy eating habits of our own.

When we don't get the love, acceptance, and approval we need to fill our hearts, some of us try to fill it up with food. "The term that I use for this is emotional eating," says well-known Christian counselor Dwight Bain, founder of The LifeWorks Group, Inc., in Orlando, Florida. "Say something happens at work that makes me angry. If I think that there's nothing I can do about it, I'll go home and eat and eat and eat. I'm not eating out of hunger or any physical desire. I'm eating because I'm upset."

In fact, "A high percentage of eating disorders like anorexia, bulimia, and overeating have a direct correlation to biochemical depression," says Dr. Jacqueline Abbott. Biochemical depression occurs when we have a deficiency in the naturally occurring chemicals in the brain.

One of the most common symptoms of depression is unhealthy eating habits, says Dr. Abbott. "It could be not wanting to eat or, more likely, eating all the time in an attempt to help soothe or calm yourself," she says.

We soon discover, though, that overeating not only fails to satisfy our emotional hunger, but it leaves us worse off than when we started. Not only do we still wrestle with the issues that led us to eat poorly in the first place; we now struggle also with being overweight and with the health problems, social challenges, and low self-esteem that weight gain may produce.

Remedies

GETTING IT RIGHT

INSTEAD OF LOOKING to food to resolve emotional issues, we can recognize that eating will not resolve the root of our problems. We can seek spiritual or emotional

Wednesday Night Special

By Jackie Scott

Every week a bunch of us have dinner. Not at the food court or the local steak house, but at church. For a few nights, at least, everyone eats healthy. That can be a struggle, as my daughter, Diane, and I know a little better than most. But we found a solution.

Five years ago, I weighed two hundred and fifty pounds. Diane weighed more than three hundred and fifty. She couldn't even use a normal scale. When I met my husband, Brett, in college, I was a svelte 127. But I thought nothing of eating fast food every day. I never exercised and eventually my metabolism couldn't keep up with my appetite. Diane copied my eating and exercise habits. She'd just graduated from college heavier than I had ever been. How could she have a normal life?

That summer the three of us moved from Michigan to Kentucky for Brett's new job. Lexington was wonderful. We joined the church choir and made new friends. But my weight caused some embarrassing situations. Such as when I visited the DMV to get a Kentucky license.

"Age?" the woman asked. "Forty-seven," I replied. "Height?" "Five-two." "Weight?" I stared at the floor. "One-seventy-five," I mumbled. The woman gave me a look but didn't say anything. I knew what she was thinking: Yeah, right.

I told Brett what had happened. "Maybe now is the perfect time for all of us to go on a diet," Brett said. We'd tried all the fad diets before. We didn't need a diet; we needed a miracle.

In church that week I prayed, God, please help Diane and me lose weight. Please let it be different this time. Soon as I finished, a thought jumped into my head. What will you do differently this time? Why had all our diets failed? Why had we?

Reading everything I could find about losing weight, I learned that it all seemed to come down to two things: calories and exercise. We burn about eighteen hundred calories a day; those who eat fewer calories than they burn lose weight. Simple. Most diets cut too many calories. We're starving! That's not healthy. The key was making smart food choices.

Diane and I started cooking our own calorie-conscious meals. We studied nutrition labels on every package. We walked. Whenever one of us was tempted to eat an entire bag of chips, we had the other to keep us in line. We were losing weight slowly and steadily. Eventually, I'd lost almost a hundred pounds. Diane had lost nearly two hundred!

"You guys look great!" our choir buddy David told Brett one morning after church. Then he turned serious. "I wish I could lose weight. The doctor says I'm at risk for another stroke. I've been praying for a miracle." The same miracle I prayed for.

I called him up. "We're making dinner tonight," I said. "Why don't you and your wife join us?"

We started cooking and eating meals with David and his wife, Jackie. They lost weight. Soon, other people in the choir were asking, "Hey, can we join you guys, too?"

That's how our dinners got started. We cooked healthy meals and served them at church five days a week. Chicken simmered in a honey-mustard glaze. Creamy orzo pilaf and roasted asparagus. Soon, everyone got involved. Later we took over the regular dinners before Wednesday night services for the whole congregation. Not only were we eating better, but we were encouraging one another in good habits. Just what a church should do. The minister himself came up to thank me. "My wife lost sixty-five pounds! She's so happy, confident, full of energy. We're all eating healthier."

We also put together a cookbook so everyone could make healthy meals at home. Maybe some eating education will help people change their lives, as it did ours. Diane just got married to a wonderful guy. I don't need to fib about my weight anymore. God gave us good food to eat; we just have to make the right choices.

help for spiritual and emotional issues, and view eating as part of the way we care for ourselves physically. Separating the physical and emotional aspects of our lives will enable us to manage our weight and live healthy lives while we deal with emotional issues on an emotional level.

"We are talking about healthy eating and regular exercise as opposed to compulsive overeating," says Bain. "We are talking about freedom from food."

Here are some suggestions for putting food in its rightful place in our lives.

Keep a food diary. This will tell us when and why we're eating. "In other words, what was the motivation behind our eating?" says Bain. "Were we eating because we were hungry or because we were lonely? Because our bodies required fuel to go out and exercise or because we were bored, angry, or stressed out and just couldn't stop?"

Recognize and respond to physical hunger. Forget diet shakes, fat-loss pills, and fat-free products. Instead, learn to recognize the difference between when your emotions are seeking comfort through food and when your body is truly hungry. When we are really hungry, we feel it physically. When we grab a candy bar or sugary beverage because we want to feel happier or to calm down, that's emotional eating.

If we eat the right foods and eat them slowly, our bodies will let us know when they are full. When we are truly hungry, we should enjoy healthy, nourishing meals or snacks, and when we feel full, we should stop eating.

Slow down. Eating more slowly allows food time to hit our bloodstreams, which in turn allows our blood sugar levels to rise, triggering the brain's appetite center and producing a feeling of fullness so we don't overeat, says Elizabeth Lee Vliet, M.D., diplomat of the American Board of Psychiatry and Neurology, founder of Hormone Health Strategies medical practices in Tucson, Arizona, and Dallas, Texas, and founder and medical director of HER Place: Health Enhancement and Renewal for Women, Inc.

Taking smaller bites, chewing food thoroughly, drinking water or other beverages more frequently, and engaging in conversation during meals help us slow the pace of our eating.

Enjoy it. God created food to nourish and strengthen us, and we are to receive it with thanksgiving. When we sit down to a meal, we should savor and enjoy it, recognizing that it is intended to benefit us.

Take emotional pain to God. If we're having problems at work or in our relationships or if we're feeling emotional or spiritually barren, we shouldn't turn to snacks. We should turn to God instead of to food. Food can't solve these problems. God can.

Join a group. Many weight-loss programs and groups are available today. Getting involved in a weight-loss group can help improve our chances of success during those first crucial months, says Bain. "A lot of people who have struggled for years with weight problems wonder, can I do this? That's where resources and people in a weight-loss group can step in the gap early on and help out."

· PART 3 ·

Navigating Relationships

Arguing

Many years ago, my children got into a rut of picking on and arguing with each other. One would say something snarly, and the other would verbally poke back. Then "He started it!" and "I'm only doing what she does!" kicked in, and we were in a bad cycle. The longer it went on, the more uncontrollable it became.

One day I was in an upscale grocery store because the regular supermarket was out of something I needed. As I waited to check out, I noticed a tube-shaped container of small, fancy chocolates. Things like that were not in my budget, but I bought them anyway.

At home I gathered the children together and showed them my purchase. "Ooooh! Why did you buy those, Mama?" my older son asked.

"They're argument stoppers," I told them. They looked startled. "Do you want to try one?" They nodded, and I gave them each a piece of chocolate. It was sweet, and tasted very good.

"Here's the deal," I said. "Whoever stops an argument gets one." I paused, and then added drily, "Even if it's Mom."

Over the next few days, I used a different strategy to interrupt petulance in our home. Whenever a spat started I simply called out, "Who's going to stop this argument?" Miraculously, everyone went silent.

It didn't take long to get back to normal discourse. By the time we were out of chocolates, we had climbed out of our rut and returned to civil interaction. It helped to have a reminder that there is something far sweeter than a scathing rebuttal or tart comeback: treating others the way God asks. —Julia Attaway

How to Fight Fair

WHETHER WE ARE NATURALLY wired to confront others and do not mind disagreements or are born peacemakers who want to avoid conflict at all costs, we're all bound to find ourselves involved in an occasional argument.

As an argument becomes heated, the voice of reason in our heads that says, "DON'T SAY THAT!" can get overwhelmed by a raging emotion that says "SAY IT!" If we're not careful, what starts as a rational discussion can degenerate into verbal abuse and name-calling. "It's okay for people to express their views," says the Reverend Terry S. Wise, Ph.D., J.D., D.Min., professor, senior executive,

minister, consultant, conference speaker, and author of *Conflict Scenarios.* "What's not okay is the destructive way that we share them sometimes. There's room to disagree and do it in a manner that glorifies God."

It's hard to imagine people taking our remarks seriously when we're snarling, yapping, or being sarcastic. Such sniping and griping is not only unpleasant: research shows that frequent, nasty arguing permanently damages our relationships. Couples who learn to fight fair—because every marriage has conflict—seem to stay together longer. Those who don't often end up in divorce court.

Remedies
CURBING CONFLICTS

IF WE WANT TO improve our relationships and learn to handle arguments better, here's what to do.

Pick our battles. Even before a conflict erupts, we need to decide if the issue is really worth the time, energy, and stress on

our relationships. If not, we need to move on, says Dr. Wise.

If we choose to press the issue, we also need to know when it's smart to back off. "If you're really upset and I can hear it in your tone of voice and see it in your facial expression, I will suggest that we postpone our discussion until you're calm enough to listen," says Cheryl Cutrona, executive director of the Good Shepherd Mediation Program in Philadelphia.

Play a role. When we don't see eye-to-eye with someone and that causes controversy, it helps to visualize the conflict from the other person's perspective. "One way is to look at the conflict as if you're watching a play," says Cutrona. "Stage the conflict in your mind and cast yourself as the other person. Script each character's response to various words, phrases, and strategies. Choose what you predict will work best before you actually approach the other person."

Hold a family meeting. When the bickering involves a spouse or child, we can address the issue at a family summit, in an atmosphere of calm, honest sharing. "Sit around the kitchen table and talk about how each person was affected by the situation. Listen for feelings. Then brainstorm ways to handle similar situations differently in the future," says Cutrona.

Appreciate variety. All of us have different personalities, communication styles, even mannerisms—some more appealing than others. If we begin to see this as a strength, recognizing that others' abilities actually complement our weaknesses, we're likely to have fewer feuds. "Diversity is not something that divides or threatens us but should unite us to do the work that each of us is called to do," says Dr. Wise.

Give thanks. The next time we're tempted to yell at someone for not seeing things our way or for pointing out one of our shortcomings, we might want to thank that person for sharing a perspective we have yet to consider, says Dr. Wise. The Bible puts it this way: "Let the righteous strike me; *It shall be* a kindness. And let him rebuke me; *It shall be* as excellent oil; Let my head not refuse it" (Psalm 141:5 NKJV). Constructive criticism may sting, but it can also help us grow and learn to do better in the future. Offered in the right spirit, it can be a gift, and we would be wise to receive it and appreciate it.

Look in the mirror. Before we speak negatively to others concerning their flaws, it's always a good idea to take a long, hard look at our own. Jesus said, "Do not judge, or you too will be judged" (Matthew 7:1 NIV) and " . . . Why do you look at the speck in your brother's eye, but do not consider the plank in your own eye?" (Matthew 7:3 NKJV). "Rarely do we find this kind of self-examination prior to verbal outbursts," says Dr. Wise. If we did, we'd definitely have fewer of them.

Why Don't We?

BY LINDA HARRIS

When Bob and I started married life, we decided to set aside time every week to talk about our concerns—money, responsibilities, in-laws, whatever. It was a good plan, but we seemed to go at it the wrong way. More often than not, one of us became defensive or too emotional and we ended up arguing. Gradually we drifted away from our weekly talks.

One day I told a close friend how disappointed I was about this.

"Try a 'conversation jar,'" she said promptly.

"What's that?"

"Just a kind of holding place to give you both time to think and pray," she replied. "Keep an empty jar handy. When you or Bob think of something you'd like to talk over in your discussion time, write it on a piece of paper and drop it in the jar. Then each of you can read the notes in advance and know what's on the other one's mind. Nobody feels 'on the spot.' You can be more objective."

Such a simple idea! When Bob and I tried it, we found that this little grace period of preview and prayer before we talked made us more sensitive to each other's needs and feelings—and to God's intentions for our marriage.

HOW TO DEFUSE AN ARGUMENT

Some people are just spoiling for a fight, no matter how hard we try to avoid it (and sometimes we incite the fight). Here's what to do when an argument begins to escalate.

Avoid statements beginning with "you." Nothing accelerates verbal conflict quicker than accusing statements like "You make me so mad!" Or "You are the problem!" What makes matters worse is to include generalities such as "You always mess up the kitchen!" Or "You never pick up your socks!"

"'You' messages are the verbal equivalent of pointing your finger at somebody," says Dr. Wise. Generalities are even worse, since no one ever does anything *all* the time, even if we think that is the case. When tempted to engage in verbal finger-pointing or to generalize, we'd do well to remember the first part of Ephesians 4:15: "...speaking the truth in love..."

Trade "you" for "I." Using "I" statements allows us to speak nonconfrontationally and from the heart. For those reasons, "I" statements are difficult to challenge. For example: "I really get frustrated when I come home and find clothes all over the bedroom floor."

"When we teach this technique, a lot of people say, 'Look, if I have a problem and want to express it, I'm not going to pussyfoot around with these little 'I' messages. It isn't real,'" says Cutrona. "But we also talk about consequences and what happens if we don't express ourselves the right way. The other person becomes defensive and before you know it, the conflict escalates."

Avoid personal attacks. Name-calling is inappropriate in an argument between two mature people, but it's important to remember that we should not speak negatively about the other person's parents, spouse, and children, either. Sinking to that level can damage the foundation of the relationship, says Dr. Wise. We can and should ask for forgiveness after saying something hurtful, but verbal wounds, like all wounds, take time to heal and often leave scars. Remember: "A soft answer turns away wrath, But a harsh word stirs up anger. The tongue of the wise uses knowledge rightly, But the mouth of fools pours forth foolishness" (Proverbs 15:1–2 NKJV).

FINDING SOLUTIONS

Once we've learned to minimize the emotional intensity in a situation, we can try these tips to find solutions for our problems.

Stick to the issue. In an argument, we can be tempted to launch personal attacks against the other person, sometimes bringing up things that happened weeks, months, or even decades ago. "It's our natural tendency. Somebody brings up something that we don't want to talk about, so we say, 'Hey, what about when you did this?'" says Anne Bachle Fifer, J.D., attorney, Christian mediator, arbitrator, and mediation trainer in Grand Rapids, Michigan. It may be that an old issue needs to be addressed at some point. But if a conflict is raging, don't push it now. Instead, focus on the conflict at hand and resolve the issue causing trouble today.

Finding Rest
LETTING TIME PASS
BY MARCI ALBORGHETTI

But I say to you that if you are angry with a brother or sister, you will be liable to judgment; and if you insult a brother or sister, you will be liable to the council..." (Matthew 5:22 NRSV).

I remember the first real fight my husband and I had. I have no idea what it was about, but I remember feeling angry and upset because we'd never argued much before.

My voice was raised; Charlie's wasn't. It hardly ever is. But he was giving back as good as he got, until at one point he abruptly left the room. I sat in the living room, caught between crying over the fact that we were fighting and steaming over what we were arguing about. I waited for him to return, becoming more distressed even as I marshaled my arguments for the next volley. The house was utterly quiet. Finally I yelled into the silence, "So that's it? You think that just because you walk away, it's over?"

When Charlie didn't reply, I jumped up and charged down the hall. The bedroom door was closed. I barged in, drawing breath for my opening verbal assault, and found him—fast asleep. It was about 7:00 p.m. and still light outside. The blinds were drawn, and he was in bed, under the blankets, gently snoring. I couldn't believe it! I spent the next hour pacing and fuming. Was this how every dispute was going to end? With his falling asleep?

More often than not, the answer's been yes. Over the years I've come to appreciate this, because when he got up the next morning, he was no longer angry, and I'd had enough time to think about whether it was worth it to continue fighting. It wasn't. Usually, it isn't.

Father, thank You for reminding me that when I rest in Your steadfast love, I rob anger of its power.

Set some ground rules. If both people agree to talk out the matter causing trouble, setting ground rules for the discussion will help keep peace, says Cutrona. "For example, I might know you well enough to say, 'When you're angry, you yell and scream. I, on the other hand, become intimidated when someone yells at me. So for me to be able to negotiate equally with you, I'm going to need you to use a lower tone of voice.' And if you agree, then I might say, 'Is there anything you would like me to do to make you more comfortable in this situation?'"

Aim for win-win. Instead of seeking to win an argument for your own sake, consider a solution that will help both parties gain something: a win-win.

"That's what we should be aiming for, when both people are satisfied by the outcome," says Cutrona. How does win-win work? Simple: You get to pick the restaurant, and I get to pick the movie. If we're just going to the movies? You choose it this time, and I'll choose it next time.

Change your approach. One sure sign that the discussion is unproductive is when we repeat ourselves. "It's one of my rules as a mediator: When you hear yourself saying the same things or you can sense that you're covering the same ground, then it's time to stop and see if you can get to a different plane or see if you can discuss it at a different time," says Fifer.

In other words, instead of going around and around, try to approach the problem from a different angle or offer a solution.

See a mediator. Most people rarely run into an argument they can't resolve, but it does happen. While some people might be tempted to wash their hands of the whole affair, the Bible is clear: we're to seek reconciliation. "Leave your gift there in front of the altar. First go and be reconciled to them; then come and offer your gift" (Matthew 5:24 NIV). How? Seek the help of a third party, such as a pastor, an elder, a Christian counselor, or a trained mediator.

"Unfortunately, it may not be enough to just pray through it," says Dr. Wise. "The Lord has given Christian mediators the training and experience to help both parties come to a mutually satisfying solution that is both good for the relationship and glorifies the Lord as well."

You were taught, with regard to your former way of life, to put off your old self, which is being corrupted by its deceitful desires; to be made new in the attitude of your minds; and to put on the new self, created to be like God in true righteousness and holiness. Therefore each of you must put off falsehood and speak truthfully to your neighbor, for we are all members of one body. "In your anger do not sin": Do not let the sun go down while you are still angry, and do not give the devil a foothold. Anyone who has been stealing must steal no longer, but must work, doing something useful with their own hands, that they may have something to share with those in need. Do not let any unwholesome talk come out of your mouths, but only what is helpful for building others up according to their needs, that it may benefit those who listen. And do not grieve the Holy Spirit of God, with Whom you were sealed for the day of redemption. Get rid of all bitterness, rage and anger, brawling and slander, along with every form of malice. Be kind and compassionate to one another, forgiving each other, just as in Christ God forgave you.

—EPHESIANS 4:22–32 NIV

CHILDREN

From the Mouths of Babes

"It was a Fourth of July celebration and I was at a fireworks display with some colleagues of mine and their young daughter," says Iris Yob, Ed.D., professor emerita and contributing faculty member at the Richard W. Riley College of Education and Leadership at Walden University in Minneapolis, Minnesota, and author of *Keys to Teaching Children about God.* "When the first of the great explosions lit up the sky and we all oohed and aahed, the little girl asked no one in particular, 'Do you think that was high enough to touch God?' What ensued was a lively exploration of how God could be up above, looking over us and also down below, sitting in our midst, right there with us. The child was both the teacher and the student. She enriched us all, but only because we respected the wisdom of her question."

Guiding Them Toward Adulthood

IN A FAMILY, the primary job of children is to prepare to leave, and the primary job of parents is to equip them to do so.

From the first gulp of air to the first gulp of food, from the first classroom to the first apartment, childhood is about departure. And the road that leads our children toward independent lives is marked by joy and anger, by sharing and secrets, and by emotional changes and growth that alter our relationships fundamentally.

"The parent-child relationship is profoundly spiritual if for no other reason than that it must constantly deal with the reality of love and loss for both parties," said the late pastoral counselor Dr. John Boyle, founding director of the Lorene Replogle Counseling Center at Chicago's Fourth Presbyterian Church. "We may love our kids, and they us, but we lose them to adulthood, the world, and the inevitability of independence. Parenthood is a full-time job and one that changes as our children grow."

How can we maintain loving, supportive, nurturing relationships during this time together? How can we help our children develop the faith and character to make the right choices as they grow?

Remedies
HELPING CHILDREN REACH INDEPENDENCE

THE FIRST STEP IN letting children grow is letting them go. We must accept that our children will have goals and ambitions that don't always match ours, and we must give them the freedom to seek their own paths, says the Reverend Mahan Siler, S.T.D., M.Div., pastor and congregational consultant. "There's a tremendous danger in investing in our kids the obligation to satisfy our unmet needs and unfinished dreams, to become what we wanted but failed to become, to make the money or earn the degree or star in the big game," Siler says. "We need to allow them to become their own independent beings, even if that means questioning some of the values or ideals that we've tried to instill in them. Better that they try to be children of God than 'chips off the ol' block.'"

If their searching leads to difficult relationships and rebellion at home, we should remember that these, too, will likely pass. "The rebellious years, usually the adolescent years, represent turbulent times in the lives of our children. They are feeling a tremendous urge to separate from their families, if only symbolically," says Dr. Yob. "They're trying to discover their own identities, which may also include their own faith—a relationship with God on their own terms. We need to keep in mind that this is a transition time in their lives, not a permanent state of existence."

Letting children rebel, letting them venture out in order to define themselves, is a tremendous act of faith on the part of the parent, noted Dr. Boyle. "The father of the prodigal son (Luke 15:11–32) let that boy go irrespective of what he may have been feeling internally. All he had to lean on was faith in God to protect his boy and faith in himself as a parent who tried to instill in his son the knowledge that he would always be loved and could always come home. His effectiveness as a loving father should not be dismissed by his son's willingness to rebel but vindicated by his willingness to return."

So how does a family survive the rough spots, the inevitable times of conflict between parents and children?

Find comfort in others. Often when our children are in rebellion, our greatest anxiety comes from feeling alone in the struggle, says Siler. If we find ourselves questioning, we should search out other parents who are going or have gone through similar situations, he says. Not only can they relieve the guilt we feel when we assume our children are the only ones prone to rebellion, but their collective wisdom can help us learn how to deal with some of our children's independent ways. Our pastors can help us find other parents we can speak to, and perhaps even bring us together to share our common concerns.

Allow children their doubts. If our children rebel against their faith and we try to repress it, there is a good chance that the rebellion will deepen, if only as a matter of principle, says Dr. Yob. "It ceases to be an exploration of alternative values and becomes instead a tug-of-war between our desire to impose obedience and their demand to assert independence.

"The first order of business is to give children the space they need to question the assumptions we've taught. I remember a young girl who, when being put to bed by her grandmother, was asked, 'What do you want to say to Jesus tonight?' She answered, 'I don't want to say anything. I don't believe in Jesus anymore!' The grandmother, instead of resisting the girl's anger, responded by saying, 'All right, you just lie quietly while I pray,' and then proceeded to offer a prayer that acknowledged how angry and dismayed we can become at God when things upset us and God seems so far away. It was a brilliant way to affirm the girl's search for answers while at the same time allowing for God's presence to be acknowledged."

A Perfect Cast

By Mike Frezon

My fifteen-year-old son Andy and I perched on the rough wooden seats of the old blue motorboat. Although we didn't always see eye-to-eye, fishing was one thing we could agree about. "Here's where we caught the lunker," Andy said, staring into the murky depths.

"Yup," I said as we cast our lines.

There wasn't a lot of talking. Fishing is quiet time, and I was still stewing over the battle Andy and I had had that morning. It started out with a simple request: "You need to take out the trash, Andy."

"Sure, Dad," he said distractedly, scrolling through his phone.

"And what about all these clothes on the floor? Didn't I ask you to pick them up?"

He nodded and muttered, "In a minute." Which only reminded me of the many times I'd asked him to straighten up his room. "Now!" I barked, wondering if his headphones had damaged his hearing.

In the light of the setting sun I looked at Andy with his huge feet and the hint of stubble on his chin. *He's a good kid,* I told myself. If only he'd listen. Soon, he'd be out in the world. I was running out of chances to make much of a difference in his life. I pulled in my line, hooked some more bait, and recast. I picked my spot, flicked my wrist, and nodded with satisfaction. That was the kind of skill I'd learned from my dad, a perfect cast.

Andy slouched in the back of the boat, his baseball cap tugged low. He pulled in his line, pierced a wriggly shiner on his hook, and recast. And then I saw it: the flick of the wrist, the nod of satisfaction. A perfect cast.

I leaned back and watched my line. Yes, Lord, I thought. Sometimes we can make a difference without words. Andy put his feet up and shot me a grin. Two bobbers softly nodded in the waves.

Picture God as a parent. Because the biblical God is often presented with metaphors (judge, bridegroom, tender of the vineyard), we can try envisioning Him as a parent who shares many of the same frustrations and anxieties we feel about our children, says Dr. Yob. When we pray to the parent God, we can ask to feel His empathy for us, His love for our children, and His guidance through the storms all families ultimately weather.

HELPING CHILDREN BUILD FAITH

Our children's faith development parallels their physical development. It matures and reshapes itself as our children acquire deeper understanding of their places in the world. "Children are always inquisitive," says Dr. Yob. "It's just that over the years, the nature of their inquiry changes and becomes more complex, and we as parents must be adaptable to these changes." Dr. Yob offers these specific suggestions to help equip our children with the tools of prayer and spiritual curiosity.

Model prayerful behavior. Children are more apt to establish a prayer life when they are accustomed to seeing us pray.

Encourage freedom and creativity. When children begin to pray, we can quench their spontaneity if we give them a lot of instructions. Instead, we should encourage them to experience the freedom of simply talking to God in language that makes them comfortable.

Give them choices. Young children can be given choices about how they pray: "Do you want to pray out loud or quietly? Together with me or by yourself? What sort of things do you want to talk to God about? What are you angry or happy or sad about?" Older children can be granted more leeway in their spiritual lives: "When you come to church, would you like to sit with us or with your friends? Would you rather attend the youth service or the adult worship service?"

Respect their questions. Children's curiosity often opens up lots of questions, which parents should applaud and explore. "I remember a mother and her daughter walking by a nativity scene one Christmas season," recalls Dr. Yob. "The child asked her mother if the baby in the cradle was a boy baby or a girl baby. When the mother answered, 'It's a boy; Jesus came to Earth as a boy,' the dismayed daughter quickly responded with 'Well, that's no good, we need a girl in there, too!' It launched a delightfully rich discussion between them about the male and female qualities of God."

Our journey as parents may be trying. It may test our resolve and our patience. But we can take comfort in knowing we're not traveling alone. "For me, it all comes down to Philippians 2:1," said Dr. Boyle. "We are literally encouraged in Christ. Christ instills in us the courage to be parents by assuring us that God is the partner in our labors, and we encourage our children to believe that with God's help and our love, they are better able to find their rightful places in the world."

· HEALING WORDS ·

Coming of Age

The clock of life seems to turn so unexpectedly.

Is anyone ever truly ready?

And now the clock turns for us, my child and me.

Teenagers feel they are ready for anything, but that only makes me more apprehensive.

They lose the innocence of the child, but do not have the experience of age.

But coming of age is going beyond all that to the coming into God on their own.

To decide for themselves to rely on Him in good times and in bad.

Today my prayer is for the parent to let go and the new adult to hold on.

All to trust in God.

All to go in peace.

—JoAnn Barrett

ENEMIES

Here is an explicit blueprint for gracious living. Ideally, Christians should live graciously with other people, hold no bitterness, and not demonstrate malice or ill will. Christians should be kind, tenderhearted, and forgiving. Nevertheless, not all relationships go well and occasionally people will view us as their enemies for some reason (often based on a misunderstanding) or position themselves as our enemies. When this happens, we need to avoid developing feelings of resentment toward those people.

Instead of allowing ourselves to harbor resentment, we can use a spiritual action strategy: do something good for our enemies. This can be accomplished by speaking well of them and in every way being just as nice to them as they have been mean to us. If we fight back, hostility will deepen. But if we give them good for evil, they will be so baffled and curious about our attitudes toward them that in due time we may actually win them over. The greatest thing to do with an enemy is to make him or her a friend.

Breaking Down the Walls of Hate

THE TROUBLE SEEMED TO start over their father's health. Brother and sister had different ideas about the kind of care Dad should receive. When he finally died, leaving them each with an equal share of the family homestead, the conflict grew more intense: brother wanted to keep his half, sister wanted to sell. By the time they reached the counselor's office, they hadn't spoken anything but angry words to each other in four years.

"There was a lot of animosity," says Anne Bachle Fifer. "The estate was standing open. Taxes were overdue because they couldn't agree on who was going to pay them. It was a mess."

But during the first few sessions with the mediator, something amazing happened. With some coaching, the sister revealed that she had always resented that her brother got to work with their father while she had to hang around the house doing "women's work." Then her brother recalled that he would have rather stayed at the house anyway because the father made him feel like he never could do anything right. Finally, they both agreed that Dad had been pretty cantankerous and that maybe some of their more recent conflict had more to do with him than with each other.

On the fourth visit, the sister tearfully dropped a bombshell: she wanted to settle immediately, and she wanted to do it exactly the way her brother had suggested. Today, the two siblings share the farm equally and

amicably. "Ultimately, they realized that their sibling wasn't the enemy," says Fifer. "They discovered that they really had a common bond, much stronger than what divided them."

HOW HATE HURTS US

If the common bond with someone we know feels strained, or if we notice ourselves beginning to avoid the person, there's a good chance that we've developed an enemy. And whether it's a neighbor, business associate, friend, or even spouse—it's likely that anger and bitterness didn't develop overnight.

Like bricks added to a wall, things like forgiven insults that aren't forgiven, insensitivity, or outright betrayal build until there's such an emotional barrier that we can't bear to speak to or even look at the other person.

This kind of attitude makes us miserable and even has a negative impact on our relationships with other people and with God. When we have an enemy, we lose our peace and joy in life. Over time, such relational pain and stress can also damage our mental and physical health.

What Prayer Can Do

By Eric Youngberg

I loved my new job, but I couldn't stand my boss. He was popular with my colleagues, but the truth was he worked only while his supervisor was on the floor. His projects piled up on my desk. To make matters worse, he took credit for my ideas while blaming me for his mistakes.

One morning on the way to work, I popped a Bible cassette into the car stereo. "But I say unto you which hear, Love your enemies, do good to them which hate you, Bless them that curse you, and pray for them which despitefully use you," the narrator said, reading Luke 6:27, 28 (KJV). I pressed Rewind.

I gripped the wheel tighter, waiting to hear the words again. What am I going to do about my boss, God? He's driving me crazy, but I can't just quit. My wife and kids are counting on me.

As I played the tape a second time, Scripture sank in—and I got an idea. Instead of complaining about the boss, I would pray for him.

When I arrived at the office I concentrated on doing my best, without worrying about who received credit for the work. As the days passed, my boss didn't change, but gradually things got better. My shoulders didn't tighten when he swaggered in to toss me his files. I could relax and tackle any project because I didn't concentrate on the man's faults.

We still had our moments, but pretty soon I didn't think of him as my persecutor. And though prayer doesn't always make problems disappear, let me tell you the good news: Not only did the prayers change my perspective, but a month later my difficult boss was transferred.

Remedies
THE SCRIPTURAL SOLUTION

WHEN IT COMES TO dealing with others, especially our so-called enemies, the Bible is clear. As Jesus hung beaten and humiliated on the cross, He uttered these amazing, healing words: "Father, forgive them; for they know not what they do" (Luke 23:34 KJV). And they weren't just words: He expects us to follow His example.

But the Bible doesn't simply urge us to follow Jesus' example, it tells us how to do it. Here's a step-by-step guide to letting the healing begin.

Get the heart ready. One of the best ways to prepare for reconciliation is to make sure that we're not harboring resentment, unforgiveness, or similar sins in our lives, because those are the starting points of resentment, the building blocks of an adversarial relationship. We need to ask God how we have hurt others and choose to forgive the hurts they have caused us.

Go alone. There's probably no lonelier walk than the one to the front door of someone with whom we're angry. But there are good reasons we should take these steps alone. Among them, the Bible says:

"Moreover if your brother sins against you, go and tell him his fault between you and him alone. If he hears you, you have gained your brother" (Matthew 18:15 NKJV).

"Going in private is to our benefit," says Fifer. "We may not have the facts right or we might have misunderstood something, and that could be very embarrassing if we brought it up in front of a group of people and then found out that we're in error."

Go for it. We're face-to-face with someone we have been at odds with for a long time. If appropriate, and as hard as it may be, we should probably start the conversation by owning up to our share of the problem. James 5:16 says, "Confess *your* trespasses to one another, and pray for one another, that you may be healed" (NKJV).

Here's one possible introduction: "I just want to tell you that I'm troubled by the condition of our relationship and want to take responsibility for my part of the problem." From there, we need to apologize and ask forgiveness for specifics: "I'm sorry I gossiped about your personal problems.

How to Love the Unloving

By Bethanne Walker*

It became a sore point in my life, nagging at me daily. Never had I known a person who openly disliked me. And to make matters worse, this woman was my father's new wife.

They married a short time after Mother's death. My husband and I felt it was too soon, but Dad convinced us he was in love. So, with high expectations, we made a special effort to include her in our family.

Dad's life and home had been built on the open-arms policy, but all that soon changed. We were no longer welcome to drop by the small house. Even our phone calls were intercepted by an impatient "What do you want with him?"

As the months went by, I continued to make friendly overtures. After all, I had always tried to be a decent person. Why should someone simply not like me? But when we met in town, my stepmother would ignore my efforts at conversation, or even pretend she didn't see me.

Christmas arrived, and thinking it was a good time to set things right, I took a homemade mincemeat pie to my father and stepmother. I felt a little better after the short visit. Her cool reception had been warmed somewhat by Dad's enthusiastic thanks. But before I could get off the porch, I heard her say, "No, I don't like mincemeat pie! And you probably don't, either. You just won't tell her."

For the first time in my life I felt like throwing a pie in someone's face. But I knew anger wouldn't help—nor my tears of frustration. Because of either her jealousy or her plain unwillingness to share this man, we were being shoved out.

It hurt even more to watch my children. The two-year-old began to relate to the couple who babysat her as her grandparents. Our young son begged to see his "papa," who had lavished affection on him since birth. Our teenage daughter looked the other way when we passed their house, aching about something that I couldn't change—or even explain.

One morning I sat down as usual for devotions. The Bible verse for the day read, "For if ye love them which love you, what thank have ye? for sinners also love those that love them" (Luke 6:32 KJV). I bristled with indignation. Some people you just can't love! I insisted. But I knew, as God's child, that loving those who loved me was nothing special. That was easy. But to love someone who apparently hated me—that would be God's way.

How can I? I wondered. I glanced over more of the Scripture passage in front of me (Luke 6:27–28)—and the guidelines were right there!

1. "Love your enemies..." I began to try to look at my stepmother through God's eyes and focus on good qualities. "She treasures my dad," I told myself. "She takes excellent care of Mother's cat. She's a spotless housekeeper, and she nurses her invalid mother."

2. "...do good to them which hate you..." Since I couldn't approach my stepmother in person, I started sending a sunny card or tiny gift from time to time, signing myself "Someone who cares." I hoped this might lift her on a bad day.

3. "...pray for them which despitefully use you." This was tough! But it got easier each day. I prayed out loud, so I could hear my own voice asking God to bless her, to love her through me.

Today, from my practical earthly viewpoint, I can see no change in the situation. But by following these three steps, I am sometimes lifted to a higher view where I do see a gradual change—not in my stepmother, perhaps, but in me. I am learning a different kind of love, loving without expecting something in return. It's difficult to put into action and slow to grow. But staggering in its practical and spiritual potential.

Name has been changed.

Will you forgive me?" Or "I never should have taken your idea without giving you credit for it. I was greedy, and I'm sorry."

"The goal isn't to rebuke them, make them feel like a worm, or make yourself look like a saint. The goal is to restore that person to fellowship. And by confessing our mistakes, it opens the door for them to do that, too," says Fifer.

Be patient. "It's difficult when people feel passionate about how they have been wronged," explains Dr. Terry Wise. "You can't say, 'Okay, Mary, you have to forgive me—and do it right now.' Sometimes you have to let people vent. But in the end, when they feel like there's been some movement, and they open up and begin to see that they've been viewing the conflict from their own perspective and that you have some legitimate issues, too, then you're going to get restoration."

If the other person does not respond positively, at least you will know you took the right steps to initiate reconciliation.

Try again, and take a friend along. If our first attempt to mend a relationship fails, we should not lose hope. The Bible says to go back again and bring a friend (Matthew 18:16). "In this type of situation, we want a peacemaker, someone whom other people would look at and say, 'This

individual is out for our best interests—not for himself, not for his agenda—he really can be trusted,'" says Dr. Wise. "We need someone who is mutually respected and has a lot of wisdom and tact, someone who brings calm to the situation."

Seek help from the church community if needed. If the person with whom we're having trouble is a member of our church or a local congregation, we can pursue the next step: "And if he refuses to hear them, tell *it* to the church" (Matthew 18:17 NKJV). "Different churches implement this differently, but the goal is still restoration of the relationship," says Fifer.

Call in a mediator. Like with the brother and sister divided over the family farm, the situation may be serious enough that it's time to call in a professional mediator. "Skilled mediators can be of tremendous help because they're able to identify the key issues," says Dr. Wise. "One of the first things that I do with certain conflicts is let each side state its position and allow them to be antagonistic. We keep it in check so that they aren't trying to kill each other, but at the same time, it gets kind of ugly. Once they get a taste of the futility and know that they aren't going anywhere, they can begin to work on common interests and a mutually agreeable solution.

It's not just communicating, it's directed communication."

Take communion together. When a nasty, long-standing dispute has finally been laid to rest, why not celebrate? And what better way than eating a meal or taking communion together? Highly symbolic and often deeply moving, celebrating communion may just bury the problem forever. "Depending on the situation, this can really bring some closure to it," says Dr. Wise. "It's a powerful and vivid illustration of what the Christian life is all about."

· HEALING WORDS ·

Changing Enemies into Friends

Father, today as I struggled to forgive someone who has caused me great pain, I came upon this quote by Henry Wadsworth Longfellow: "If we could read the secret history of our enemies, we should find in each man's life sorrow and suffering enough to disarm all hostility." And in my head, O Lord, I accept the truth in that statement. Yet, without Your help, it is impossible to convince my bruised and battered heart. I need a clearer vision, God, so that I might look with eyes of love upon this person, whom I perceive to be my enemy. Please reveal to me the part that I have played in this experience, and give me the grace to face it honestly. Realizing that my thoughts and actions ripple out to affect all of humanity, I desire now to release this grievance from my life, knowing that my reward will come in the form of greater harmony for myself, and all of mankind.

—LIBBIE ADAMS

FRIENDSHIP

Finding Friendship with God

What's true of our friendships with one another is equally true of our sense of kinship with God. "An added dimension of the quality of human relationships is the fact that they can often help shape our faith, our relationship to God," observes Carole Bohn, Ed.D., associate professor of counseling psychology and religion at Boston University School of Theology.

Put another way, our understanding of God reflects our experiences of life. "If, for instance, we've raised our children in a home in which punishment was doled out liberally and love intermittently, chances are that they're not only going to find opening themselves to other human beings difficult, but will probably also develop an image of God as punitive and dictatorial," says Dr. Bohn. "If, however, they're raised in an atmosphere of love, acceptance, and protection, they're more likely to believe in a God Who will care for them unconditionally."

Building the Ties That Bind

WE EXIST IN A WORLD that depends on relationships, closeness, and camaraderie. Yet sometimes the structure breaks down. Sometimes we feel incapable of nurturing the kinds of friendships that offer us support, understanding, pleasure, and companionship. When that occurs, our lives are a bit emptier, our souls less fulfilled. Even our health can be affected.

In fact, in a five-year-long study of heart disease patients, those who had neither a friend nor a spouse were three times more likely to die than people involved in strong relationships, according to Redford B. Williams, M.D., professor and chief of behavioral medicine in the Psychiatry and Behavioral Sciences Department at Duke University Medical Center in Durham, North Carolina.

"The capacity to form relationships is critical to our survival as human beings," says Dr. Bohn. Even the Bible agrees: "It is not good that the man should be alone" (Genesis 2:18 RSV).

THE ROOT OF THE PROBLEM

So relationships are essential. We can accept that. Then why do some of us have such a hard time fostering them? One possibility is the way we were raised. "When we are born, we must form a relationship of trust with our mothers and then with the rest of the family members," says Dr. Bohn. "We need these people to care for us and sustain us, and very often the texture of these first relationships will go far in determining how well we will be able to form the other relationships we will need later in life."

In other words, trust begets trust. "When a child is cared for in a loving, nurturing, and supportive environment, that child is likely to have an easier time developing intimate relationships than one who is brought up in an atmosphere of indifference or neglect," says Dr. Bohn. "Just as relationships are vital to our existence, the quality of our earliest relationships is vital in shaping the quality of our later ones."

But our relationships with our parents aren't the only reason we may find forming connections difficult. Other life experiences may either help us or hinder us as we seek to build relationships with others. For example, moving from place to place during childhood and not being able to be part of a group for months or years at a time can have a negative impact on relationships later in life. Similarly, memories of being ostracized or criticized for physical characteristics, learning or developmental challenges, social awkwardness, or lack of athletic abilities during school years may linger into adulthood, making it hard to trust others and experience genuine friendship with them. Many factors in our early lives affect whether or not we can build and maintain healthy friendships later.

Some people are also naturally shy or reserved, or are happier than others spending time alone. For them, developing friendships is often a challenge, but it's one they can overcome.

Whatever the cause of any struggle to make and keep friends, we shouldn't feel embarrassed or ashamed if relationships don't come easily, says Dr. Bohn. Nor should we try to fix blame. Instead, we can fix the problem through steps like these.

Look inside. If we tend to avoid intimacy, we should explore what makes us uncomfortable by talking with a therapist or counselor or asking ourselves tough questions, such as "What am I afraid will happen if I allow myself to draw close to this particular person?" or conversely "What part of me am I protecting by steering clear of this person and why do I think I need to protect myself?" says Dr. Bohn. "By facing fears in this way, we may actually reduce their power over us" (to find a Christian counselor, contact the American Association of Christian Counselors at aacc.net).

Look for safe terrain. When we seek relationships, we should start with settings in which we feel secure, such as groups and organizations that reflect our values, beliefs, and interests. "We're far more likely to be open to the possibility of intimate relationships in such contexts," says Dr. Bohn. What types of places might be good? "Church fellowships, volunteer organizations, hiking clubs, and cultural societies. Even twelve-step meetings have proven a wonderful place for people to meet one another."

Take a first step. When we're ready to seek friends, we should start simply, perhaps smiling or saying hello to someone. Once we feel comfortable, we can engage in longer conversations and then perhaps ask someone to have coffee or share a meal. We can also start by asking questions of people, which is a great way to initiate verbal interaction and begin to get to know one another.

Accept rejection. Some people are more open to friendship for various reasons. Some people feel overwhelmed with personal or family issues and view friendships as a drain. Others are focused on hobbies or projects and happy to give their time and attention to those things. If someone does not want to be friends with us, we should resist the temptation to take the rejection personally, understand that it's about that person and not about us, and move on to someone else.

Isaac's servants dug in the valley and discovered a well of fresh water there. —Genesis 26:19 (NIV)

Sometimes my husband, Bill, and I like to banter ideas around. Most often we end up trading outrageous puns, but sometimes we surprise ourselves with deeper thoughts. Last week we were headed over New Market Gap in Virginia's Blue Ridge Mountains when one such moment occurred. Usually when we crest Massanutten Mountain and start down the east side, we have long vistas of Page Valley and the Blue Ridge winding southward. On this day, however, summer haze had removed any hint of hills or mountains.

"Hey, they took the mountains away!" I exclaimed. "Maybe someone had enough faith to speak to them as Jesus said in Matthew 21:21, and we'll have to go to the beach to find them!"

"Well, the valley is nice," Bill commented. "Maybe God wanted us to focus on it today."

"Now, why would that be?" I asked with a grin.

"Well," Bill said slowly as he eased the van down through the curves, "it's pretty in its own way...and it's where the people are."

Where the people are, I thought. Although mountaintop experiences are nice, it's in relationships where life becomes real, especially the life of growing faith. And relationships, like Bill's and mine, are not always mountaintop times. Yet in the valleys are the wells, the places of refreshing, like Isaac's.

As if finishing my train of thought, Bill added, "And if it weren't for the valleys, we couldn't appreciate the mountains."

Today, Lord, I need a well of fresh water in my relationship with _____ _____ (Fill in name). Clear the air and show us Your magnificent mountain-range plans for us. —ROBERTA ROGERS

NOURISHING RELATIONSHIPS

Once we enter the realm of relationships, we'll want to know how best to thrive in it, which, according to experts, means understanding that a relationship is a two-way street. If all we seek is our own gratification, we're likely to end up with nothing but our own frustration. To develop healthy relationships, we can try some of these tips.

Love ourselves. Good relationships start with solid foundations based on our own happiness and security. If we enter relationships in misery, then "we'll view our friends with jealousy, which breeds resentment and anger, which in turn destroys friendships," says Sharon Scott, founder of LifeSkills for Positive Living, based in McKinney, Texas. How can we be happy? By treating ourselves well, says Scott. "Take yourself out to dinner, or to horseback riding lessons, or to a movie. Treat yourself to what you enjoy. Be good to yourself. And write a journal entry each evening describing one thing you are pleased with about yourself that day," she suggests.

Love our neighbors. How much? As much as we love ourselves, says Father Kurt Stasiak, a Benedictine priest and professor emeritus of sacramental and liturgical theology at Saint Meinrad School of Theology in Saint Meinrad, Indiana. "The goal for Christians is not to give to others so that we receive something in return but to give as much as we possibly can because that is the right and good thing to do."

Use solitude. Time spent alone can prepare us for more enriching times with others. Solitude can be thought of as an extended form of prayer, says Dr. Bohn, because it offers us an opportunity to pause, reflect, give thanks, and understand our current needs so that we can be better friends when we then reengage with the people we care about.

Adds Dr. Miller, "In solitude, we want consciously not to do things—not watch television, not clean house, not do things that distract us. Simply think about what our lives look like at this very moment and why our friends are important to us."

FEEDING FRIENDSHIPS

In addition to a healthy attitude, relationships require a healthy dose of human effort. "They're a little like a house plant," says Scott. "They don't just jump up and tell us they need attention. But if we ignore them for too long, they wither, atrophy, and maybe even die."

Unfortunately, for many of us, activities and concerns compete for the time that

Y
ou have blessed the work of his hands..."—Job 1:10 (NIV).

It's been a full year since I took knitting lessons at our local yarn shop. I'd like to tell you that knitting came easily for me and that I was able to give my family handmade items for their birthdays. But the truth is, I haven't been the quickest learner. And I'm prone to sticking my knitting in the top of my closet for months at a time. But I am working on a project: a scarf, ice blue with charcoal flecks. Inch by painfully slow inch, I'd made my way through two skeins of yarn when disaster struck: a knot—huge, hairy, impossible! I had no idea what to do.

Then I thought of Sue. Sue has been knitting since she was seven years old and creates the most wonderful sweaters and shawls. When I took my snarled yarn to her, she gave one look at the mangled mess, smiled, and said, "I can fix this." I watched in awe as she did. In and out, over and back, again and again—slowly the tangles disappeared into smooth blue lines.

"I thought you'd cut it," I said as she handed my restored project back to me.

Sue shook her head. "Never cut what you can untie."

It was good advice; advice I could apply to some difficult relationships that had plagued me lately. Maybe with patience—and skill—these things, too, could be restored.

It was something to think about while I knit.

Keep me, Lord, from being in a hurry to sever what You would have me work through. —MARY LOU CARNEY

we would otherwise give to our relationships. There are jobs to be done, children to be raised, groceries to be purchased, and mortgages to be paid. "We're pulled in any number of directions, with any number of what we perceive as urgent issues that deserve our immediate attention," notes Scott, "and inevitably, relationships suffer." How can we correct this? Experts have some suggestions.

Work out a schedule. We can formally schedule time each month for people who are important to us but we wouldn't see otherwise, suggests Dr. Bohn. "My husband

and I have been part of a dinner group that has met monthly for twenty years. All the people in that group mean a great deal to us, but without the scheduled meeting, we'd probably never see half of them," she notes.

Make resolutions. "Resolve to limit both your own activities and those of your children," advises Scott, "so that you have time for friends. Don't overbook, or you'll spend all your time driving yourself and your children from one event to the next. For example, I limit myself to two volunteer activities for a duration of one year each. Most recently, that involved nursing-home visitations and volunteer work with homeless animals. I politely say no to other commitments."

Anticipate change. When one member of a relationship undergoes a life transition, such as marriage, divorce, or a new career, both members need to talk it through. "I remained single many years beyond my friends. When they began having babies, it really put us in different worlds," Scott recalls. "We didn't know what to talk about at first because our interests were now so different. We talked about it and agreed to maintain our friendships with visits, perhaps less frequent, yet filled with our old selves."

Pray with friends. We don't set out to pray solely to build relationships. But lifting our worries and concerns to God with another person forges a powerful bond, says Father Stasiak. "Prayer can hold people together," he says. Not only that, but praying with and for others is an act of service commanded by Scripture: "Carry each other's burdens, and in this way you will fulfill the law of Christ" (Galatians 6:2 NIV).

· HEALING WORDS ·

For Special People

Lord, I want to pause today and thank You for the blessing of people in my life who are willing to be vulnerable and open, who are willing to accept me as I am, who are willing to question me when I am wrong and gently point me back to You.
Thank You for allowing them to love me through Your power.
—DOLPHUS WEARY

MARITAL PROBLEMS

Marriage in Crisis

Like storms, troubled marriages send their dark clouds before them. Judging from the disturbing trend evident in the Guideposts mail, an alarmingly increasing percentage of married couples wait until the storm strikes before making efforts to protect their homes. A storm-damaged house can easily be repaired; a troubled marriage, damaged by the storms of daily life, can be irreparable.

Guideposts editors researched the factors beneath the problems in marriage and realized the problems—sex, alcoholism, infidelity or adultery, money, in-laws, children, broken trust, religion, boredom, open battle—were merely symptoms of something more serious.

Staff members of the American Foundation of Religion and Psychiatry gave us the benefits of their knowledge and experience. Religious leaders, judges, lawyers, marriage counselors, and physicians shared with us their insight and wisdom acquired over many years.

As our research progressed, two underlying factors in marital crises became obvious simply by their prevalence. First was the inability of the husband and wife to communicate with each other honestly and with love early enough in the gathering storm. Second was the immaturity of the husband or wife or both—men and women who rushed into marriage not with outstretched arms, accepting adult responsibilities, but with outstretched hands, like greedy children expecting gifts.

The passing months also brought to light other marital factors:

1. A happy, meaningful married life requires self-denial and sacrifice by both parties.
2. Love is the most confused and misused word in any language. Love in marriage is elusive and ever-changing, easy to lose but almost always retrievable.
3. When God's role in married life is willfully or neglectfully disregarded, the marriage is being built on thunderclouds that can break into fatal storms when the slightest change in human temperatures occurs.

RECOVERING THE MAGIC

Pastors know what plagues and dooms marriages. They counsel couples all the time. The two biggest problems are lack of effective communication skills and lack of commitment to drive the relationship through the inevitable rough and tough terrain.

"Marriage breakdowns don't occur because of 'differences'; they happen because a couple can't seem to handle those differences. Relationships don't cause conflicts; they bring out whatever incompleteness we have in us anyway," explains the Reverend Rowland Croucher, D.Min., founding director of John Mark Ministries, serving pastors, ex-pastors, church leaders, and their spouses throughout Australia and elsewhere.

Anyone who has experienced marriage knows that living "happily ever after" requires work. It requires sensitive, dignified discussion of touchy issues. It requires a willingness to resolve conflict amicably. And it requires a solid commitment to do both by both partners.

If those things were easy and automatic, more than half of all marriages would not end in divorce, notes Michael J. McManus, president/founder of Marriage Savers in Potomac, Maryland, syndicated columnist, and author of

> *Marriage Savers.* Fortunately, many communities and churches offer programs teaching constructive communication for couples, ways to resolve conflicts amicably and fairly, says McManus, whose nonprofit organization has helped establish programs in more than one hundred metropolitan areas in America.
>
> —Editors of Guideposts

Researching Reasons

THE REASONS CITED FOR divorce are legion and vary from relationship to relationship, everything from alcoholism and unfaithfulness to unrealistic expectations about marriage to falling out of love. But research suggests that miscommunication and, more specifically, poor conflict-resolution skills are probably at the root of most failed marriages. Whether characterized by sniping and griping that slowly erode respect or explosive episodes that cripple intimacy, these are the acts that can inflict the deepest, hardest-to-heal wounds.

"Very vicious, very painful cycles get started when a partner says something and the other person gets hurt. And when they're hurt, they often respond by some sort of automatic counterattack," says Dr. William Richardson, Ph.D., professor of marriage and family therapy and clinical director of the Center for Marriage and Family Therapy

at Reformed Theological Seminary in Jackson, Mississippi. "When this reactive, offensive-defensive communication spins out of control for years, the relationship becomes such a painful place to be that the partners naturally withdraw from each other."

For some, the loneliness and pain caused by such estrangement is the gateway to an affair. Others simply walk away. And though they may look back from time to time, they simply never come back. The Bible, of course, has plenty to say about proper communication. "Those who consider themselves religious and yet do not keep a tight rein on their tongues deceive themselves, and their religion is worthless" (James 1:26 NIV).

GOOD LOVE GONE BAD

Of all the damage caused by marital infidelity, it's no surprise that among the most painful is the loss of trust. It may also be the hardest to repair. But the hard work of restoring a marriage must begin with a careful and honest examination of what went wrong. And often, the problems and issues go beyond simple sexual attraction.

Frequent, angry fighting, for example, can destroy intimacy between a couple, forcing a spouse to first withdraw and then search elsewhere, says Dr. Richardson. Also, sexual addiction and lust put us at risk for one-night stands.

As we get older, major life and career changes are more likely to damage our marital foundations and open the door to affairs, according to Leslie Parrott, Ph.D. and Les Parrott, Ph.D., cofounders of the Center for Relationship Development at Seattle Pacific University in Washington, and authors of *Saving Your Marriage before It Starts.*

For example, a woman who joins the work world after years of devoted—and often unrecognized—care for her family might find the admiration of a male colleague seductive. And a man in midlife who may not get many pats on the back at home might feel ripe for an indiscretion if the office secretary laughs at his jokes and generally makes him feel attractive.

In fact, the deficits created in a marriage by familiarity and neglect are hard to overstate. "When counseling, we'll often ask a couple, 'If you could change something about your marriage, what would it be?' In most cases, the man will say, 'I wish my wife were more concerned about sex,'" says Rob Parsons, founder of Care for the Family based in Cardiff, Wales. "When we turn to the woman, she will often say, 'Affection. I want him to listen to me when I talk to him. I wish sometimes he would touch me in a nonsexual way. I wish when we're shopping he would sometimes hold my hand rather than walking a mile ahead of me.'"

When a couple is committed to their marriage with a special kind of dedication called agape love—the highest form of love described in the Bible—research shows, two amazing things happen: they spend less time seriously thinking about what it would be like to be with somebody else, and when they're attracted to someone else, they perceive it as a threat to their marriage, says Scott Stanley, Ph.D., research professor in psychology and codirector of the Center for Marital and Family Studies at the University of Denver, Colorado, and coauthor of *A Lasting Promise* and *The Heart of Commitment.* "Agape love doesn't mean that they're always happy, but they are dedicated to Christ-like unconditional

This Thing Called Prayer

BY HAZEL MCCAFFERY

Before we were married, Phil and I were like most couples in love—we hoped we'd never fight or let ourselves fall into the trap of petty quarreling. Right from the start as newlyweds we committed ourselves to praying together. We promised that we would hold hands and say the Lord's Prayer together every day.

Of course, as in many marriages, there have been times of worry and anger, when prayer was difficult, or when one of us was stubborn and wanted nothing so much as to go to bed without even a "good night." But each night, Phil or I would reach for the other's hand. "Better say our prayers now..."

It's not easy to go to sleep angry at somebody if the two of you are holding hands and praying to the Lord.

At least that's what Phil and I have found to be true during the fifty years we've been married!

love that keeps on giving, even when it's not too easy."

When confronted with even the possibility of an affair, a person with this type of commitment starts looking more at the negatives than the positives in the new person, to protect the commitment to his spouse. What's more, folks with this type of commitment seem to be less likely to neglect their mates, says Dr. Stanley.

Dr. Stanley notes, "In the Bible, the often-quoted passage on divorce says, '...guard yourself in your spirit, and do not break faith with the wife of your youth'" (Malachi 2:15 AMP). "The word *guard* in Hebrew literally means 'hedge.' And they're not talking about wimpy American hedges. They're talking about hedges that work like the walls of a fort. God is saying that part of guarding our commitment in marriage is tending that hedge. And that starts with having a forgiving spirit toward our spouses, while maintaining it means keeping our thought lives—that seemingly secret realm where we ponder, mull, consider, entertain, and fantasize—as pure as possible."

Remedies
WE HAVE TO TALK

GOOD COMMUNICATION IS CRUCIAL for a healthy marriage. So, regularly, we should assess how we talk to our spouses—what we look like when we speak, how we act, the tone we use, and more, says the Reverend Steve Carr, senior pastor of Calvary Chapel in Arroyo Grande, California and author of *Married and How to Stay That Way.* Here is some of Carr's advice.

Be proactive. Waiting patiently doesn't mean sitting on our hands. In the meantime, we should be working with a pastor, a small support group, or a counselor to resolve the personal problems that we contributed to the relationship's demise. Not only that, but we can also enlist our spouse in our reconciliation efforts. "We need one another," says Dr. Richardson. "If there are two parties who are willing to say, 'Yes, I have done these things that have hurt my spouse and our relationship,' and if they are willing to say, 'I am willing to do things to contribute to the reconciliation and growth of this relationship,' relationships can be saved."

Assess the attitude. Consider not what we say so much as how we say it. Are we being sarcastic, arrogant, superior, or indignant? Are we resentful, bitter, or unforgiving? Are we indifferent or apathetic? Are we harsh? Are we deceitful? If the answer to any of these is yes, an attitude adjustment may be in order.

Watch the words: King Solomon said, "A soft answer turns away wrath, but a harsh word stirs up anger" (Proverbs 15:1 NRSV). "Harsh, condemning words are incredibly destructive," says Pastor Carr. We need to think of how we feel when someone condemns or belittles us and then remember Apostle Paul's instruction to husbands (though it applies to both spouses): "…love your wives and never treat them harshly" (Colossians 3:19 NRSV).

Also, we must avoid using exaggeration, particularly the kind of exaggeration found in accusations like "You always do this" or "You never do what I ask." Steve Carr says, "Always, never, or every time are like gasoline on the fire of an argument."

Stick to the present. Don't bring up past failures or grievances. "That kind of ammunition should never be used to win an argument," says Carr. "If you have forgiven your spouse for a past failure, then it should be off-limits."

Hold the tongue. Interrupting and finishing our spouses' sentences suggests that we are not listening. It's impolite and fuels anger. "…be swift to hear, slow to speak, slow to wrath" (James 1:19 KJV).

Curb the anger. Some people learn to use anger to manipulate their spouses and control conversations. "They know that the spouse will cower and retreat once the rage appears," says Pastor Carr. This tends to discourage and destroy intimate, direct, and honest communication and, thus, relationships.

Uncontrolled anger is equally noxious and needs to be curbed. "No one wants to communicate the deepest things of the heart with someone who rages out of control in an angry fit," says Carr. If we cannot control our anger, we should seek counseling, he urges.

Confess, but not for just confession's sake. "A confession should be designed to care for the person receiving it, not to just unburden the person giving it," says Dr. Les Parrott. "And it's really hard sometimes for the person to not just confess to unburden himself. More than the words, we should check the motivation of our hearts."

Call in experienced counsel. Coming clean with our spouses is important, but in some cases, it may not be wise to attempt it alone. "Often, in the heat of the exchange, the couple doesn't hear each other and a priest or pastor or counselor can act as a calming force, a diffusing force, to slow the conversation down, if need be, and to reiterate what has been said. It's my experience that this type of intervention can make things safer and can diffuse what could erupt into a bad situation," says Dr. Mark Ginter, theologian, consulting ethicist, Catholic education administrator, evangelization coach, parish missionary, motivational speaker, researcher, and author.

No matter what counsel we choose, we need to make sure that the person has experience working with couples who are overcoming conflicts. "You don't want someone who just says, 'You've done wrong; let's just pray about it,' and that's it. Praying

Introducing prayer to a prayerless marriage can seem awkward, but there are some simple steps we can take. Daily prayer is the key to a successful marital prayer life. Here are some ways to incorporate prayer into marriage.

Keep it short. When beginning prayer together, we need to keep the entire daily sessions to no more than five minutes, and select a daily agreed-upon time, whatever best fits the schedule.

Pray back and forth. Both spouses should have a chance to pray. Sometimes, as this happens, each one's prayers will build on the other's, creating a fuller picture of our hopes for our marriage.

Pray for personal needs, for mates, and for the marriage. After praying for our personal needs, we need to thank God for our mates and for the strengths they have that we admire. We can pray for tender hearts, forgiveness, and growth in the relationship. If time allows, it's always also a good idea to pray for our children, extended families, and people with particular challenges or needs.

Remember the Bible's instruction. "Husbands, love your wives, as Christ loved the church and gave himself up for her, that he might sanctify her, having cleansed her by the washing of water with the word, so that he might present the church to himself in splendor, without spot or wrinkle or any such thing, that she might be holy and without blemish" (Ephesians 5:25–27 ESV).

is important, but there's other work that needs to be done," says Dr. Stanley.

Be patient. Just because we declare our intentions to reconcile doesn't mean that our spouses will readily admit the error of their ways and come running back. "Sometimes the spouse will say no and then see some hope in the other person and begin to say yes. But that can take time—a long time of waiting," says Dr. Richardson. "You're trying to demonstrate that you're genuine."

COMMUNICATING LOVE

If we commit with our spouses to keep our marriages alive and healthy, not just during the easy times but also during the tense and tough times, then we have taken giant steps, says McManus.

Marriage, says Dr. Croucher, "is a commitment of one imperfect person to another imperfect person. The person to whom we are relating is made in God's image. He or she is like God, so we should treat our spouse with courtesy and dignity even when we don't feel like it."

We have to love our partners even when they are mad, when they frown at us, and when they hold us in contempt. Love requires a spiritual commitment, says McManus. In fact, he says, 1 Corinthians defines love as requiring an act of will in fifteen different ways: "Love is patient, love is kind. It does not envy, it does not boast, it is not proud. It does not dishonor others, it is not self-seeking, it is not easily angered, it keeps no record of wrongs. Love does not delight in evil but rejoices with the truth. It always protects, always trusts, always hopes, always perseveres" (1 Corinthians 13:4–7 NIV).

For healthy marriages, couples must assure each other that divorce is not an option, says McManus.

"Too many times, partners do the opposite and in arguments threaten to leave or to divorce," says Pastor Carr. "When people are threatening to destroy the marriage, they can never build it because the other partner doesn't have any security. In the Bible, God says, 'I will never leave you or forsake you' (Hebrews 13:5 NRSV). How much more we need to make that commitment to each other."

We must communicate commitment, love, and respect every day to strengthen and build our marriages, recommends McManus.

Pray together. This doesn't have to be a long, dreaded ritual. Five minutes is a good place to begin, says Carr. Just do it. Daily. (See "Inspiring Reflection" and "Practical Advice" sections in this chapter for encouragement and direction on how to pray together.)

Offer loving acceptance and forgiveness. Acceptance is not something that our spouses should have to earn from us. "I love my wife before she changes or whether she changes or not," explains Dr. Croucher. "Nothing is unforgivable. Nothing will ever stop me from loving her. She can utterly count on that. A good marriage is the union of two good forgivers. It is three parts love and seven parts forgiveness."

Expect and encourage growth and change. A healthy marriage, says Dr. Croucher, includes "a commitment to grow, to become the persons that God intends us to be. Growing couples set growth goals: to read a good book and discuss it, to go away every year on a retreat, to pray together, or to take a course together." Besides doing things together, spouses should help each other grow and develop in their own unique ways.

Be brutally honest. But only about ourselves. We need to acknowledge our faults, mistakes, and failures with our partners. We should apologize for hurtful behaviors and actions. We should tell our mates that we "truly want to change in these areas," says Carr. Communication will leap forward.

Relinquish control. We shouldn't tell our spouses what to wear, how to wear their hair, or what to do. Discuss things, yes. Offer opinions, sure. But our partners must be allowed free choice and personal freedom, says Carr.

Put spouses first. We should keep our spouses as the priority in the marriage in every action that we take. In everything we say and in everything we do, we must demonstrate that the person to whom we are committed is really the priority," says Carr.

Our spouses and their needs, concerns, and plans must always come first, ahead of our parents, children, in-laws, neighbors, and jobs. "The marriage and the time with one another must always be top priority, and that must be clear," says Carr.

Communicating that communicates love, and a loving, caring commitment.

Start small and deliver. For those of us who cheated, it could take months or years of promise-keeping and persistent behavior before our spouses truly trust us again. In other words, flowers or cooking our spouses' favorite meals every week are nice, but coming home on time, calling when we say we will, and being truthful are probably more important. "It comes back to the issue of empathy—trying to understand what our partners need right now and gently letting our partners know that we value the relationship," says Dr. Les Parrott.

Marital Conflict

Prince of Peace,

Your Word says that in marriage

the two become one flesh.

But today we feel

more two than one.

I'm tired of division,

of the clash of wills,

of combat.

Bring reconciliation to

our fractured relationship.

Plant seeds of healing in us

and nurture their growth.

Enable us to know a love that

is stronger than

we've ever known before.

Thank you for

marrying us to each other...

Thank you most of all

for loving us.

—NORM NELSON, FROM *"THANK YOU MOST OF ALL FOR LOVING ME"*

· PART 4 ·

Finding Support for Emotional Challenges

ANGER

> **· FAITH BUILDER ·**
>
> Where do we turn for words and feelings that express our deepest negative emotions without cursing or doing something worse? I suggest we read the Psalms. They capture raw, honest, and vivid feelings of living in the real world as they integrate praise, pleading, prayer, and even a desire to see others harmed—feelings we all have felt, but seek to refrain from acting on.
>
> Human emotions need to be expressed, but how we express them matters.
> —Pablo Diaz

How to Tame the Beast

Everyone knows that good people aren't supposed to get angry, right? At least that's what many of us believe. We think we are supposed to stuff our negative feelings and keep our mouths shut when we are angry. But when we look to the Bible, we see a different approach toward dealing with our anger.

There are 455 references to anger in the Old Testament, and of those, 375 refer to God's anger. "Anger is clearly not a sin," says Dr. Gary J. Oliver, executive director of the Center for Healthy Relationships at John Brown University and coauthor of *When Anger Hits Home.* "If it is, then God is in serious trouble." In fact, the Bible records several incidents when Jesus himself was angry.

Yes, we are allowed, even expected, to be angry sometimes. Righteous indignation, among other things, eventually helped free the slaves, defeat Hitler, and further the civil rights movement. It's how we handle our anger—or don't handle it—that gets us into physical and emotional trouble. "Moral outrage can be a powerful, positive force, but it has to be controlled," says Pastor David Roper, cofounder of Idaho Mountain Ministries.

So what's the difference between healthy and destructive anger? The simple answer is that anytime we think about harming someone else—with our tongues or otherwise—we've probably crossed the line, says Pastor Roper.

THE DARK SIDE OF ANGER

Though we think of anger as by far the most powerful of human emotions, it's actually a secondary emotion. "Underneath anger is either fear, hurt, or frustration," says Dr. Oliver. "We need to understand what our anger is really about, or we won't be expressing the core emotion."

We also need to understand how damaging anger can be and how it can take years off our lives. Anger has been linked to a long list of health problems ranging from depression, high blood pressure, heart disease, arthritis, and stress to drug and alcohol abuse and obesity.

Not only that, but women who suppress anger have been found to have higher breast cancer rates and unhappier marriages and are two times more likely to die prematurely than those who directly expressed their anger. Angry men don't get off any easier: they're twice as likely to die from cardiovascular disease.

That's not the only way that anger kills. After all, most murders aren't "premeditated acts of violence, but crimes of passion committed in moments of uncontrolled frenzy," says Pastor Roper. "Although we probably move in incremental, escalating steps, when anger intensifies, it can become uncontrolled rage." The Bible urges a different way of dealing with anger: "My dear brothers and sisters, take note of this: Everyone should be quick to listen, slow to speak and slow to become angry, because human anger does not produce the righteousness that God desires" (James 1:19–20 NIV).

Dealing with a Teenage Meltdown

By Julia Attaway

My almost-a-teenager had a rough afternoon and spoke angry words he should not have uttered. Afterward, when I felt peace returning, I commented, "You said some pretty unkind things earlier."

"I was angry," he replied, with a curt nod.

"Angry enough to say things that hurt others," I countered.

"I can't help what I say when I'm mad!" he protested.

I let that statement hang in the air for a few moments so he could hear it before responding, quietly, "I'm not sure that's true."

"Well, it's not my fault!" he blustered.

"Hmmm," I said, and waited. Eventually, I said, "I'd bet that even when you are very angry, there is still a part of you that is aware of what you are doing."

He nodded warily. "I'm glad you know that," I continued, "for the part of your brain that sees it is the part that can prevent you from saying the nasty stuff. If you want to control it, that is."

"Sometimes I don't want to!" He scowled. "Sometimes I'm hurt and just want to hurt others!"

Right. We've all been there. And still...

"Buddy," I said, gently, "if you can observe yourself wanting to hurt others, you're not completely out of control. You can rein it in. I know that about you, because I know it about myself. Not that I always do stop it, but if I'm honest with myself, I know I can."

He nodded, reluctantly. There was a long, long silence. And then, "I'm sorry, Mama," my son said.

Remedies
QUENCHING THE FURY

THERE'S PLENTY OF SOUND advice on how to handle anger effectively and, as a result, lives the mandate of Ephesians: "In your anger do not sin" (Ephesians 4:26 NIV). Here's how it's done.

Express and explain it. Since suppressed anger is bound to ignite someday like dry timber, it's probably best to express it early, preferably with some kind of "I" statement. Instead of the typical accusatory approach ("You're making me angry!"), we should "own" our reaction to events. "I sometimes say to my wife, 'You know, this conversation is bugging me. I'm feeling angry now. Let's take a break,'" says Pastor Roper.

But we shouldn't stop there, cautions Dr. Oliver. We then need to identify for the other person the emotion underneath the anger. "If I say, 'What you did really hurt me or really frustrated me,' you can do something about that. Otherwise, just expressing anger is no more effective than rearranging the deck chairs on the *Titanic*," he says.

Go to God. If we can't quite identify the true source of our anger, the Bible promises that God will help if we will only pray. The need for prayer is more urgent if the discussion has degenerated into arguing or fighting. "If I were in a situation like that, I'd say something like 'My sense is that either I'm not doing a good job of communicating right now or you're not hearing, and so we're only going to shed a lot more heat than light. Let's stop and pray together,'" says Dr. Oliver. "And then I would say, 'Lord, the desire of my heart right now with so-and-so is not to blame or trash or dump on him, and so I would pray that you would help me communicate more clearly.' If the other person is unwilling to pray, pray something similar silently."

Take a time-out. If our hearts aren't in it, sometimes even prayer can't immediately diffuse angry situations. That's probably the right time to take a time-out. "Depending on the circumstance, a time-out might be short enough to simply say the alphabet backwards or long enough to take a walk or even work in the yard—anything that gives me enough time to permit my emotions to stabilize," says Dr. Oliver. When that is needed, it's necessary to reengage eventually. "You don't want to leave the other person hanging," he says. One guideline for the length of the time-out: it takes, on average, twenty minutes for the stress hormones released during an angry outburst to work their way through our systems, he says.

Seek to understand. One of the first things we forget when we're angry is that we're dealing with another person who may not agree with us but deserves our understanding. "Our old dog barks and bites and is a ferocious terror to strangers, but I understand her," says Pastor Roper. "She was abused by a man when she was a pup before we got her and reacts adversely to men. It's important to recognize the latent forces that lie within us and in other people's anger. It helps us to be more understanding and patient with them."

Forgive. Forgiveness is the best way to end just about any problem, including anger. And it's healthy, too. Studies show that anger has been implicated in a variety of health problems, including depression and high blood pressure. But how do we do it? Not by serving as doormats, but by choosing not to hold the offense against the offender and by not punishing the person for what he or she has done. See the section entitled "Forgiveness" in Part 6 of this book.

Write a letter. Pouring our feelings out onto paper is a good way to release them without harming ourselves or anyone else. When we finish writing, often the best thing to do is simply throw away the letter, says Dr. Oliver.

What if the person with whom we're angry is unavailable—or gone for good—such as an abusive ex-spouse or a deceased parent? We can still forgive. We can go to a quiet place with an empty chair across from us and then talk as if the person were sitting there. We can explain why we're angry. When we've poured out our hearts, we can choose to forgive, says Dr. Oliver.

Do it now. A verse from the Bible reads: "Do not let the sun go down while you are still angry, and do not give the devil a foothold" (Ephesians 4:26–27 NIV). Letting anger settle into our hearts over a period of time is dangerous to our emotions and bad for our health. The best way to handle it is to resolve it as quickly as possible.

Resist the temptation to defend yourself. We may have our anger under control, but we need to remember that careless words or actions can raise the ire of others. When our angry words or actions cause pain for other people, we should not defend ourselves. In fact, often one of the best ways to diffuse an angry situation when someone confronts us about our anger is to say, "You're right. I know that must have hurt you, and I'm sorry."

Eight Steps to Help Control Anger

By Norman Vincent Peale

If you become angry easily, if you are quick to resent somebody—or a remark—then you may be a person who is seldom in control of situations. When you give in to anger, the situation controls you, the other person has the upper hand, and you spend much of your time hating yourself and hating the other person involved.

What is the antidote? Obviously it is to fill the mind with attitudes of good will, forgiveness, love, and the spirit of imperturbability. Following is an eight-point plan to help you control angry emotions:

1. Anger often erupts from an accumulation of minor irritations. At the point when you feel a situation building up, force yourself to sit down and make a list of everything that irritates you, no matter how inconsequential it seems. This will help dry up the tiny rivulets that feed the great river of anger.

2. Make each separate irritation a special object of prayer. Gain a spiritual victory over each, one at a time. By working away at each small annoyance in this way, you weaken the emotion of anger to the point where you can control it.

3. Go to someone you trust and pour out your grievance to him or her. If you prefer not to tell anyone what is bothering you, write it in a letter to a friend. Then tear up the letter. Think of this as a technique to air your grievances without damaging a relationship.

4. If you feel anger rising inside you, despite efforts to control it in advance, train yourself to say, "I will make a fool of myself. I will lose friends. I am only hurting myself. I must control myself."

5. Remember that anger is an emotion, and an emotion always is warm, even hot. Therefore, to reduce an angry emotion, cool it. To do this, understand that in anger, fists tend to clench, voices raise, muscles tense. Oppose the heat of these actions with coolness. By an act of will, keep the hands from clenching. Hold your fingers out straight. Reduce your tone of voice; bring it down to a whisper. It is difficult to argue in a whisper. Slump in a chair, or lie down if possible. It is difficult to be angry while lying down.

6. Instead of counting to ten when anger begins to surge, try saying the first ten words of the Lord's Prayer: "Our Father Who art in heaven, hallowed be Thy name." Repeat it several times in the full flush of emotion.

7. If, despite all efforts to control it, you blow up in anger, try to straighten out the situation as soon as possible. Avoid brooding or feeling sorry for yourself. Deal with the hurt with a prayer and begin again to work on the little things that were responsible for the blow-up in the first place.

8. Finally, realize that the undisciplined urge that flames to the surface in you can be tamed only by allowing Jesus Christ to take control. Therefore, make it a practice to say this prayer often, "Lord, even as You can convert a person's morals, so now I ask You to convert my nerves. As You give power over the sins of the flesh, so give me power over the sins of the disposition. Bring my temper under Your control. Pour Your healing peace in my nervous system as well as in my soul."

If you find yourself continually losing your temper, repeat this prayer several times each day. It might be helpful to type it into your phone, print it on a card, and keep it where you can see it often.

Reprinted and adapted from Dr. Peale's book *The Power of Positive Thinking* (Englewood Cliffs: Prentice-Hall)

Put the situation in perspective. Anger often causes us to view situations as worse than they really are. If we can calm down long enough to see our circumstances realistically, we can usually handle them in a constructive—not destructive—manner.

Think about good things, not about how angry you are. The Bible doesn't say, "focus on your anger." It doesn't say, "beat yourself up" or "drive yourself crazy." It says to focus on whatever is true, noble, right, pure, admirable, excellent, or praiseworthy (Philippians 4:8).

Avoid extremes. Some people cause even more trouble for themselves by throwing around words such as *always, never,* and *every* when they're angry or in an argument. Some classic examples: "Why do you always do that?" or "You never listen to me!"

Not only are such generalizations rarely true; they're also infuriating to hear, says Dr. Oliver. "And what are the three core emotions of anger? Fear, hurt, and frustration. If I communicate in ways that frustrate you, then you will probably respond in frustration or anger as well. The result is misunderstanding and hurt feelings. In one interaction, we can find ourselves about a mile off course."

Carry a STOP! card. The purpose of a STOP! card is to help put the brakes on emotional situations that are careening out of control.

To make a STOP! card, simply write "STOP!" in big red letters on one side of a three-by-five-inch index card. Then, says Dr. Oliver, write a Bible verse on the other side, such as: "For the weapons of our warfare *are* not carnal but mighty in God for pulling down strongholds, casting down arguments and every high thing that exalts itself against the knowledge of God, bringing every thought into captivity to the obedience of Christ" (2 Corinthians 10:4–5 NKJV).

Then, when we feel anger building, we can pull the STOP! card out of our wallets or purses, says Dr. Oliver, and say to ourselves, "STOP! I'm making this emotion, this thought, captive to the obedience of Christ." This isn't something to wave in another person's face. This is for us.

Lower expectations. In some cases, our spouses, friends, or coworkers simply will not change their ways. Instead of staying angry all the time, we should state our cases, lower our expectations, and hope for the best. To put it bluntly, the other person's problem doesn't have to be—nor should it be—a main focus of our lives. When we let that problem go, it can have a positive effect on both of us.

Find a healthy outlet. Anger can be the fuel for social change, if we allow it. Mothers Against Drunk Driving, for example, was founded by women whose family members had been killed by drunk drivers. Channeling our anger into Christian service may very well make the world a better place instead of making us bitter, says Pastor Roper.

Go the other way—for now. What if we've repeatedly made an honest effort to resolve a problem and the other person is still angry with us? If the story about Paul and Barnabas—two solid believers—in Acts 15 is any indication, it may take some time and maturity before we're able to work together again. They had to split up for a time after a disagreement, but they later reconciled. If spending time apart from someone with whom we are angry seems wise, we should do so with the hope and goal of eventual reconciliation.

· HEALING WORDS ·

Beyond Martyrdom

Lord, there's an ogre that's living in my "house." It was a little creature at first, but—I must admit—I was the one who invited it in.
You see, my neighbor made an unkind remark: "Your wash on the line makes the neighborhood unattractive."
Okay for you. There are other neighbors I can have coffee with.
I rehashed my former friend's words over and over, and silently retaliated with more and more words of my own.
After all, what she said was completely unjustified.
For a while I enjoyed my martyrdom. But now I want this despot out of my soul's "house." The monster has taken over.
I know You've been waiting to rid me of this ruler; you just wanted my permission.
Lord, cleanse my mind of my resentment.
And, while You're at it, give me the willingness to go to my neighbor and make amends.
—ISABEL WOLSELEY

ANXIETY AND FEAR

· FAITH BUILDER ·

Gratitude doesn't come automatically to me when a big, ugly fear blocks my vision: I have to go looking for it. I embark on the search because the mere fact that I am living with fear tells me that I am not seeing my life as God does.
—JULIA ATTAWAY

Overcoming Anxiety

SHOTS TERRIFY ME. I hate needles. So when I took my ten-year-old marmalade cat, Red, to the vet not long ago because he'd lost a lot of weight, I didn't want to hear about shots. "He's got diabetes," the doctor said, gently stroking Red. "He'll need a specially formulated cat food from now on, and you'll have to give him insulin twice a day."

"In his food?" I asked.

"No, by injection."

No, not that! I thought. I could never stick a needle into my precious cat. "Here's how," the vet said. "Pinch the fur on the back of his neck, insert the needle, and press the plunger. There's nothing to it." He handed me some disposable syringes and a bottle of insulin.

I nodded, pretending to agree. Back home I thought, *This will never work. Maybe I can hire a nurse.* I had memories of nurses puncturing me, doctors trying to distract me, the nausea and anxiety that came with the sting of a needle. How could I do this to Red? Then again, how could I not? His health was at stake. "Red," I finally called through gritted teeth. He came running, trusting.

He purred at my touch and looked at me quizzically.

"This is good for you," I whispered. Then I prayed, *God, I trust you with my fears…just the way Red trusts me.* I closed my eyes and plunged in the needle. Red didn't even flinch. He was totally calm.

Twice a day I had to give Red shots, and every time he came running (it probably helped that I did it just before mealtime). He put on weight again and his coat got its old shine back. As for me, twice a day I got into the practice of praying. I still don't like needles, but they don't terrify me anymore. I know where to put my fears—and how to shrink them down to a more manageable size. —B. J. TAYLOR

WHEN WORRY AND FEAR GO AWRY

Healthy fear, as well as common sense, is what keeps us from stepping up to a podium to address thousands without being prepared. But if we refuse even to be a part of the crowd because we're afraid people will stare at us, we likely have a form of anxiety or a phobia.

If we do struggle with fear or anxiety, we shouldn't feel alone. According to the Anxiety and Depression Association of America (adaa.org), some 40 million adults in the United States are affected by anxiety, making it the most common mental illness in the country. From chronic worrying, which experts call generalized anxiety disorder, to panic attacks, most anxiety disorders seem to have the same root cause: unrealistic, overwhelming fears that can not only paralyze the mind but also cause serious physical problems, says the late William Backus, Ph.D., founder of the Center for Christian Psychological Services and author of *Telling Yourself the Truth* and *The Healing Power of a Healthy Mind.*

THE GOOD SIDE OF WORRY

For all the trouble it can cause, a certain amount of worry or anxiety can be healthy. Concern over what the boss will say if we're repeatedly late to work helps us get up and out of bed in the morning so we won't lose our jobs. Fear of a car accident reminds us to look both ways before crossing the street.

A bit of anxiety over how we'll fare against the competition stimulates our adrenal glands, improving blood flow, concentration, and other aspects that are key to enhanced performance, according to Dr. Gary J. Oliver.

When anxiety goes bad, it gets ugly fast. The sudden feelings of terror associated

Fear No More

BY NORMAN VINCENT PEALE

I sought the Lord, and He heard me, and delivered me from all my fears." —Psalm 34:4 (KJV).

There are two kinds of fear: normal fear and abnormal fear. Normal fear is necessary for our protection and for the exercise of a sensible caution. But abnormal fear is something altogether different. Sad indeed are the people who walk day and night in the terror of abnormal fear. It is one of the most crippling afflictions of our day, producing painful symptoms, such as depression and anxiety. In some cases, fear can cause actual physical illness. We are not supposed to be afraid of anything. The only fear we should have is the fear of God and the fear of doing wrong. That is not fear in the sense of being scared; but, rather, it is an awed respect of God and of what is right. We should walk unafraid. But, as that is not easy, we have to consciously build up our faith.

POSITIVE ACTION STEP #1: PRACTICE AFFIRMATION

You have known some people, no doubt, who have become absolutely fearless. And these are people of profound faith. "That is what I would like to be," you may say. "I am tired of being afraid of illness and of other people and of possible catastrophes. I want to know how to be free of fear always." The first thing all of us must realize about fear is that most of the things we are afraid of probably will never really happen. If we let our fears dominate, they could cripple our lives.

One absolute and positive way to let go of your fears is to practice the form of prayer known as affirmation: not the prayer of asking, but the prayer of affirming. Believe that God loves you and that He watches over you. Believe that He is taking care of you this very moment and, therefore, you need not be afraid. Do not say, "O Lord, please deliver me from fear. I am so tired of being upset and anxious." Rather, affirm that He is already doing it, and you will drop fear.

One of the elders of our church, an intelligent, dedicated man, told me about his experience in the hospital. At one point in his illness, fear gripped him with icy fingers. "But," he said, "I was told that many people were praying for me. So I began to affirm that these prayers were taking effect and that the Lord was hearing my own prayers. And I had a wonderful experience, for, as I affirmed this, all of a sudden every vestige of fear seemed to leave me. I was at peace and rest, and felt absolutely confident."

Positive Action Step #2: Stand Up to Fear

Fear can't be evaded. And it can't be avoided. It has to be met head-on. If you're not willing to go to the heart of what it is you are afraid of, that fear will haunt you constantly. President Theodore Roosevelt once said, "I have often been afraid, but I wouldn't give in to it. I made myself act as though I was not afraid, and gradually my fear disappeared." Action is the only answer.

Fear of trying something new, after all, is normal. When children enter a new school, or when people start a new job, they are bound to be fearful. But, if they act with confidence and faith, their fears vanish. And they have that glowing sense of accomplishment that comes with trying something new and succeeding. I am sure that you can't sit inside a space shuttle and run through a countdown without some feelings of uncertainty. But, if you accept these feelings as normal, you can deal with them.

Positive Action Step #3: Let Fear Motivate You

Kenneth McFarland, a wonderful speaker, told the story about a man who worked until midnight every night, and customarily walked home afterward. One beautiful moonlit night, he thought he would walk through the cemetery, rather than around it, because the way was shorter. This he did for several nights, until the moon began to wane. By then he knew the path through the cemetery and even though it was absolutely dark, he felt he could walk through safely.

But one night, as he came along the path in the darkness, his feet suddenly went out from under him, and the man found himself grabbing dirt and sliding into a newly dug grave. He tried his best to get out, but he was too short and the grave was too deep. All he accomplished was to pull a lot of loose dirt down on himself. Being a practical man, he reasoned that the gravediggers would come back the next morning. So he pulled his coat around him, huddled into a corner of the grave, and tried to sleep.

An hour later, another wandering citizen came along through the cemetery. All of a sudden this other man slid into the grave—at the other end—and started making futile efforts to climb out. Finally, as the second man stood contemplating his situation, our first friend, speaking in the darkness, said, "Boy, you'll never get out that way." But the second man did—like a shot!

You see, this second man (and for that matter, the first one, too) had the potential for getting out of that hole; but the potential needed motivation. This story illustrates, if rather crudely, that resident in you, in me, and in every person is the potential for lifting ourselves up out of defeat. It just needs a force to be applied.

There are two primary forces in this world, fear and faith. Fear can move you to destructiveness or sickness or failure. Only in rare instances will it motivate you to accomplishment, but faith is a greater force. Faith can drive itself into your consciousness and set you free from fear forever.

with panic attacks often trigger chest pains, heart palpitations, shortness of breath, dizziness, abdominal discomfort, and even fear of death. Those who have obsessive-compulsive disorders, also considered forms of anxiety, often find themselves performing bizarre rituals, like cleaning part of the house or washing their hands dozens or even hundreds of times a day. Post-traumatic stress disorder, a form of anxiety caused by traumatic events, such as rape, exposure to war, abuse, or other forms of violence, can result in nightmares, flashbacks, numb emotions, depression, and feelings of anger, irritability, and distraction.

For some people with anxiety, the relief provided by drug therapy is a welcome respite from paralyzing fear or tormenting worry, and a health practitioner can determine who would benefit from this treatment if any of the symptoms mentioned above are present. Early religious believers, although certainly not immune from anxiety and worry, didn't have that luxury.

But whether facing hostile Romans, hungry lions, or fiery furnaces, they often used faith, prayer, and wisdom from Scripture to overcome. These coping mechanisms are still powerful today.

Remedies
PUTTING THE PROBLEM TO REST

"A KEY TO OVERCOMING worry is to choose to make the God-given emotion of anxiety work for you rather than against you," says Dr. Oliver. "Before Christ was able to heal the paralyzed man at the pool of Bethesda, He asked him: 'Do you want to be made whole?' That's the same question that He asks each of us today." Here's some good advice for dealing with anxiety and fear from a Christian perspective.

Do one day at a time. Jesus covered several important topics during the Sermon on the Mount. Is it a coincidence that He devoted as much time or more to worry and anxiety, or is He trying to tell us something? "Therefore do not worry about tomorrow, for tomorrow will worry about its own things. Sufficient for the day *is* its own trouble," Jesus concludes (Matthew 6:34 NKJV).

POSITIVE ACTION STEPS

1. Practice Affirmation
2. Stand Up to Fear
3. Let Fear Motivate You

POSITIVE AFFIRMATION
Respect God, do what is right, and you will walk unafraid.

"I find it interesting that 'one day at a time' has become the motto of many recovery programs," says Dr. Oliver. "Remember that worry usually involves reaching into and borrowing potential problems from tomorrow. One friend told me, 'Yesterday is a canceled check, tomorrow is a promissory note. Today is cash. Spend it wisely.' That's sound biblical advice."

Eliminate avoidance behavior. Often those who experience anxiety try to avoid whatever they view as the source of their problems. Unfortunately, this approach can make the problems worse, so much so that psychologists have given it a name: avoidance behavior.

"Suppose I'm a kid who doesn't want to go to school because all the others are picking on me. And I tell my mom and she says, 'Aw, honey, you stay home today.' Guess what happens to the knot that I had in my stomach? It goes away. That's the reward," says Dr. Backus. "But that kind of avoidance in the long run will cause anxiety to get worse. The anxiety response is strengthened by avoidance behavior."

Face the fear. Ending avoidance behavior is a big step toward recovery. Challenging anxieties or worries to see if they are realistic is another. "One of the best ways to abandon the merry-go-round of worry is to simply jump off and do something," says Dr. Oliver. Have you been anxious about making that important phone call for weeks or months? Start dialing—it's probably nowhere near as bad as you think, he says.

Lest we forget, this advice also has some scriptural basis: "...ask, and it will be given to you; seek, and you will find; knock, and it will be opened to you" (Luke 11:9 NKJV).

Study the Psalms. Soldiers have carried copies into battle; business leaders and secretaries keep framed passages on their desks. For more than four thousand years, the Psalms have helped provide an unparalleled sense of peace in times of anxiety and fear. "Just thumb through them. One of my favorites is 'What time I am afraid, I will trust in thee' [Psalm 56:3 KJV]. Or the twenty-third Psalm: 'The Lord is my shepherd; I shall not want. He maketh me to lie down in green pastures: he leadeth me beside the still waters. He restoreth my soul...,'" says Dr. Backus. "Now, I know this isn't magic, and it doesn't immediately banish every wisp of fear, but it sure makes it possible to tolerate it—to know that you have the greatest power in the universe available to you during this difficulty."

Pray for peace of mind. Prayer has a way of "clarifying our worries," says Dr. Oliver.

The following verses have helped many people gain victory over fear and worry.

Hence we can confidently say, "The Lord is my helper; I will not be afraid. What can anyone do to me?" (Hebrews 13:6 ISV).

Nobody can really hurt you. We do not stand alone in this world, for we can turn to God and He will always help us. Fill your mind with thoughts of God; get in harmony with His will; eliminate from your mind all feelings contrary to love; practice simple trust. Practice thinking less about your worries and more about God. Instead of thinking how difficult your problem is, think about how great and powerful God is. This will change your psychology; but more than that, it releases spiritual power into your mind. That will enable you to meet your situation intelligently and creatively. Repeat this text when you are afraid.

Have no anxiety about anything, but in everything by prayer and supplication with thanksgiving let your requests be made known to God. —Philippians 4:6 (RSV)

This method of dealing with anxiety is fourfold: prayer, supplication, thanksgiving, and telling God what you want. When you are worried, stop thinking emotionally and talking in an anxious manner and pray. Ask God to relieve you of your fears and show you how to handle the problem that causes the fear. Then, immediately upon asking Him, give thanks, thus expressing your belief that He is answering your prayer, for He is.

When you lie down, you will not be afraid. When you rest, your sleep will be peaceful. —Proverbs 3:24 (ERV)

It is important when dealing with worry to go to sleep at night in the right manner. If you retire with a mind filled with fearful thoughts, you will have only superficial sleep, for beneath the surface, anxieties are disturbing you in the deep subconscious. Therefore when you lie down to sleep, think of God as being with you and watching over you. Place the cares of the day in His hands. Every night

> say this verse to yourself before you go to sleep. Then, instead of fears in your subconscious, faith in God's presence will develop a confident approach to your anxiety. —NORMAN VINCENT PEALE

"God can help us weed out the outrageous and irrational fears from the legitimate and rational concerns. He can help us identify the real issues." Best of all, prayer works. In one study, twenty out of twenty-two people who practiced prayer or meditation to reduce moderate to severe anxiety showed marked improvement after three months.

Listen to music that will help you focus on God. Listening to Christian praise music that reminds us of God's grace, goodness, power, and majesty is perfect for those moments when we're feeling anxious and fearful, says Dr. Oliver.

Focus on the positive. The Apostle Paul in his letters wrote frequently of the need to focus our minds on the good things in life, not the bad. "Whatever is true," he wrote to the Philippians, "whatever is honorable, whatever is commendable, if there is anything worthy of praise, think about these things."

To turn our minds away from our fears, Wilford Wooten, a licensed marriage, family, and child counselor and former director of the counseling department at Focus on the Family, recommends making a list of pleasant thoughts and memories and adding to it regularly. "When we're tempted to start dwelling on something negative," he says, "we'll have something that's good and true to put in our minds to replace it with."

Watch your mouth. While we're getting our thoughts right, it's also a good idea to control our speech, whether we are talking to ourselves or others. "Anxiety weighs down the heart, but a kind word cheers it up" (Proverbs 12:25 NIV).

Know when to get help. Fears can develop into debilitating phobias if left unchecked. It's important to realize this and seek professional help if we feel that we're having a hard time handling our fears. How can we know? When a fear becomes immobilizing or interferes with our normal functions, says Wooten, it's time for us to seek counseling.

Acknowledge fear, then take it on. A fear faced is often a fear defeated, Wooten says. He quotes a saying he once had on his office wall: "Boats are safe anchored in the harbor, but that's not what boats are made for." People of faith have lots of things to do for the Lord, he says. Sitting at home afraid isn't among them.

Tune out bad news. The bad news reported on television and online do not do our peace of mind any good and can cause us to worry or be afraid of things we wouldn't have thought of had we not seen them or read about them.

Seek strength in numbers. We can do much to allay our worries and fears if we wrap ourselves tightly in a network of fellow Christians by attending services regularly, participating in church social activities, and doing volunteer service.

· HEALING WORDS ·

Overcoming Anxiety and Fear Through Scripture

Several Bible verses remind us that no matter how anxiety producing a situation may be, God is always with us to help us.

Teaching them to observe all things whatsoever I have commanded you: and, lo, I am with you always, even unto the end of the world. Amen.

—MATTHEW 28:20 KJV

So do not fear, for I am with you; do not be dismayed, for I am your God. I will strengthen you and help you; I will uphold you with my righteous right hand.

—ISAIAH 41:10 NIV

Ye are of God, little children, and have overcome them: because greater is he that is in you, than he that is in the world.

—1 JOHN 4:4 KJV

But they that wait upon the LORD shall renew their strength; they shall mount up with wings as eagles; they shall run, and not be weary; and they shall walk, and not faint.

—ISAIAH 40:31 KJV

There is no fear in love; but perfect love casteth out fear: because fear hath torment. He that feareth is not made perfect in love.

—1 JOHN 4:18 KJV

Create in me a clean heart, O God; and renew a right spirit within me.
—PSALM 51:10 KJV

Immediately he made the disciples get into the boat and go on ahead to the other side, while he dismissed the crowds. And after he had dismissed the crowds, he went up the mountain by himself to pray. When evening came, he was there alone, but by this time the boat, battered by the waves, was far from the land, for the wind was against them. And early in the morning he came walking toward them on the sea. But when the disciples saw him walking on the sea, they were terrified, saying, "It is a ghost!" And they cried out in fear. But immediately Jesus spoke to them and said, "Take heart, it is I; do not be afraid." Peter answered him, "Lord, if it is you, command me to come to you on the water." He said, "Come."
—MATTHEW 14:22–29 NRSV

Depression

A Battle with Darkness

A PARENT DIES. A spouse leaves. A child is lost.

We are devastated, sad, morose, frantic—but are we depressed? We may think so. We may say so. But doctors, psychologists, counselors, and therapists might not classify it that way. They say we are supposed to be disturbed when bad things happen. But feeling normal sadness and hopelessness is not the same as clinical depression. Depression is more than deep disappointment.

Depression is crippling despondency with a combination of symptoms that may include lethargy, listlessness, physical pain, hopelessness, loss of appetite, and others.

Depression may also include morbid thoughts or, in critical (emergency) cases, suicidal thinking, talk, threats, or attempts. In fact, depression is the number-one cause of suicide, says Christian psychiatrist and theologian Paul Meier, M.D., psychiatrist, ordained minister, founder of Meier Clinics, cofounder of the board of physicians, called Physicians Resource Council, to advise the Focus on the Family on medical issues, author, and lecturer.

Depression is a black cloud that doesn't blow away, dissipate, or lift as it should. When depression hits, our brain chemistry goes awry. The chemicals that regulate our senses of well-being, joy, pleasure, our sex drive, and our ability to concentrate vary and wane, says Dr. Meier.

Depression may develop following an emotional trauma. Or it may develop because something else causes our feel-good brain chemicals to be depleted. Here are some things that drain them.

- Stress and anxiety
- Poor eating habits or poor nutritional choices
- Lack of sleep
- Lack of exercise
- Side effects from prescription and/or over-the-counter medications
- Feeling unloved
- Feeling helpless, lost, or worthless
- Feeling guilty over unconfessed wrong-doing
- In a small percentage of cases, a physical defect depletes the pleasure-producing brain chemicals or otherwise interferes with their operation

Regardless of the trigger, once depression sets in and our brain chemistry changes, we can end up feeling empty and thoroughly hopeless.

Untreated, depression can ruin lives, limit lives, and take lives. Yes, depression is a physical condition and a curse. But it is not a sin. There is no Eleventh Commandment saying "Thou shall not be depressed," says lecturer and ordained Episcopalian priest Harold Ivan Smith, D.Min., Ed.S., counselor, grief educator, public speaker, workshop facilitator, trainer, and faculty member at St. Luke's Hospital in Kansas City, Missouri, and Carondolet Medical Institute in Eau Clare, Wisconsin.

Jesus, Elijah, Job, Jeremiah, and other saints appear to have been depressed, according to today's standards, sometimes to the point of being suicidal, says Dr. Smith. Elijah, trembling in fear, "sat down under a juniper tree; and he requested for himself that he might die" (1 Kings 19:4 NASB). Jesus, in the Garden of Gethsemane, said to his disciples, "my soul is deeply grieved to the point of death" (Mark 14:34 NASB).

We need not let depression or guilt about feeling depressed devastate us. We can climb out of it, one positive, constructive, certain step at a time. And we can take steps to ameliorate and manage depression so it will never again be so threatening or consuming.

HELP IS AVAILABLE

Many types of help are available for those with depression. Some is self-help. Some is professional help. All is of God, says Dr. Smith. God may bring us books, online videos, podcasts, groups, friends, helpers, counselors, doctors, or medications.

But if we're in deep despair, feeling hopeless, the immediate action we should take is get to a professional therapist, says Dr. Meier.

"Run to counseling," urges psychologist and author Dr. Michele Novotni, assistant professor of counseling at Eastern College in St. Davids, Pennsylvania, and licensed psychologist. A good therapist can quickly assess the depth of our depression and can help us immediately begin to break the downward spiral. A good counselor will not start preaching to us, accusing us of having hidden sin in our lives, or otherwise make us feel guilty or shameful.

A good counselor may refer us to someone who will prescribe antidepressant medication. Medication can make all the difference in the world. Antidepressant medications are not "happy pills," explains

Dr. Novotni. They simply help coax wayward, depressed brain chemistry back to relative normality. Those who use antidepressant medication still feel sadness when confronted with sad events. But with the proper medication (experimentation to find the right medication is often necessary, since reactions are quite individualized), people are much less likely to sink into a deep, life-threatening despondency that seems impossible to overcome or interferes with our ability to function effectively.

Medication and other positive measures can give us the boost we need so we can find our balance, says Dr. Novotni. Then, when we're in a stronger and clearer frame of mind, we can tackle the tough issues that may be at the root of our depression. That is when we are better able to examine our pain, deep-rooted guilt or secrets, or repressed inappropriate behaviors. "Jesus often healed first, and then had people restored to service to God. But He didn't tell them, get right with God and then I'll heal you," she says.

Some people need medication only for a single brief period, or several brief periods, to recover or maintain equilibrium. Others need it for longer periods of time. Give medication a fair chance, doctors say. Many drugs take up to eight weeks to fully kick in, so patience is necessary.

How to Rise up over Depression

By Marion Bond West

When I approached my third year of widowhood and the last of my four children was about to leave home, I felt very melancholy. It wasn't the first time I had felt depressed, but it was bad enough to keep me awake for entire nights. I seldom laughed and I seemed haunted by thoughts of "how it used to be." All my anticipation for life was gone. Finally, like a drowning person, I cried out, "Do something, God!"

The next day I happened to see a small ad in my church paper for a secretary at the church counseling center. I had the strangest feeling that God was telling me to answer that ad. My church was twenty-five miles away, in downtown Atlanta, and I hated driving downtown. Furthermore, I wasn't a secretary and hadn't worked outside the home in twenty-eight years. But in spite of my reluctance, I still felt God nudging me.

I got the job. And I was a disaster. I made one mistake after another—even wrote down phone numbers wrong! I had the feeling that everyone would be relieved if I quit—including me. The one good thing about it was that I began to take an interest in the people who came in for counseling. I prayed for them. I began to notice their progress and rejoice over their victories.

Slowly, things changed for me. I was exhausted when I got home, but content at night, and sleep came again. So did laughter. I began to anticipate the next day. After several months I began to understand why God had wanted me to take the job. Doing something difficult—something for which maybe I wasn't even qualified—had helped me because I was helping someone else.

I've learned some things about depression since then: that you can't escape by running away, that it can attack men and even children. I know, too, that if depression persists, it's wise to seek professional help.

But I've also learned there are things you can do on your own to confront depression:

1. **Arm yourself for the battle.** I read encouraging passages of Scripture and try to memorize them (Isaiah 61:3 or 40:31, or Psalm 34:17, for instance). I also read from a favorite book, *My Utmost for His Highest*, by Oswald Chambers. Or I listen to inspirational music, sometimes singing along. Of course, I sometimes don't feel like turning on the music, but I realize this is a battle, and in order to win it, I have to do some things I may not feel like doing.

2. **Try to pinpoint why you are depressed.** For instance, I miss being a wife, and I think that if I were a wife again, I wouldn't be depressed. But I must remember that I was a wife for twenty-five years, and there were often times when I felt depressed then. I explain to myself that people, circumstances, and things don't make one really happy. Joy comes from choosing to believe that God is working in my life in all circumstances.

3. **Do something for someone else.** Dr. Karl Menninger of the famous Menninger Clinic once said there's one sure way to avoid having a breakdown, a solution so simple that almost no one will believe it works. You simply walk out your front door and find someone—anyone—who needs help, and you help him or her.

Reaching out, reminding ourselves that we're not alone, is the first step back. We may not be immune from ever feeling depressed, but our powerful God is always standing ready to help us fight the battle against it. After all, He promises us that "sorrow and mourning shall flee away" (Isaiah 51:11 KJV).

Even if we aren't seriously depressed or if we are against taking medication, a therapist can help speed our recovery, says Dr. Novotni. A counselor can listen to us describe our lives and often identify distorted thinking patterns that we can correct to ease our depressive episodes or reduce their frequency, she says. To find a good counselor, she suggests:

- Asking friends for referrals.
- Interviewing potential therapists over the phone or in person before making a decision.
- Looking for a comfortable, positive rapport.

- Asking, once we meet a therapist: Is this therapist listening? Is this therapist empathic, understanding, and relating to my important values? Is this therapist inspiring and encouraging?
- Realizing we may need to visit several therapists until we find the right one for us and can begin to build an effective working relationship.

Getting treatment can be a matter of success or failure, a future filled with bright, promising days or with melancholy and struggle, life or death. Get help, and don't shy away from therapy, urges Dr. Meier.

Remedies
CLIMB TOWARD THE LIGHT

DEFEATING DEPRESSION and reigniting life can be an exciting prospect and project. It does require a vigilant and ongoing effort for many of us. And it does require that we start somewhere. If we haven't started already, why not start now?

We can do a lot ourselves and/or with the help of a counselor. Here are some exercises that can help us both get better now and stave off future depression.

Monitor thinking. Dr. Meier recommends that we identify and change critical, angry, resentful, painful, self-effacing, and gloomy thoughts. All of these are negative and fuel depression, particularly angry thoughts. If we change our thinking, we will see our moods begin to lift.

We talk to ourselves mentally at a rate of five to ten times the speed with which we talk with our mouths, says Dr. Meier. We talk inwardly with images, concepts, and ideas. We need to try to catch the negatives in our minds and refocus them on positives.

How should we think? Dr. Meier cites this passage: "…whatever things are true, whatever things *are* noble, whatever things *are* just, whatever things *are* pure, whatever things *are* lovely, whatever things *are* of good report, if *there is* any virtue and if *there is* anything praiseworthy—meditate on these things" (Philippians 4:8 NKJV).

Confront anger. We need to make sure we're in touch with our anger and are handling it biblically. Obey Ephesians 4:26–27, Dr. Meier says. "'Be angry and do not sin': do not let the sun go down on your wrath…" (NKJV).

"If you hang on to your anger, Ephesians 4:27 says, you give Satan a foothold in your life," says Dr. Meier. "Leviticus 19:17–19 says that if you're angry at your neighbor, tell him how you feel. But don't get vengeance on him. Just tell him that you're angry." Vengeance belongs to God, as Romans 12:19 says, notes Dr. Meier. "We need to turn all vengeance over to God. Basically, we need to be aware of our anger. We need to verbalize it. The anger can be at God. It can be at others. It can be at ourselves. We need to take our anger to God. We need to trust Him to take care of it."

Release resentment. Let it go. Easier said than done? Yes, but harboring resentment is self-punishment. We replay over and over a hurt we feel someone else inflicted on us, and that makes us feel awful again and again, says Dr. Smith. We can't change the past, but we can change how we choose to perceive it now. Forgive, as Jesus instructs. Release the matter to God. Ask for a healing change of perspective.

Ask for help. When darkness descends, call friends and loved ones and ask for help with basic needs such as food, shelter, cleaning—because all of these can be nearly impossible to cope with in the midst of major depression, says Dr. Novotni. And having friends and people we love around helps lift our moods.

Seek social support. The last thing we should do when we are depressed is to isolate ourselves. Numerous medical and sociological studies show that regular, positive social interaction—the greater number of different types of contacts, the better—tends to enhance our overall well-being and limit depressive episodes in our lives, says heart specialist and best-selling author Dean Ornish, M.D., clinical professor of medicine at the University of California, San Francisco, and founder and president of the nonprofit Preventive Medicine

Noteworthy

By Ann Kochenberger

Depression hit me out of nowhere, just like before. One day I was myself and the next I was consumed by sadness and anxiety. I lost my appetite for everything—food, sleep, reading, working around the house. My brother and sister-in-law thought it would be beneficial if I moved back to my home state of Mississippi to stay with my family.

"Think of this as a rainstorm you are driving through," Fran told me at their house. "It seems never-ending. But it will end. The sun will shine again."

I pretended I was getting better. I smiled and acted like I was happy. Fran saw through it. She encouraged me to get involved in the household routine, sensing when to push me and when not to. We talked a lot, but her notes to me each day meant the most.

"Went to the market. When I get back let's take the dog for a walk. Love, Fran."

"Yoga at 1:00. Love it if you came. Fran."

Those notes gave me a boost. People cared and wanted me to get well. Before long I wanted to get well, too. For my husband, for my family, for myself—and most of all for my friend Fran.

Research Institute, who has conducted such studies.

Some studies indicate that we get a healthy emotional boost from our spiritual communities; that is, from interacting with groups of people and individuals we feel comfortable with and enjoy being around and who inspire and encourage us and share our values, says Dr. Ornish.

Going to church also seems to help, says Dr. Dale A. Matthews, who has published studies of the effects of religiosity on well-being and depression. The research demonstrates that the benefits from simple church attendance go beyond social support. Attending church regularly seems to help people develop better coping skills and greater self-control.

In addition, joining a small group at church or agreeing to meet once a week with another friend or two, even if it's just for coffee, can help provide someone with whom to share our struggles.

Deal with depression cognitively. Widely used cognitive therapy, pioneered by Aaron T. Beck, M.D., in the 1950s, has been proven to help in curing and coping with depression, says Dr. Novotni.

Dr. Beck identified specific distorted thinking patterns in which we all engage at times that confound and confuse things. An example is a tendency that we sometimes have to contrast ourselves with people who are more successful and, in the process, condemn ourselves as failures. Rather, we could recognize how well we've done compared with people who have accomplished less. Another distorted thinking pattern is to blow a little thing all out of proportion and let it ruin our whole morning, afternoon, day, or week.

Cognitive therapy teaches us to recognize and constructively counter many common distorted-thought spirals. Therapists can help us with this.

Reduce stress. Learn calming methods of breathing, praying, and meditating, advises Dr. Meier.

Talk to a counselor or clergy person. When we are depressed, we can always seek support from a Christian counselor, clergy member, or other health professional. The bottom line is that we need help. If we are depressed to the point of considering suicide, we should call a suicide prevention hotline, which can be found on the Internet. Suicide hotlines offer a nonjudgmental safe space to talk about one's darkest thoughts and provide help that could save a life.

Pray. There is unlimited power in prayer, and it's an effective course of action for people who are depressed or desperate enough to consider ending their lives.

"Jesus says, 'Come unto me, all ye that labour and are heavy laden, and I will give you rest'" (Matthew 11:28 KJV).

Meditate on Scripture. The Bible is filled with verses that can provide comfort and encouragement in times of distress, for example: Psalm 23, Psalm 40:1–2, Psalm 91, John 14:1–6, or Proverbs 3:5.

"Isaiah chapter 55," suggests Father Kurt Stasiak, "has a beautiful image: just as the rain comes down from the heavens and doesn't return to the sky until it does what it is supposed to do, namely water the earth, so God's Word is not going to come down and return to God frustrated—if we take time, it will take root and make a difference" (Isaiah 55:10–11).

And finally, Jeremiah 29:11, about which Father Stasiak says, "This passage reminds us that we just need to trust God that He has a purpose and plan—and He has the power."

· HEALING WORDS ·

The Lord is my shepherd; I shall not want. He makes me to lie down in green pastures; He leads me beside the still waters. He restores my soul; He leads me in the paths of righteousness For His name's sake. Yea, though I walk through the valley of the shadow of death, I will fear no evil; For You are with me; Your rod and Your staff, they comfort me. You prepare a table before me in the presence of my enemies; You anoint my head with oil; My cup runs over. Surely goodness and mercy shall follow me All the days of my life; And I will dwell in the house of the Lord Forever.
—Psalm 23 NKJV

*I waited patiently for the Lord; And He inclined to me, And heard my cry.
He also brought me up out of a horrible pit, Out of the miry clay,
And set my feet upon a rock, And established my steps.*
—Psalm 40:1–2 NKJV

DISCOURAGEMENT AND HOPELESSNESS

What Prayer Can Do

I'm a nurse, and I was helping out at a community health fair one morning, even though a blinding headache had kept me awake for the third night in a row. I've suffered from chronic pain for nearly three decades, and I had tried everything to treat it. I had recently made an appointment with yet another pain management specialist, only to cancel it. "What's the use? Nothing will help," I said to myself. I'd even stopped praying about it. The hopelessness was nearly as bad as the pain.

That day at the health fair we were offering flu vaccines. "You're at high risk for the flu," I explained to an elderly gentleman.

"I'm not taking one of those shots," he insisted. "My wife got one last year and she got the worst case of the flu you ever did see."

I told him the vaccine had nothing to do with his wife's bout of the flu, but to no avail. "Convincing some people to do what's in their own best interest is like pulling teeth," I complained to a colleague.

Yet hadn't I been just as stubborn? I had canceled my appointment with a new doctor. I'd turned away from God when He didn't take away my pain. But isn't prayer a kind of inoculation against difficulties? It offers protection against not just illness, but also doubt, fear, and hopelessness.

I rescheduled the appointment. Thanks to some new treatments, my pain is manageable these days. I still recommend flu shots to patients, but I also like to remember the best preventive medicine: the power of prayer. —ROBERTA L. MESSNER

Faith and Hope Are the Best Defense

CONSIDER THE CASE OF Thomas Edison.

He publicly announced in 1878, boldly and unequivocally, that he was going to invent an electric incandescent bulb that would light homes worldwide. He solicited funding from New York's financial elite. Many invested, joining him in forming the Edison Electric Light Company (later known as General Electric).

A key to creating this incandescent bulb, Edison determined, was finding the right filament fiber, one that wouldn't burn too quickly. He was sure that he'd find it soon. He tested fiber after fiber. He failed to find a fiber that would work. He failed more than six thousand times.

Do you think he was a little discouraged? Humiliated? Hopeless, even?

Apparently not Thomas Alva Edison. Sometime after the six thousandth fiber, he discovered that carbonized filaments from cotton thread worked well.

Within the span of thirteen months, Edison actually built 1,199 light bulbs that did not work. Then he invented the one that did. And from that one came the ones that light the world today. What kind of mind-set does it take to fail six thousand times, or 1,199 times, or a combined total of 7,199 times and still keep at it?

It's a genius mind-set, a saintly mind-set that we all should cultivate, says Dr. Paul Meier.

KEEP ON KEEPING ON

The Bible teaches us to keep hope alive, says Dr. Meier. We are to be diligent; we are to learn from our mistakes; and as 2 Timothy 2:15 says, we are to be workmen that have no need to be ashamed.

But wait. What about when we're certain that we've hit the wall, come to the end of the line, feel let down, feel that someone—or God, for that matter—has failed us?

Obviously, we feel disappointment. Obviously, we feel discouragement. And that's fine, says Dr. Meier. But it's not acceptable for us to let it cripple us. Instead, we need to follow the example of Thomas Edison and endure. Ideally, we run the race to win the prize, as the Apostle Paul instructs. That's what faith is all about. It's about holding on in the face of disappointment and discouragement: "...faith is the substance of things hoped for, the evidence of things not seen" (Hebrews 11:1 KJV).

Sure, we will be disappointed in life. We will feel the disappointment. And it will hurt. We just can't surrender to it, says Dr. Mel Lawrenz.

Remedies

THE APOSTLE PAUL SAYS in Romans 5:3–5 that if we believe in God and the promises that God has made to take care of us, then we can "...rejoice in our sufferings, knowing that suffering produces endurance, and endurance produces character, and character produces hope, and hope does not disappoint us..." (RSV).

So we may not feel like rejoicing. But certainly, we can build our character by keeping a constructive attitude. Here are some great ways to do that.

Think prayerfully and carefully. Being in a state of discouragement clouds our outlook and hampers our ability to make good choices, says Dr. Lawrenz. Making poor choices only leads to greater discouragement and despair. Spend time in spiritual reflection, seeking positive choices that will lead to positive outcomes.

Look for the lesson. If we look, we'll find a lesson in everything that happens to us. Sometimes it is not evident immediately, but it's there. We need to be patient and look for it while holding hope. That's faith.

"When I get up in the morning," says Dr. Meier, "I ask God, 'If I have a flat tire or whatever else it is that may go wrong today, help me to learn from it. Help me to grow from it. Help me realize that everything that happens is good.

Caller ID

BY LISA BRINKWORTH

They'll hire some young college grad," Dave told me. "Not an old guy like me." I'd never seen my husband so discouraged. He'd been doing great work as a field applicator for a farming co-op for ten years, but when a higher position opened up, the company said they were looking to make an outside hire. After a few weeks of searching, they finally let him take a skill test to be considered. Dave felt sure he'd passed but didn't think it would change their minds.

"If it's meant to be, God will open the door," I told him. "All we can do is pray."

The next day, we came home from running errands to the sound of the phone ringing. I was wrestling off my wet boots, so I asked Dave to get it. He usually lets calls go to voice mail, but I'd been expecting a call from the phone company and I didn't want to miss it. Unfortunately, Dave didn't pick up in time.

"Who was it?" I asked.

"Fervent Prayer," Dave answered.

"Fervent what?"

"The caller ID says Fervent Prayer!"

That's crazy, I thought, and took a look. Dave wasn't kidding. *Fervent Prayer,* clear as day on the tiny caller ID screen.

I dialed the phone company. They *had* just called. The woman couldn't explain the message on our caller ID. It didn't pop up when she called again later.

"How often do you answer the phone?" I asked Dave. "Maybe God's trying to tell you something."

The next few days, we prayed fervently, all right, every second we got, just like the caller ID said. And two weeks later, Dave's boss offered him the promotion.

Everything works together for good.' I wake up expecting not to have everything go perfectly. Then, when it doesn't, I'm not disappointed. So when something goes wrong, I just say, 'What can I learn from this experience?'"

Be patient and persevere. When we feel discouraged or hopeless, those are times we need to persevere and be patient until things change. James 1:12 says, "Blessed is anyone who endures temptation. Such a one has stood the test and will receive the crown of life that the Lord has promised to those who love him" (NRSV).

Circumstances are always in the process of changing, even if we aren't able to see any change on the horizon. Hope means leaning into the future based on God's faithfulness in the past. Since He has carried us through before, we can know that He'll be there to do it again.

Seek encouragement and hope. Turn to inspirational writings, people, and Bible verses. It is hard to remain discouraged when we surround ourselves with hope. Visit, call, and talk with positive, proactive, affirming, upbeat people, recommends Dr. Michele Novotni. "Encouragement," she says, "basically means 'offering courage' or 'supplying energy to others to help them go on.'" When we need it,

we should seek it. When others need it, we should give it.

"Encouragement can help build self-confidence and stimulate courage, which is the will to act even when you're scared or discouraged, when you feel like you can't go on," says Dr. Novotni. It is something that we all need at times. And it is something that we all need to share at times. The world is not divided into two classes of people: helpers and people who need help. All of us are actually both at differing times. By recognizing this, we build understanding and empathy and are better able to cope with our own dark times and better able to help others with theirs. And that's living our faith, she says.

Look inside. Since cynicism and negativism—opposites of hope—are learned behaviors that we may have picked up at home, we may simply have to develop new behaviors, like viewing problems as opportunities to grow, strengthen our characters, or make deep-seated change.

"Do you know anybody whom you really look up to as having tremendous character, not with just a public front but someone who is really high in integrity and strength of character?" asks the late Dr. William Backus. "And if you do, does that person have a life history of everything being easy? I'd guess that it's marked with various kinds of suffering. We don't like to think about it, but as Paul said, suffering produces positive traits."

Look at the facts. As it turns out, many depressed people don't have lives worse than the other guy; it's their interpretation that's flawed, says Dr. Backus.

"If you say that your future is hopeless, what is your evidence for that? What makes you think so? How can you say that if you don't know? Has the idea of a hopeless future made you feel better? Does it make you happy? Is it fun to wake up in the morning, look at the day, and say that the day is going to be terrible? And if it isn't, why don't you try talking yourself out of that and telling yourself the truth? Dr. Backus says. Finally, approaching a problem rationally is very effective for many.

HELPING SOMEONE WHO IS DISCOURAGED

Remember what it feels like to be discouraged, says Dr. Novotni. Then we'll begin to understand what our friends, loved ones, or acquaintances are going through. Here's how she says we can help them.

Treat them as equals. "When someone is discouraged, they don't need all these people who want to tell them exactly what it is they should do. That up-down relationship feels very uncomfortable to most people. That almost makes them dig deeper into the hole. It's as though everybody else knows how to do this. The truth is, each of us is going to go through times where we struggle," Dr. Novotni points out.

Listen to them. Let them express what they are feeling. Don't try to fix the problem.

Locate the problem. "It usually falls in a particular area of life: friendships, work, making a contribution to life, achieving intimacy, having loving relationships, money, self-acceptance, or problems in the spiritual dimension," says Dr. Novotni.

By encouraging a person to identify the problem area causing the discouragement, we help them keep it in perspective. It's one problem, not their whole life.

Offer encouragement. Be positive, upbeat, helpful, inspiring. Offer hope. Show respect and admiration. "This should be a goal of every church. It could be an intentional activity. Help people within the church to be more helpful and more encouraging of one another," she says. "There would be less of a need for professional counselors if people would really encourage one another."

Most Richly Blessed

"I asked for strength that I might achieve; I was made weak that I might learn humbly to obey. I asked for health that I might do greater things; I was given infirmity that I might do better things. I asked for riches that I might be happy; I was given poverty that I might be wise. I asked for power that I might have the praise of men; I was given weakness that I might feel the need of God. I asked for all things that I might enjoy life; I was given life that I might enjoy all things. I got nothing that I had asked for, but everything that I had hoped for. Almost despite myself, my unspoken prayers were answered; I am, among all men, most richly blessed."

—PRAYER COMPOSED BY AN UNKNOWN
CONFEDERATE SOLDIER BETWEEN 1861 AND 1865

EMOTIONAL PAIN AND HEARTACHE

Treasures Among the Ruins

After a nearly devastating loss, I began taking stock of various areas of my life. I discovered a Pandora's box of psychological liabilities and unmet expectations that held the marvelous potential to be transformed into better things.

I started the job of emotional housecleaning by taking a load of old clothes and children's things to a local charity. I cut up two high-school ski jackets of sentimental value to make my daughter a snowsuit. When the annual chore of removing the dead growth from the flower garden came around, I carefully tapped the dried seeds from the dead blooms, gathering the ingredients that would become next year's spring garden.

None of these activities was very remarkable. Some I had done before. But never in the spirit of deliberately taking something negative and extracting the very last ounce of good from it.

Gradually I was able to apply my new perspective to more volatile personal issues. I came to see error, misfortune, emotional pain, and heartache not as stumbling blocks but as influences in the current of change.

It didn't always work. To believe that all bad things can be transformed into good is a philosophy destined for disappointment. But the debris of loss

> has its usefulness. It rebuilds and changes shape. And sometimes, sparkling among the ruins, treasures can be found: courage, resolve, self-acceptance, and fresh hope. —DIANE BURTON ROBB

How to Tear Down the Walls

WHO CAN FORGET PRESIDENT Ronald Reagan standing on West German soil in Berlin, pointing to the wall that separated the city and divided the Western world from the communist Union of Soviet Socialist Republics: "Mr. Gorbachev," Reagan said, "tear down this wall!"

How often do we sense twinges of emptiness, guilt, or pain when reality slams into one of our own emotional Berlin Walls? Perhaps these twinges are signals that God is pointing to a tall, thick emotional wall that we've erected to protect ourselves from hurt and saying to us, indignantly, "Tear down this wall!"

We all have a tendency to try to insulate ourselves from emotional pain and heartache by erecting invisible barriers that keep people and circumstances at bay and cut us off from the world. It could be that we're hiding from some horrible event in our past, like sexual abuse or the sudden, tragic death of a loved one. Or it could be something as simple as an innocuous event from childhood that we've long since consciously forgotten but misinterpreted to mean that we had done or experienced something awful.

We often do this instinctively and probably hide from hurt more often than we realize, say counselors. This is an unhealthy response.

Really, it is an act of fear, says James E. Miller, D.Min.

We certainly don't need to deliberately seek out fearful situations. But we do need to realize, as the Scripture says, "…God has not given us a spirit of fear, but of power…" (2 Timothy 1:7 NKJV).

If we allow emotional wounds to send us into hiding, then we are adopting the role of victim. We are telling ourselves that we are hopeless and powerless and that our lives and futures are beyond our control. This is not a productive spiritual outlook. This is in direct opposition to faith, says Dr. Mel Lawrenz.

God's Word says, "'For I know the plans I have for you,' declares the LORD, 'plans to prosper you and not to harm you, plans to give you hope and a future. Then you will call on me and come and pray to me, and I will listen to you'" (Jeremiah 29:11–12 NIV). This verse and others like it are what we should meditate on.

Remedies
HOW TO HANDLE HEARTACHE

AT TIMES, EMOTIONAL PAIN, embarrassments, failures—in marriage, business, long-standing, valued relationships, or maybe even simply failing to impress a parent, teacher, sweetheart, or boss—can seem more than we can bear, more than we can handle. "But this is how we grow," says Dr. Michele Novotni. "Often during deep, troubled emotional events, people really grow in their relationships with God in ways that they never would have imagined," she says.

These events do affect us, bend us, and stretch us, and they do change us. The goal, says Dr. Novotni, is to change for the better, to learn and grow. These are good times for quiet spiritual soul-searching, for in-depth Bible reading, and for prayer, she says.

Here are some great ways to handle emotional injuries.

Seek support. Don't try to go it completely alone, advise counselors. "Find someone to be with you as you go through it," recommends Dr. Miller. "Yes, there are some things that you have to do yourself, that no one can do for you. But counselors have found that the one variable that matters more than any other is the kind of support system people have. Those who have the better support systems, the more complete support systems, the healthier support systems, are the most likely to really heal."

Some of us will only need one person, one close confidant; others will need a dozen. For many, support groups help.

"For almost every kind of dilemma, there is a support group," says Dr. Novotni. To find one, call hospitals, look in newspaper listings of community services, check with your doctor and pastor, or call counseling centers. Most counseling centers will know about support groups in the area.

Never Alone

By Sheryl Smith-Rodgers

The Christmas Eve service had already started by the time I pulled into the parking lot. *Good,* I thought. I slipped inside while the choir was singing "Silent Night." I kept my head down, hoping nobody would wish me a merry Christmas.

My marriage was crumbling and my life felt like a big mess. I hadn't even wanted to come to church, much less talk to anyone, but a nagging voice in my head had made me go anyway.

I made a beeline for the corner of the sanctuary. There was a pew in the back row where I knew I could be alone. Plus, I could slip out as soon as the service ended. But when I got to the pew I almost groaned out loud. A woman was already sitting there!

God, if you really want me to make it through this service, I'll need your help, I thought as I sat down in the next-to-last row. Would it be possible to make me invisible?

I kept my eyes fixed firmly on the floor as the service progressed, up through the choir's rendition of "Joy to the World." Then came the moment I had been dreading. The minister rose, spreading his arms wide. "It's time to greet one another," he said.

I turned dutifully to the woman in the pew behind me and braced myself for the inevitable smile and cheerful "Merry Christmas." But as I reached out my hand, our eyes met—and instantly I recognized the pain I saw in hers. It was the same pain I'd seen in the mirror that morning.

"Are you all right?" I asked, almost reflexively.

Struggling to hold back tears, she told me briefly about her son's troubled marriage and her hurting grandkids, his children. I told her about my own heartache. Before the minister spoke again, we'd agreed to pray for each other.

After the service, I hugged my new friend good-bye.

"I almost didn't come to church today," she said. "But something drew me."

Consult a counselor. Some of us will want to seek professional counseling, and that can really help, says Dr. Novotni.

How will we know? Dr. Novotni suggests seeing a professional if we find ourselves unable to lift out of our sadness or despondency, if we are unable to function effectively in normal day-to-day duties, or if we find ourselves telling our same sad stories over and over to the same people. A professional can help us get unstuck, steer us away from increasingly destructive behaviors, and guide us into proper treatment for depression, should it be overtaking us.

Feel the pain. We shouldn't avoid what is happening, but "go more deeply into it. We should immerse ourselves in it as we are able—as our support systems allow us to and as our health allows. We should move toward it rather than away from it," says Dr. Miller.

Take responsibility. Traditional Christian teaching says that we will be forgiven, no matter what we have done, and that we should forgive, no matter what someone else has done. Still, we must not rush forgiveness, says Dr. Lawrenz, particularly if our actions have somehow hurt someone. First, we must acknowledge what we have done and take responsibility for our actions. Then, and only then, can and should we make amends, if possible, and forgive ourselves.

Forgiveness is a gift we need to give ourselves, says Dale Ryan, Ph.D., CEO and founder of Christian Recovery International. If we've hurt someone, we're rather out of order to run to them and say, in effect, "I've hurt you terribly. So give me something valuable." Our job is to make amends with others and make peace with ourselves, he says. The others can forgive us when they are ready and able.

Seek strength in faith. We should know that God will never abandon us, asserts Dr. Lawrenz. As the Bible says, "The Lord Himself goes before you and will be with you; he will never leave you nor forsake you. Do not be afraid; do not be discouraged" (Deuteronomy 31:8 NIV). Focus on encouraging, faith-building Scriptures like "I can do all things through

Christ which strengtheneth me" (Philippians 4:13 KJV) or "We are hard pressed on every side, but not crushed; perplexed, but not in despair; persecuted, but not abandoned; struck down, but not destroyed" (2 Corinthians 4:8–9 NIV).

Set goals. We should imagine where we want to be a year or two from now, emotionally and otherwise, and hold on to that vision, suggests Dr. Novotni. We should work toward it. That's an essential part of the process of rebuilding hope.

Develop a new horizon. Each new habit formed during difficult times is like adding a pearl to a necklace. New faces, new interests, and new hobbies create new thoughts, which give strength and luster to the necklace.

· HEALING WORDS ·

Living Through the Season of Pain

We are weeping now. We will not weep forever. Someday soon, we will enjoy laughter and find joy in life again, says Dr. Harold Ivan Smith. Remember, he says, what the Bible advises.

To every thing there is a season, and a time to every purpose under the heaven...
A time to weep, and a time to laugh; a time to mourn, and a time to dance.
—ECCLESIASTES 3:1, 4 KJV

GRIEF AND THE DEATH OF A LOVED ONE

The Tomato Patch

Nothing would grow on the scarred land where the backhoe had dug up the earth on the far end of my property down by the creek. More than a year had passed since I had to put in a septic tank at my mountainside home, and I kept telling myself that it would take time for the ground to heal. The oak and hickory would reseed, the tiny acorns and nuts would sprout, but spring had come and gone, and all I could see from my dining-room window was a barren swath of brown earth and rocks. Even the wildflowers I had seeded didn't come up.

If my friend and neighbor Doris were alive, she would have been able to make something grow. On a warm day we loved to go down to the creek and watch the light play off the dancing water. Eventually, shadows would slip over the soft green hills. "I love this place just the way God made it," Doris would say in a near whisper, "with things always growing."

In her garden Doris grew lettuce, red cabbage, bell peppers, tomatoes. At the end of the previous summer—it seemed an eternity ago now—she brought me a big box of tomatoes. "Girl, there's every kind of tomato you could ever want," she said. More than I could ever eat. I had to dump the ones that spoiled down by the creek.

No one knew she was dying then. I certainly didn't. Sometimes she made excuses, "I'm just a little tired, Fran." She wouldn't go on a hike or a picnic. She wasn't outside in her garden as much. When I asked, she said she was getting over something. Nothing to worry about. Maybe if I'd known that that was her last harvest, I would have canned all those tomatoes. I wouldn't have chosen to dig a septic tank. It could have waited.

The backhoe came the same month Doris died. My heart wrenched each time the powerful teeth grasped one of the young trees and ripped it from the ground. Lord, I prayed, this is too much after the death of my friend. To lose my wooded view and my neighbor all at once. I tried to imagine what Doris would say—that the land would heal, that God would bring it back more glorious than it had been before. "Just wait," I could almost hear her say.

I was tired of waiting. I wanted Doris to be here with me, to tell me the names of the birds I saw out my window and the critters rushing through the brush. I wanted Doris to bring me the bounty from her garden. I wanted to go on walks with her down by the creek. I wanted her here to comfort me, impossible as that was.

Then one morning I looked out my window and caught sight of a small red spot at the edge of the creek. What's that? I wondered. Had something blown onto my property? I put on my boots and went down to investigate. Not till I came to the edge of the bank did I see it—a tangle of tomato vines spilling across the ground. Right where I'd dumped those spoiled ones, the fruit of Doris's last crop. Every kind of tomato you could ever want. I felt Doris close to me. I could hear her saying in a near whisper that even after a season of loss, God can heal—just as He makes dry land flourish again. —FRAN YOUNGER GREATHOUSE

A Natural and Normal Process
"JESUS WEPT" (JOHN 11:35 KJV)

THIS IS THE SHORTEST VERSE in the Bible. "Jesus wept" because His friend Lazarus had died.

God wants us to know that grief is universal; grief is real; grief is okay. We need not hide grief, and yes, Jesus grieved; yes, "Jesus wept." Exhibiting signs of grief, even long after a loss, is not a sign of weak faith, says grief educator John W. James, founder and president of Grief Recovery Institute in California and coauthor of *The Grief Recovery Handbook*. It is evidence of a feeling, caring person.

Grief is a natural and painful but healthy emotional response to profound loss of any kind, not just death. We grieve the loss of health, wealth, mobility, reputation, possessions, pride, youth, and so on. We grieve all losses, and we grieve each loss uniquely. Sometimes the process of grieving for a new loss dredges up past ones and the pain associated with them, multiplying the effect and deepening the depths of our despair and angst.

Grief is not easy to deal with, and we may be tempted to avoid it instead of embracing the pain of it, but it's a vital part of the process of healing after a loss or the death of someone we love, so we need to allow ourselves to do it.

DIVE IN

Well-meaning people may try to distract us from our grief and encourage us to suppress it, ignore it, and move beyond it. "We have a lot of what I call grief police, who say, 'Here is what you should and shouldn't do,'" says Dr. Harold Ivan Smith. Grieving people don't need to be told what to do; they need to grieve.

Grievers don't need clichés and pat answers, either, says James. Near the top of the list are comments such as "It just takes time," "Just give it time," "Your faith will see you through," and "Keep a stiff upper lip."

Grievers don't need a stiff upper lip but, rather, opportunities to fully explore their grief and how it affects them and their lives. They need to remember the meaningfulness and significance of what they have lost, to memorialize it and celebrate it, to keep alive the memory of the treasured aspects of whomever or whatever it is they have lost, say experts.

COMFORTING VERSES

At a time of profound loss, much seems uncertain to us. But God's presence is unchanging, says Dr. Mel Lawrenz. Reading the Bible, especially these verses, can help us grasp that.

Though he brings grief, he will show compassion, so great is his unfailing love.

For he does not willingly bring affliction or grief to anyone.

—Lamentations 3:32–33 NIV

Blessed are those who mourn, for they will be comforted.

—Matthew 5:4 NIV

You are filled with grief because I have said these things.

Very truly I tell you, you will weep and mourn while the world rejoices. You will grieve, but your grief will turn to joy.

—John 16:6, 20 NIV

Your sun will never set again, and your moon will wane no more; the Lord will be your everlasting light, and your days of sorrow will end.

—Isaiah 60:20 NIV

Remedies
TAKE THE PAIN TO GOD

WHEN WE'RE IN THE throes of loss, we need to seek sympathetic people, turn to God, and talk to God. We need to tell Him how we feel and ask Him what we are to do next and how we are to get from here to there. We need to express anger and disappointment. The very process of expressing disappointment is an expression of faith. We don't get mad at someone we don't believe exists, says Dr. Lawrenz.

God never says in His Word that we would not suffer losses in life or that life would not be painful sometimes. He does, however, promise to be with us through it all. As the Psalmist writes:

God is our refuge and strength, an ever-present help in trouble. Therefore we will not fear, though the earth give way and the mountains fall into the heart of the sea, though its waters roar and foam and the mountains quake with their surging.

—Psalm 46:1–3 NIV

Special Delivery

By Barbara Beamer Hodgen

I reached into the mailbox and something ruffled against my fingers. *Probably another sympathy card,* I thought.

My husband, Tom, had died recently, and sympathy cards were arriving every day.

This felt different, though. I peeked inside the box. A small note with a green ribbon was nestled between two bills. I took it out. "A journey of a thousand miles begins with a single step," it read. It had no envelope, no name. No way of telling where it had come from.

Thank you, I thought. Grief was a long unexpected journey, and I needed all the help I could get.

The notes continued to appear long after the sympathy cards had stopped. Each one with a ribbon attached and a comforting quote. "Faith is building on what you know is here so you can reach what you know is there," said one. A reminder that my faith would always be with me.

"God doesn't always still the storm, but He can calm the sailor," another read. I thought about walking along the beach with my husband in stormy weather and feeling at peace when I held his hand. *Lord, I need you to hold my hand now.*

"Spring will come! The clouds cannot stay forever!" I was grateful for the friends who would listen to me and let me cry.

Then one day, after almost a year of these daily comforting notes, the last one arrived in my mailbox: "The question is not whether we will die but how we will live."

Life would go on. All it took was a bit of kindness. The worst of my mourning was over, thanks to the help of my secret correspondent.

As for the notes, I've passed them on. May they continue to help someone else on a journey, one single step at a time.

Here are some practical things we can do to help ourselves after the death of someone we love or some other type of loss.

Find an on-call friend. We need someone sympathetic who says it's okay if we call them anytime, even at 3:00 a.m., if we're feeling desperate. We shouldn't abuse the privilege but make use of it if we really need to, says Dr. James E. Miller.

Avoid toxic people. Being around certain people simply isn't good for us. If they don't let us grieve, and if they lecture, denigrate, chide, or otherwise upset us, either intentionally or unintentionally, it's okay to avoid such people for a while if it makes us feel better, says Dr. Miller.

Some people will think that it is their duty to jolt us out of our grief, says Dr. Lawrenz. We will want to avoid them in particular.

Track thoughts. We need to record what we learn. As we go through a profound loss experience, we can learn many lessons and gain many insights. We can write these down in a notebook or journal, day by day, then reflect on them occasionally, says Dr. Miller.

Recognize the good in grief. Grief truly is a necessary, healthy process. People and cultures that recognize grief as an essential passageway handle life much better than those that try to short-circuit the process, says Dr. Lawrenz. Those who short-circuit grief actually repress it. Then it's likely to nag at them negatively for much longer and more fiercely than it would have otherwise.

Visit the grave. Some people find comfort in visiting a grave or memorial site. If so, they should visit as often as they would like to remember a loved one, pray, weep, or leave flowers as a way of honoring the memory of someone special to them.

Cry freely. If we feel like crying, we should cry. It's natural for people enduring a serious loss. Some people cry a lot, and some seldom or never cry. Whichever, we shouldn't restrain the urge.

Vent anger. Grieving people often feel anger. We need to let it out. We can yell at the walls, if necessary, or hit a pillow, clean the attic. We can even work off the angry energy in a physical way, such as exercising or chopping a cord of wood. We shouldn't repress the anger we may feel, advises Dr. Miller.

Speak up. We need to tell people what we need and want. Most don't know and are wary of saying or doing the wrong thing. We can tell them if we'd like them to go ahead and talk around us about our loss or the deceased person. If we need time alone or help with tasks, we should express that, too.

Find a support group. While not for everyone, support groups are helpful for many people. Quickly, we learn that we are not alone and that our feelings are natural. We also learn coping skills from others. In most large communities, some churches sponsor support groups, says James.

Face the pain and deal with it. We are not supposed to run or hide from our pain. In fact, we are to dive in and experience it and all the issues it raises so that we grieve fully and work our way through the hard questions that arise. Losing a loved one is supposed to hurt. There are ways to deal with that hurt effectively and help it heal. For example, we could write a letter to the deceased, expressing feelings or communicating the sentiments we wish we'd shared with the person when he or she was living; we could carry a memento of the person in our pocket or purse, create a memorial at home with photos or other memorabilia of the person, or we could make a memory album with photos and special things that remind us of the person we loved.

Be prepared for feelings of sadness. Expect memories of earlier losses to flood forth. Particularly those that we have not completely processed and those that we have not completely grieved, says James. This is an opportunity to work through them as well, he says, a time to seek completion and closure.

Accept change. When the time is right, we can give away some of the things that will never be used again or rearrange the furniture so it works well for us and anyone else who currently shares our home. At some point, we will begin to want to make some changes in our environment to make it clear that a profound change has taken place in our lives. When we feel this way, we should act on it, recognizing that it is not a way of trying to forget the person we loved, but a way of moving forward with our lives, says Dr. Miller. As God says in Isaiah 43:19 (ESV), "Behold, I am doing a new thing!"

Refuse to be isolated. During times of grief, spending some time alone is helpful, but we should not isolate ourselves from others. It's important to be with supportive friends and family members who will both honor our loss and help us move forward in appropriate ways.

Give thanks. Find something every day to be thankful for and spend some time appreciating it.

How to Grow Through Grief

By Elizabeth Sullivan-Brown

In 1974, our daughter Tricia was in an automobile accident that ended her life at the age of twenty-four. In the aftermath of grieving, over a period of months and years, I discovered that certain things helped me to grow, both as a person and in my faith.

The process of grief after the death of a loved one is highly individual, of course. But for everyone, it means change. What I learned may help you—or someone you know—make that change a positive one.

1. **Trust your instincts, even if they're "unorthodox."** No one can tell another the best way to mourn or handle funeral details. You will learn what is meaningful and comforting to you by following your heart. Despite some raised eyebrows, we chose to have Tricia's casket and ceremony in our living room at home and to ask a pastor friend to play the guitar and sing at the service. We wanted her funeral to be a reflection of her life.

   We didn't immediately remove Tricia's presence from the house by disposing of all her things—what some people call "painful reminders." Handling her possessions sometimes brought gentle tears, but it also gave me a sense of closeness to her that had a healing effect, not a distressing one.

2. **Allow yourself to feel your loss.** The Bible says "Jesus wept," rather than "Jesus cried."

   The word *wept* implies a depth of feeling. I wept. I feel I would have died without that release. Thinking and talking about Tricia helped, too. I found that going over memories of her—at this time when my feelings were especially sensitive—gradually brought helpful insights to a surprising number of areas: other personal relationships, religious beliefs, my priorities and attitudes.

One of Tricia's qualities that's more a part of our lives than before is respect for nature and all living things. We used to laugh at her for taking a bug outside instead of killing it or for showing real sorrow when a tree was cut down. In my reassessing time, I realized that her feeling for nature reflected her feelings about God and other people.

3. **Increase your exposure to spiritual teaching.** In addition to services at my own church, I began to attend those at an interdenominational church suggested by a friend. Hearing in an increased measure—about the love of God, the part of Him within us all, and the ways we can show love in daily life—helped me with spiritual growth through a time of potential depression.

I know the death of someone dear can be a positive experience, a time of growth, reexamination of values, new understanding, and change. I feel I am a better person from having known Tricia and experiencing the death of her body. Handling death in a constructive way is a tribute to the person who has passed to the other side.

THE REGIMEN OF SORROW

Grieving, quite simply, is consuming and exhausting work, notes Dr. Miller. Not only do we tire ourselves out, but we may also neglect essentials for our health and well-being, like nutrition, sleep, exercise, bill-paying, and medical care, to name a few. We do need to watch out for ourselves a bit. The following can go on our to-do lists.

Take it easy. Grieving is depleting. So it helps to give ourselves permission to rest and replenish our energy by taking naps, relaxing, and reenergizing.

Plan and complete one thing each day. Even if our grief is excruciating and our energy nil, we should plan to do something and then do it every day, says Dr. Miller. We don't need to convince ourselves to stay busy all day long; we just need to accomplish one little significant something to prove to ourselves that we are not totally at the mercy of seemingly all-engulfing grief, that we are capable of doing at least some things.

Practice self-care. Eat regularly. Eat healthfully. Get proper sleep. Missing sleep and eating poorly, excessively, or not at all affect how we think and feel both physically and emotionally, says Dr. Miller.

Expect ups and downs. We don't suddenly get over it. We may feel much better one day and then much worse the next, or even later the same day. Recovery from grief is the result of sustained effort over time, says James.

Avoid major decisions. Postpone them if at all possible. We are vulnerable when in the midst of mourning, warns Dr. Lawrenz.

Remember to breathe. "Most grievers do not breathe well," says Dr. Smith. "Practicing several minutes of deep, gentle belly breathing actually helps us release emotions and get in touch with ourselves and God."

Try to laugh. Yes, it is good to laugh later in the process of grieving. It's healthy. It's healing. It's needed, says Dr. Smith. We can rent funny videos, read funny books and comics, or watch favorite comedians to regain our sense of humor. We do sense greater hope and wider perspective when we're able to laugh a bit each day. If we have to start with just one a week, it still helps.

LET IT BE

How long does grief last? "As long as it takes," says Dr. Miller.

Other experts agree. It varies from person to person and with the nature of the relationship, from a few weeks to five or more years in some cases. Experts warn, though, that if we find ourselves not just sad but careening out of control into destructive behaviors, we should see a qualified counselor.

Dr. Lawrenz explains: "In a normal grieving experience, a person is very sad about the loss. But there is such a thing as complicated grief, where a person moves into depression and despair. You recognize it if there is long-term isolation from other people or a general downward decline of the person's ability to function in life. What that basically means is that mourning is turning into significant depression. When that occurs, he or she should seek medical or counseling help."

The Journey Home

God, slip him into eternity

on satin wings

so swift and strong

so graceful and serene

that You alone

will know the moment

of his departure.

And even as his loved ones

bend low to catch his final breath,

may the angel throng

be welcoming him home

in song.

—ALMA BARKMAN

JEALOUSY AND ENVY

It was once thought that those afflicted with envy became so unhealthy their complexions took on a greenish tinge. That's what Shakespeare was alluding to with his phrase "the green-eyed monster." Though he took a bit of poetic license, still, envy does change our inward complexions. As a friend of mine says, jealousy is comparing the inside of yourself to the outside of others. It's not so much what they have, but what you think you lack—in other words, jealousy is all wrapped up in feelings of inadequacy. Yet how on earth can I feel deprived or inadequate when all around me my life is full of God's blessings? Envy is, more than anything, a state of ingratitude.

As Proverbs 14:30 says: "A relaxed attitude lengthens a man's life; jealousy rots it away." Now, if you'll excuse me, I'm off to salsa lessons. —MARY ANN O'ROARK

Gaining a Right View of Ourselves and Others

ANGER. CHARACTER ASSASSINATION. Catty, cutting comments. Unkind jokes. Gossip. Lying. Even murder.

Jealousy shows up in many damaging ways. But where does such a toxic force get its start? Like many deep-seated emotional problems, jealousy and its alter ego, envy, tend to develop in childhood when we come to believe that resources, including our parents' love, are in short supply, says Dr. Charles Zeiders. "Jealousy is characterized by a position of lack," he says, "the belief that there is only so much beauty or talent or happiness or love to go around."

If a child wants his mother to make him feel loved, soothe a hurt, or reassure him, and Dad consistently distracts her from the task, "the child learns that in a relationship with a woman, there really isn't enough of her nurturing to go around," says Dr. Zeiders.

Or if Mom simply isn't there when the child needs her, the child may start to think, "I'm going to lose whomever I love. I'm going to be rejected," according to Everett L. Worthington, Ph.D., professor of psychology at Virginia Commonwealth University. The same dynamic can result if certain children in a family seem to get more attention than the others, he says.

Another common cause of jealousy: when parents push a child toward independence and then pull the child back because they can't bear the thought of the child not relying on them, says Dr. Worthington. That child learns to view independence as negative and undesirable.

UNDERSTANDING JEALOUSY AND ENVY

How might these childhood experiences affect our later relationships? In the case of people who feel they have been rejected, "they're always afraid they're going to lose the other person. So they're anxious and alert to any possible way this might happen, including when the other person even looks at someone else," says Dr. Worthington.

Someone who struggled with independence as a child will likely become jealous if "their romantic partner tries to make any moves toward independence," Dr. Worthington says. "This kicks in the need for a glomming-on type of dependency that's uncomfortable."

A man who is jealous over his wife's other relationships "will often be consumed by rage," says Dr. Zeiders. "He'll berate his mate and accuse her of not loving him. He's constantly on the verge of ruining the relationship by 'guilting' her for her imaginary infidelities." A jealous woman in the same situation may operate more deceptively. "She'll drop a few well-placed comments to discredit the people she thinks the husband is interested in," he says.

Even if jealousy or envy don't manifest verbally, they can spark an unhealthy sense of competition, when we constantly compare ourselves with others to see if we're as successful, intelligent, or desirable. Keeping score in this way ultimately "undermines the jealous person's ability to celebrate the good things that happen to other people or themselves," says Dr. Zeiders.

Jealousy

BY NORMAN VINCENT PEALE

How to overcome...

People who are habitually jealous of others, by this very weakness, block off the flow of creative power through their lives.

Years ago I knew a minister who became notorious for his failures. "We're not doing so well, but the Baptists down the street aren't doing any better," I once heard him say.

Despite his jealousy, this minister had an earnest desire to serve God. Someone who loved him enough finally helped him face up to his shortcomings.

In turning his weakness over to God, the minister felt the strong guidance that he should write letters to the very people he was jealous of. As a result, he has since built for himself a great following by the warm, personal messages he sends to those who achieve in any field.

All of us, by nature, can be jealous: a man and woman of each other because of the attentions, imagined or real, of a third person; a mother over the beauty of her daughter; a husband over the attention his wife gives their children; a wife over her husband's love for his business. It can happen between people in business, politics, and even social activities.

How do you recognize jealousy within yourself? It is there if you tear another person down, belittle one's accomplishments, or ignore another's achievements.

One young man in his forties complained to me recently of his high blood pressure. Through counseling, we found he had a history of jealousy toward another man. When I suggested that he pray for his rival, he said, "How can I pray for him and really mean it?"

"Pray first for sincerity and believe that this prayer will be granted," I replied. "Then pray for your rival, asking for him success, achievement, and blessings."

After he did this, all the strain seemed to drain from his body. I picked up an elastic band from my desk and drew it out to full tension. "This is the way you were a few minutes ago," I said. Then I allowed the band to return to normal. "This is the way you are now. Keep this as a reminder that you can always pray your way out of jealousy."

Here are several further suggestions:

1. Learn how to detect jealousy in yourself. Watch for telltale signs such as criticism of others.

2. Admit openly to yourself that you have a problem with jealousy.

3. Practice giving credit to others; pray regularly that your friends will be successful.

4. Write letters to people who receive awards and recognition.

5. Ask the Lord to help you; then repeat some specific prayer such as, "I can do all things through Christ which strengtheneth me" (Philippians 4:13 KJV).

Jealous and envious people may not only blame themselves for their perceived misfortunes. They're often angry with God, too. "The envious person has basically decided that God has made a mistake," says Ray Pritchard, M.Th., president of Keep Believing Ministries in Dallas, and author of *The ABC's of Wisdom* and *What a Christian Believes*. Basically, the jealous person is saying, "God didn't give me enough. He gave somebody else too much, and they don't appreciate it; they don't deserve it."

Remedies
FINDING PEACE

KING SOLOMON, THOUGHT by some to be one of the wisest men who ever lived, summarized it this way: "A heart at peace gives life to the body, but envy rots the bones" (Proverbs 14:30 NIV). One possible goal, then, is to turn our envious, jealous hearts into hearts at peace.

How? There are three important steps, says Dr. Pritchard: developing a right view of God, of ourselves, and of others.

Here are some suggestions to help that happen.

Be careful about self-talk. The way we talk to ourselves can reinforce feelings of jealousy and envy, says Dr. Backus, "If we think, 'I must get what I want in order to be happy,' it can trigger feelings that it's terrible if we don't get what we want or that doing without is intense suffering. We may even feel that if other people have what we want and we don't have it, it's unfair."

All of these attitudes are patently false. Instead, says Dr. Backus, we need to tell ourselves, "It's not terrible when my every whim isn't gratified" or "It may be uncomfortable or inconvenient to do without certain things, but I can do it."

Give others their due. The words may get caught in our throats the first few times, but praising others when they've done well can help break jealousy's power over us. "Genuine, heartfelt praise can't exist in the same heart as envy," says Dr. Pritchard.

Follow the commandment. In His infinite wisdom, God issued a commandment dealing with this specific problem that is worth following. "You shall not covet your neighbor's wife. You shall not set your desire on your neighbor's house or land, his male or female servant, his ox or donkey, or anything that belongs to your neighbor" (Deuteronomy 5:21 NIV). Yesterday's ox may be today's sports car, but the concept still applies. And the best way to avoid such jealousy is by simply being thankful for what we have, says Dr. Pritchard.

Set a new standard. If we truly believe in our faith, we know we should set our sights higher than a newer car or a bigger house than our friends or neighbors have. "As Christians, we've pledged to pattern our lives after Jesus," writes former president Jimmy Carter in *Sources of Strength*. "The real measures of success are the things that He said were important— in the words of St. Paul, the things that we cannot see, like truth, compassion, justice, service, and love."

Avoid words and actions that provoke jealousy. Even if we don't personally struggle with envy or jealousy, we may help bring it to life or perpetuate it in others with our words and deeds. For example,

The Bracelet

By Doris Haase

Jenny's birthday party had to be special this year. Her father was dead, and as her mother I wanted to make up the loss to her. So did friends and relatives. The gifts piled high. A tiny gold bracelet with "Ten Commandments" charms became her immediate favorite. She wore it as she and her cousins went out to play.

"You might lose it, Jenny," I warned. *No more losses, God,* I thought silently. *We can't stand any more losses. Even small ones.*

I joined my younger sister and her husband in the living room. They sat close together, hands entwined and smiling. The way Dave and I used to do. Their intimacy seemed complete and exclusive. I felt stirrings of pain. *They're ignoring the other guests,* I thought irritably. And then another thought came.

It isn't fair that they're together and I'm alone. There it was. Envy. The words struck like a bolt of lightning.

"Mom," Jenny called, running in. "The catch opened and I lost my bracelet. Help me find it, Mom."

Grateful for the chance to hide my face and feelings, I went outside and dug through leaves and flowers. We found the chain quickly, but one of the charms was missing. On my knees in the grass I hunted. At last a glimmer caught my eye. The tenth charm. I picked it up. Tiny engraved letters on gold: "Thou shalt not covet."

Everything became still. *Thou shalt not covet thy neighbor's happiness,* I thought. *Or thy sister's joy.* I walked slowly back into the living room and stood looking at them. I felt their love, and suddenly its warmth seemed to draw me in. Quickly, I bent down and kissed my sister's cheek.

if we fawn over someone's children in the presence of an infertile woman who is desperate for children of her own, it will likely arouse feelings of sadness or jealousy in her. Or if our spouses tend to be jealous of our relationships, we should avoid personal, private discussions with members of the opposite sex.

"My husband is a pastor, and he will never meet with a woman alone," says Mary Ellen Ashcroft, Ph.D., vicar of the Spirit of the Wilderness Episcopal Church, Grand Marais, Minnesota and author of *Temptations Women Face*. "That's treating our marriage relationship with the honor that it deserves."

Seek God's intervention. More stubborn patterns of jealousy and envy may require specific prayer to overcome. If we feel the need for greater help, we should "invite the Holy Spirit to speak the truth," says Dr. Zeiders. "Sometimes the Spirit will give us a sense that even if a parent forgot or rejected us, God has not and will not forget us. By inviting God's truth in, we learn that we are, in fact, nurtured and loved on some real and universal level by God."

Adopt God's view of gifting. Not only has God created each of us with specific gifts and talents unique to us, but He also gave them to others so we could work together to build His Kingdom. "It's the idea that the church is a body and each of us is a hand, an eye, a head, or a foot. Each of us has a place in the body," says Dr. Zeiders. "Jealousy divides the body, so we need to come together. We complement one another."

Get self-worth from God. If we have proof that our spouse has been flirting, we need to get to marriage counseling—fast. But even if our jealousy is well-founded, ultimately, we can't allow our self-esteem to be defined by someone else's sin or neglect.

"Larry Crabb wrote an important book called *The Marriage Builder*," says Dr. Worthington. "In it he argues that one of the keys to getting rid of jealousy is not trying to find security in our mates. Our security, if we have any at all, is in a loving and faithful relationship with God through Jesus. And to the extent that people can really come to believe that deep down in their hearts, they'll be better off."

Overcoming Envy

Who is *wise and understanding among you? Let him show by good conduct*
that *his works* are done *in the meekness of wisdom.*
But if you have bitter envy and self-seeking in your hearts,
do not boast and lie against the truth. This wisdom does not
descend from above, but is *earthly, sensual, demonic.*
For where envy and self-seeking exist, *confusion and every evil thing* are *there.*
—JAMES 3:13–16 NKJV

Do not envy the oppressor, and choose none of his ways;
For the perverse person is *an abomination to the Lord . . .*
—PROVERBS 3:31–32 NKJV

Let us not become conceited, provoking and envying each other.
—GALATIANS 5:26 NIV

Love is patient, love is kind. It does not envy, it does not boast, it is not proud.
It does not dishonor others, it is not self-seeking, it is not easily angered,
it keeps no record of wrongs.
Love does not delight in evil but rejoices with the truth.
It always protects, always trusts, always hopes, always perseveres.
—1 CORINTHIANS 13:4–7 NIV

LONELINESS

A World of Their Own

Being young and lonely is something I remember well. To me, the very sound of loneliness is lonesome—the little word only hidden in "loneliness" always reminds me that I was an only child. When I was six years old, my family moved to a small town where the children had already formed tight circles of friendship. So I invented children and animals to play with; I learned to read early and found company in books. But sometimes, still, I felt so lonely that I would go out and hug trees....

It was a sunny, wind-washed morning when I left Guideposts' offices and set out by taxi for Manhattan's Upper West Side to interview Madeleine L'Engle. As the cab wove its way north through Central Park, I went over my notes. Like me, Madeleine had been an only child. Her parents, already middle-aged when she was born in 1918, were preoccupied with problems. Her father's lungs had been damaged by mustard gas during World War I, and his illness absorbed her mother's attention. Except for Sundays, the adults ate by themselves, and the little girl spent a good deal of time alone, eating her meals in her room.

At school, gawky, awkward Madeleine was unpopular with the other children. One of her legs was slightly shorter than the other, making her inept at sports. Teachers assumed she was clumsy mentally as well as physically, and in fact, bright but bored, she made a poor showing in class.

By the time Madeleine was twelve, her father's condition had deteriorated so much that the family left their home in New York City in search of pollution-free air in Switzerland. There was no appropriate school in their remote Alpine village, so Madeleine was placed in a Swiss boarding school, where she was desperately unhappy....

My cab let me out at the Cathedral of St. John the Divine. In a parklike area next to the cathedral I followed a tree-lined path to the diocesan house. There Madeleine L'Engle uses the handsome, high-ceilinged library as an office in exchange for her services as librarian. Tall, slender, gray-haired, she greeted me warmly and introduced me to Dr. Charlotte, a golden retriever who was keeping her company. Then we settled comfortably at a refectory table.

"I'm interested in the children you write about," I said. "They're kids with problems and self-doubts, yet they're achievers, too."

Madeleine nodded. "That's because they don't give up. They do things they think they can't do."

"You didn't give up, either," I said. "You had some harsh experiences as a child. What kept you going?"

The answer came without hesitation. "Trust in God. For me, God was the One Who took the side of the underdog. In the Bible, you notice, the people He chooses are always the flawed ones, the failures. That was important to me because I was not a successful child. I found my acceptance didn't come from peers, but it did come from God. I didn't have to win relay races to be loved by God."

Loneliness. I'd assumed it was something some children simply had to endure. But that was before I met Madeleine L'Engle. Before I began to see that parents can make a crucial difference in their children's lives by loving them as they are. By reading Bible stories. By telling them, "God loves you so much. He's even there with you when you're alone." —NANCY SCHRAFFENBERGER

A Force That Won't Let Go

WHAT IS LONELINESS?

"It's a sleepless night that never ends, spent with a phone that never rings, waiting for a sun that never comes up."

"It's a numbing nothingness, neither warm nor cool, as though all my nerve endings have gone limp, and the only thing that reminds me I'm alive is the inconsolable ache that I feel in my heart."

"Loneliness is the rest of the choir singing 'Joyful, Joyful, We Adore Thee' and me welling up inside, finding it absolutely impossible to connect to the words, let alone sing them."

There are few things more poignant, more wrenching than being caught in a web of loneliness, as these testimonies from three parishioners at New York City's Riverside Church attest. Loneliness can leave us drained, defeated, weary, and depressed. It can rob us of motivation. And, says Dr. Joan Kavanaugh, D.Min., psychotherapist in private practice in New York City and ordained minister in the United Church of Christ, "in a culture such as ours that puts such a premium on relationships, we also feel ashamed, as though it is some kind of stigma, a sign of personal failure. The refrain that I hear so often from people I treat is 'What's wrong with me?'"

There isn't necessarily anything wrong, says Dr. Kavanaugh. There is no reason to feel ashamed. Loneliness is a normal, even an expected part of a full life. Once we understand this, and once we understand what causes loneliness, we can take steps to find our way out of it.

Remedies
THE ROOT OF THE PROBLEM

THE FIRST STEP IN overcoming loneliness is realizing what it isn't, says Alison Boden, M.Div., Dean of Religious Life and of the Chapel at Princeton University. "It isn't simply a state of being alone. In fact, we can find ourselves feeling terribly lonely even when we're surrounded by others just as easily as we can find ourselves quite

Ten Steps to End Your Loneliness

By Norman Vincent Peale

1. **Realize that lots of other people are lonely, too.** Look around for those who seem to be alone and show an interest in them. You will be surprised how quickly many such people will come to depend upon you, and this will help alleviate your own loneliness.

2. **Study yourself to discover why you have so few friends.** Honestly analyze. Ask what it is that fails to attract other people. Are you dull in conversation, hard to get along with, critical, not neat and attractive in dress, deficient in intellectual interest or other factors? Consider consulting a trusted friend, pastor, or counselor regarding this issue.

3. **Study and develop the art of being a good conversationalist.** Read books, learn to ask questions, and stay informed about current events. You can talk about all of these things with others.

4. **Learn how to tell a happy story.** Make a list of such stories and be alert in conversation to recognize the place where such stories would add a unique touch. When you tell a story, put your whole self into it. Then let the other person tell one. Give him or her genuine interest and appreciation. Always try to bring the other person out rather than calling attention to yourself.

5. **Develop a prayer list.** Every day pray for those on your list. Whether you ever become close to these people or not, by praying for them you are sharing your deepest personality with them and thus they are your friends.

6. **Look for opportunities to bring encouragement, especially to those who suffer sickness, sorrow, or disappointment.** Call, write, or visit them and offer support and friendship. Also, join in people's successes and joys by sending a message of affirmation or congratulations when good things happen to them.

7. **Practice developing a great mental storehouse of pleasant and happy thoughts, memories, ideas, and experiences.** When you are alone, draw them one by one in the center of your consciousness and live them over, or meditate upon their rich meaning.

8. **Live with a consciousness of Christ.** Would you be lonely if you could actually spend a day with Christ? It would be the one supreme day of your life on earth. You can do this, for He is with you always. Talk to Him just as you would to a friend sitting beside you. And listen. The more you do this, the more real He will become. Christ in you will irresistibly attract people to you, for you will have something to share and they will recognize that fact.

9. **Go around doing good in Christ's name.** But don't act pious. Be normal and genuine, happy and self-forgetting, as Jesus was and is.

10. **Learn the magnificent art of friendliness by association with the greatest Friend of all.** Whoever learns friendship from Him gains and keeps the affection and devotion of others and will no longer be lonely.

content and fulfilled when we have only ourselves to keep us company," she says.

If loneliness can occur even in a crowd, then what triggers it? It could be some loss, such as the death of a loved one, the break-up of a relationship, or a child leaving home. And it could be a chronic condition that stays with us, says Dr. Kavanaugh, "like gum stuck to the sole of a shoe. The unifying theme for both is that it is a profound sense of alienation, disconnection, not belonging, or not feeling a part of a loving community."

Regardless of how universal it is, loneliness is a condition most of us would rather live without. So what do we do when we encounter it in our own lives, when, to play on Dr. Kavanaugh's words, loneliness sticks to our souls? Try some of these tips.

Listen to loneliness. Figure out why it's there. It's providing a warning that something's not right, and we need to heed that warning, says Dr. Kavanaugh. "When we're lonely, we no longer trust in the security and durability of loving relationships, including our relationships with God, so we don't let anyone get too close to us," she says. "By exploring where our loneliness originates, we can grow beyond our suspicions and dare to trust again."

Dr. Kavanaugh says we can begin examining our loneliness by making a list of the important people in our lives and then next to each name writing one word that characterizes the current state of the relationship, one word or phrase describing where we want that relationship to go, one word or phrase describing what we might be doing to prevent the relationship from getting there, and one word or phrase describing what we can do to move the relationship along. For example, we might write the word *spouse* and use the word *distance* to characterize the relationship. Then we might describe our goal with the word *intimacy* and use the phrase "afraid to talk" to describe what's preventing the intimacy. Finally, after analyzing this string, we might use the phrase "risk showing my real feelings" to describe one possible solution.

Don't fight it; join it. One of the great fears with loneliness is that it will grow and overwhelm us. It doesn't have to play out that way. Our immediate impulse might be to lash out or try to resist the feeling—to try to push loneliness away. We are better off to experience it, explore its roots, and trust that it won't kill us.

One way to do this is to meditate on Psalm 23:4 "Even though I walk through the valley of the shadow of death, I fear no evil; for thou art with me." Repeat this verse to yourself until you trust the promise that God is with you through every valley.

Find strength in God. Even when life seems loneliest for us, we can take solace in knowing that God is always there as a friend and guide. Job learned this lesson, though he did go through a period of doubt along the way. "Here was a guy who believed that as long as he prospered God was close to him, but as soon as calamity befell him, he was sure that he'd been abandoned," says Dr. Kavanaugh. "Only when he suffered through his torment, presented himself to God, and heard God's answer did he learn that no matter what his lot, God was with him. He was never alone. That's strong testimony."

Find God in good works. We draw closer to God by drawing closer to one another, says the Reverend Marc Mullinax, Ph.D., by placing a phone call to a long-lost relative, by spending a day at a local drop-in center for troubled kids, or by shoveling snow for an elderly neighbor. These tasks are not only worthwhile in and of

His Mysterious Ways

BY IRMA LEVESQUE

I grew up in rural New Hampshire, eldest daughter in a family of six children. In our chaotic household I found refuge in make-believe, often pretending that I was a beautiful girl named "Joan Bishop" (Joan from Joan of Arc and Bishop from the English translation of my French last name). I never told anyone else about Joan Bishop. It was a secret between God and me.

Little girls grow up, though, and the day came when I bade good-bye to Joan Bishop…and to God. I moved to New York, got caught up in a fiercely competitive line of work, and gradually found my personal life getting lonelier and lonelier. In time I knew I wanted to return to God, but I hesitated. Would He welcome me back?

One Sunday morning I could not stay away any longer. I went to Grace Church nearby. I walked down the north aisle, past the old pews, each with its own waist-high door and tiny brass nameplates, relics from the last century when parishioners purchased their seats. I chose an empty pew and closed the door behind me.

"Please, God," I began to pray, "I'm lonely and afraid. Are You here? Is this the place for me? Will these people all around me take me in?" I wanted God's assurance that I should stay in that church, but no assurance seemed to come. Suddenly I felt an overpowering urge to leave.

Hastily gathering up my coat and scarf, I opened the pew door and stepped into the aisle. As I turned to shut the old door, my eyes were drawn to its tiny brass nameplate. The plate read: J. Bishop.

I returned to my seat. I was home again.

themselves but are also good for us because they connect us with people.

Find intimacy through prayer. Prayer, says Dr. Kavanaugh, helps us "go deeper into ourselves. We can ask God for the power to discern how we might be unwittingly encouraging loneliness and what power we have to cope with it or see ourselves through it."

Find intimacy through outreach. Praying can be an effective treatment for loneliness, but it works best if we use it as a bridge to others, says Elizabeth Tener, M.S.W., L.I.C.S.W., C.A.R.T., psychotherapist, pastoral counselor, and addiction counselor at CAB Health and Recovery in Salem, Massachusetts. God often works through others to answer our prayers, but we're usually the ones who have to take the steps to make it happen. So by all means, we should pray, she says, but then we should find someone to talk to, be it a friend or professional counselor. We need to share feelings and develop intimacy with them. Even though we may not feel like doing so at first, we should make the effort to join a group, church, or club that has similar interests or problems as we do. We need to get out and be among people.

Be open to change. Lonely people are often fearful and quick to find fault with themselves and others. To help overcome these feelings, Tener recommends beginning each day with this simple prayer: "Lord, keep my heart gentle, open, and receptive to others."

LETTING LONELINESS WEAVE ITS COURSE

There's an old story about a young man whose frustrated prayer went like this: "God, give me patience, and give it to me right now!" We're sure to feel a sense of urgency when we're lonely. But we must accept that curing the problem will take time. And, says Tener, when we pray, "we need to know what not to expect. One of my patients was terribly lonely because she had a very difficult time getting close to people. She prayed, 'God, give me friends!' She was literally seeking divine intervention, a bolt from the blue. For her, learning to pray meant learning how to ask God's help in discovering what she had to do to relieve her loneliness."

Of course, none of us is immune to loneliness. It isn't necessarily a bad thing. In fact experiencing loneliness is a normal part of life; it's part of being human. During lonely times, it may be helpful to turn to Psalm 13, which begins, "How long, O Lord? Wilt thou forget me for ever?" and ends with "I will sing to the

Lord, because he has dealt bountifully with me" (RSV). These words speak to the journey of allowing our loneliness to draw us toward Him.

Pieces of a Greater Spirit

There are diversities of gifts, but the same Spirit.
There are differences of ministries, but the same Lord.
And there are diversities of activities, but it is the same God Who works all in all.
But the manifestation of the Spirit is given to each one for the profit of all:
for to one is given the word of wisdom through the Spirit, to another
the word of knowledge through the same Spirit,
to another faith by the same Spirit, to another gifts of healings by the same Spirit,
to another the working of miracles, to another prophecy, to another discerning of spirits, to another different kinds of tongues, to another the interpretation of tongues.
But one and the same Spirit works all these things, distributing
to each one individually as He wills.
For as the body is one and has many members, but all the members of
that one body, being many, are one body, so also is Christ.
For by one Spirit we were all baptized into one body—whether Jews or Greeks,
whether slaves or free—and have all been made to drink into one Spirit.

—1 Corinthians 12:4–13 NKJV

PRIDE

The Wrong Kind of Pride

It was close to midnight, and I found myself outside the door of the small chapel. Why was I here? What was the matter with me? One force inside cautioned, "Go easy, Len, or you'll make a fool of yourself." Another force urged me on. "What are you afraid of—a life that will have some cutting edge to it?"

And then I suddenly had an indescribable longing to go inside to the altar and surrender myself to God.

But at the very same moment, two things held me back. First, the thought of kneeling at an altar repelled me. All my life I had resisted it. It was uncomfortable; it went against the image of nonchalance.

The second thing was that I could see another person—a girl—in the chapel, sitting in meditation. How could I possibly go up to the altar and kneel in front of her? My pride was so misplaced that what that girl thought of me was more important than what God thought.

This became my "moment of truth." A pride, built up so carefully through the years, was now assaulted by a new and compelling emotion. Slowly, as if some power inside me were taking each leg and moving it forward step by step, I walked down the aisle to the altar. For one last moment, I stood there, my knees rigid, my body tense.

Then the knees bent easily and I knelt. Words came out in a hoarse whisper, "Jesus, I am here kneeling on this altar to tell You I want something I haven't got. I don't really know what it all means yet. But I'm willing to find out. So I give . . . yes, surrender, my life to You."

At the word *surrender* I felt an almost instantaneous feeling of release . . . joy . . . a kind of cleansing.

The next morning, however, I knew that there was still a step to be taken. And for me a very difficult one. Somehow the validity of the experience depended on reporting it to the group. I had to go on record.

It was a role I never could have imagined for myself as, hesitatingly, I reported what had happened. Then came the discovery of a new and disconcerting factor. I had lost the rigid control of my emotions: my voice broke. Tears filled my eyes.

Yet soon, all this became unimportant amid the response from the group . . . the warmth of new friends whose closeness I feel today as poignantly as then . . . the overwhelming feeling of love and aliveness everywhere.

Fourteen years later, there have been occasions when the urge to flee from God nearly overwhelmed me. Yet I have never once been able to get very far away from that experience of surrender—when the barrier of pride was torn down and God came fully into my life. —LEONARD LESOURD

The Cure: Learning to be Humble

IS IT WRONG TO be proud that we've maintained our sleek figure after our friends have lost theirs? Is it wrong to be proud of the job and position that we've attained or the good works that we do? It is, if we feel like we've done it all on our own, say theologians. Such an attitude demonstrates a sense of vanity, arrogance, haughtiness, or whatever you want to call it, suggesting a dangerous independence from God.

St. Augustine's Prayer Book defines pride this way: "It is the refusal to recognize our status as creatures, dependent on God for our existence, and placed by Him in a specific relationship to the rest of His creation."

In fact, this kind of attitude puts us in direct opposition to God and in worse shape spiritually than someone whom we may view as wretched and sinful, but who is contrite. "As the Bible says, 'God opposes the proud but shows favor to the humble. Humble yourselves, therefore, under God's mighty hand, that he may lift you up in due time'" (1 Peter 5:5–6 NIV).

Maybe that's what Solomon meant when he wrote these famous words: "Pride goes before destruction, a haughty spirit before a fall" (Proverbs 16:18 NIV).

CHOOSING OUR OWN WAY

But of all the truly nasty sins around, such as murder or adultery, how could God think that pride is so bad? For one thing, people who do things that are really wrong often are repentant, deeply sorry that it ever happened, willing to make amends and then change their ways. Proud people, on the other hand, simply don't think that they have done anything wrong, and therefore have no need for God, let alone His love or forgiveness. And, as the Bible says, God has no tolerance whatsoever for that kind of attitude.

Consider the fate of Nebuchadnezzar, perhaps one of the best examples of pride run amok in holy writ. At one time the ruler of the known world, Nebuchadnezzar thought that he was so important that people should worship him. For his arrogance, he earned a special comeuppance: he lost his sanity and ended up living in the wilderness, grazing like a cow in a field for several years (Daniel 4:33).

This seemed to change His Highness's tune. When released from his punishment, he said, "Now I, Nebuchadnezzar, praise and exalt and glorify the King of heaven, because everything he does is right and all his ways are just. And those who walk in pride he is able to humble" (Daniel 4:37 NIV).

Remedies
LIVE THE HUMBLE LIFE

PRIDE IS CLEARLY BAD and wrong—number one among the seven deadly sins. So how do we defeat it? Maybe by not trying to, says Dr. Everett L. Worthington. "I used to think that you should try to defeat pride. But I have come to the

No Easy Way

By Fred W. Norman

Early in my ministry, I entered into a prolonged and bitter argument with one of my church members. I lost a night's sleep over it. Neither of us, of course, had accomplished a thing.

The key to the situation was the word *humility*. Since to be humble closely resembles being humiliated, we usually rebel against this. We are even embarrassed when we recognize true humility in another, embarrassed because it impresses on us just how far we have allowed our pride to lead us. Such was the case with me following the argument with the parishioner.

The morning after our discussion, our doorbell rang; there stood this same lady. Before I could say anything she blurted out, "I'm sorry about last night. I shouldn't have made such a fuss. Here's a chicken as a peace offering." And she walked away.

Everyone in our small community knew about the argument; many of them were on my side. But that morning my antagonist walked up onto the parsonage porch in full view of the people in the bank, the grocery store, and the post office—and apologized, even when she was convinced her position was right!

At that moment she won me as a friend and taught me something I've never forgotten.

Humility does not mean an admission of error that is not felt, nor a weak compromise. Simply stated, it does mean understanding and kindness. It comes with real difficulty, but nothing could possibly be more rewarding.

conclusion that that's not the way to go about it. That is just another form of a pride trip." The trick, he explains, is to forget about pride and concentrate on living humbly. "Nineteenth-century Christian author and pastor Andrew Murray wrote: 'Humility is not thinking of one's self to be less than one is. Humility is not thinking of oneself at all.'"

Such humility is exactly what Jesus demonstrates through His teaching, His attitude, His very life. Remember when He washed the disciples' feet? Jesus wasn't demonstrating the importance of good hygiene. He was making a powerful point: the greatest of all isn't the most prideful; he's servant of all.

The Lord therefore set us an example and teaches that the greatest in the Kingdom is the one who is the least.

Not only that, but when we take off our masks of pride and perfection and are open and humble about our own problems, others become more willing to admit their failings, says Dr. David Stoop, That, in turn, means there's even less pressure for us to try to act perfect, which helps everyone be more humble in the long run.

Make no mistake, trading pride for humility can be challenging. After all, some of us are already prideful over how

humble we are. But here are some suggestions to get us on the right track.

Serve somebody. Nothing cures a case of pride quicker than humbling ourselves with simple tasks of serving, like cleaning the bathrooms of a church, washing dishes in a soup kitchen, or assisting a disabled person, says Dr. Stoop. Not only is it exactly what Jesus would do, but it's also a reminder to be thankful for all that God has given us. After Jesus washed the disciples' feet, He said, "I have set you an example that you should do as I have done for you.... Now that you know these things, you will be blessed if you do them" (John 13:15, 17 NIV).

Make amends. Have a friendship that's on the rocks because of someone's prideful refusal to admit a mistake or wrongdoing? The biblical prescription is simple: "Go—to the point of exhaustion—and give your neighbor no rest! Allow no sleep to your eyes, no slumber to your eyelids" (Proverbs 6:3–4 NIV). Even if they're too proud to respond, at least we'll have done the right thing, says Dr. Ray Pritchard.

Learn from the tax collector. If we're proud of our religiosity, the story that Jesus tells about the tax collector and the Pharisee can set us straight: "Two

When pride comes, so does shame, but wisdom brings humility. —Proverbs 11:2 (CEB)

My friend Ann is a pastor of a small church in Brooklyn, New York. Their actual membership is about fifty, but on nights when they offer a hot meal to the homeless or on food-pantry afternoons, their numbers swell to two hundred or more.

I happened to be there the day the local food-surplus organization delivered three tons of fresh green beans to the front lawn of this little church. Have you ever seen three tons of green beans? I'm six foot five, and the stack of crates towered over me! All afternoon, volunteers rotated in and out, cooking the meal for that night's dinner or bagging the fresh beans two pounds at a time for the food pantry the next day.

At one point I found myself bagging beans with an actor who, in a few hours, would be performing his role in a Broadway play. "What does it feel like to come onstage at the end of the play with the audience standing and clapping?" I asked him.

"Actually, I get more satisfaction from working here," he said, "because it's not about people saying thank you to me for something I've done. It's about me saying thank You to God through what I'm doing. That's what gives me the deepest satisfaction."

Since that day, I've adjusted the way I think. It's not simply about doing good and being recognized for it; it's about intentionally asking how I might use part of my skill that day to say thank You to God. That subtle change has filled my soul in profound ways.

Thank You, God, for opportunities daily to say thanks through my actions for the great gifts You've given. —JEFF JAPINGA men went up to the temple to pray, one a Pharisee and the other a tax collector. The Pharisee stood by himself and prayed: 'God, I thank you that I am not like other people—robbers, evildoers, adulterers—or even like this tax collector. I fast twice a week and give a tenth of all I get'" (Luke 18:10–12 NIV).

"But the tax collector stood at a distance. He would not even look up to heaven, but beat his breast and said, 'God, have mercy on me, a sinner'" (Luke 18:13 NIV).

The tax collector, not the Pharisee, went home "justified before God," says Jesus. "For all those who exalt themselves will be humbled, and those who humble themselves will be exalted" (Luke 18:14 NIV).

Look at Jesus. Sometimes, when our lives seem to be going better than those around us, we can start to feel pretty important. The quickest way to shut that down is to compare ourselves with the king of humility, Jesus. In *Sources of Strength*, former president Jimmy Carter suggests that we ask ourselves, "Have I lived in a way that is truly compatible with the teaching of the humble, human, yet all-loving and all-knowing God I have pledged to

follow?" The answer, he says, "can be troubling, even humiliating—though humbling may be a better word."

Be thankful. The Bible teaches us: "And whatever you do, whether in word or in deed, do it all in the name of the Lord Jesus, giving thanks to God the Father through him" (Colossians 3:17 NIV). It also advises: "...give thanks in all circumstances; for this is God's will for you in Christ Jesus" (1 Thessalonians 5:18 NIV). Giving thanks to God or being thankful helps us keep humble because it reminds us that God has given us all we have, says The Reverend Slag-Yang Tan. One simple way to develop a more thankful spirit in ourselves and our loved ones is to say grace when we gather for meals.

Get closer to God. "No matter how great our achievements or success, getting closer to God can help us see more clearly how great He is and how small we really are," says Dr. Tan. The story of Job in the Old Testament is a good example. He had this to say after encountering the might of God: "My ears had heard of you but now my eyes have seen you. Therefore I despise myself and repent in dust and ashes" (Job 42:5–6 NIV).

When I Get a Little Power

Humble me, Lord, when I think I know what I'm doing—I still have a lot to learn.

Humble me, Lord, after I solve a big problem—I create as many as I solve.

Humble me, Lord, when I stand too tall—I am only dust at Your feet.

Humble me, Lord, if pride shows on my face—a proud face is an ugly one.

Humble me, Lord, when I receive words of praise—let me give that praise to You.

Humble me, Lord, when I look down on others—You are the only and final judge.

Humble me, Lord, if I'm given human power—Yours is the Kingdom, the Power, the Glory.

Humble me, Lord, especially when I succeed—I couldn't have done it without You.

—LISA MARIE ROVITO

STRESS

Stress Test

I was charging down the sidewalk at my usual Saturday morning much-to-be-done pace when my wife said from behind me, "Heel!"—her little way of telling me to slow down. I stopped and turned. Julee was grinning at a woman with a bag on her arm, which read "Too blessed to be stressed."

Everywhere we go these days, someone is telling us how to relieve the stress in our lives, warning us against too much pressure building up. Do we live in the Age of Stress? I can't recall my parents ever using the word, except perhaps to stress something important they expected of me (and that could stress me out). They got tired and they worried, but they never called it stress. Of course, they lived in a time when there was only one phone company.

Meditation, massage, acupressure, reflexology, herbal tea, vitamins and mineral supplements, even pet therapy. You name it and people are trying to use it to beat stress.

Except maybe that woman with the bag. She reminded me that even in the maelstrom of modern life, when I can imagine so much going wrong, I can still be as tranquil as a lazy summer breeze. For at any given moment on any given day, an amazing number of things are going perfectly right in the world, from the love of our families to the turning of the tides. And we are blessed to be here.

Finding Relief through Faith

A LIGHTER LOAD. Renewed strength. Rest for our weary minds and souls.

Yes, these ideas sound good, too good to be true if we're caught in the jittery, irritable, and overwhelming world of stress. But it is possible to bring our lives under control, to better cope with the anxiety and tension that stress causes. How? By using prayer, our faith, and biblical principles written thousands of years ago to manage and even reduce the stressors in our lives.

In fact, studies show that people who pray regularly and have a deep commitment to religion may be uniquely equipped to handle pressure, according to the late David B. Larson, M.D., psychiatrist, founder and director of the National Institute for Healthcare Research, and leader in the field of religion and health research. Strong faith, he continues, can help people cope with stress because it can help us slow down our automatic responses to stressful events and make us less likely to rush to judgment.

Dr. Everett L. Worthington agrees. "When we recognize that God is ultimately in control, that's going to change how we react to most situations."

WHERE IT ALL STARTS

Although a variety of factors trigger stress, it's no surprise that some of its most damaging sources are traumatic events beyond our control, such as the death of a loved one, divorce, separation, or chronic illness. When we experience two or more of these events at the same time, we may feel so physically and mentally devastated that we literally have trouble getting out of bed, according to Dr. Charles Zeiders.

More insidiously, we can bring on stress by our own desires—our demands for more money, better jobs, more recognition, bigger houses, or more of whatever, says Dr. Zeiders. Other causes include career

He Makes Winds His Messengers

By Judy Spence

Camping out in the woods for a week was supposed to relax me. But while my husband slept, I stared into the inky darkness and worried. One daughter battled rheumatoid arthritis; the other was recently divorced and trying to start a business.

Life was so much simpler when the girls were young, I thought. If they couldn't sleep at night I'd tell them to imagine themselves outdoors in a peaceful place with flowers blowing in the breeze. Now, wide awake myself, I pulled the covers up to my neck. Wind whipped around our pop-up trailer, swaying it from side to side. Even vacation was stressful.

I sat up and anxiously peered out into the wild night. *Lord, I'm so afraid.* Strong winds could easily blow over this trailer.

How little control I had over anything—the weather, my daughters' lives, even my ability to sleep through the night.

And just like that, the trailer stopped rocking. The wind turned calm. Trees stood still. I closed my eyes and pictured flowers gently blowing in the breeze, content with the assurance that the One Who calmed the wind in the trees could also handle the worries in my life. Maybe I wasn't always completely in control, but I knew someone Who was.

and financial problems, the tension that comes from raising children and teenagers, trouble with neighbors, bitterness, and weight gain.

Whatever the trigger, stress takes a heavy toll, and not just because we toss and turn and can't sleep at night. During a crisis, our bodies produce adrenaline, epinephrine, and other chemicals that heighten our senses and quicken our reactions, essentially putting us on red alert.

This can come in handy if we need to pull a grandchild out of the way of a speeding car or confront other sudden dangers. But people under constant stress never stop producing the stuff, setting themselves up for serious health problems. These include headaches, high blood pressure, irritable bowel syndrome, ulcers, panic attacks, muscular tension, insomnia, chest pains, and heart problems, says Grant Correll, M.D., fellow in the American Academy of Family Practice and global health outreach team leader with the Christian Medical and Dental Associations.

"Whether stress is the primary diagnosis or whether it's masked by another one of these medical problems, a very large percentage of people I see have stress-related problems," says Dr. Correll.

So how do we turn off energy-sapping levels of stress? Try these prescriptions.

Don't sweat the small stuff. It's the title of a best-selling book, but it has always been solid biblical advice. "Consider how the wild flowers grow," Jesus says. "They do not labor or spin. Yet I tell you, not even Solomon in all his splendor was dressed like one of these. If that is how God clothes

the grass of the field, which is here today, and tomorrow is thrown into the fire, how much more will he clothe you—you of little faith!" (Luke 12:27–28 NIV). In the light of eternity, it's *all* small stuff.

Learn from the early Christians. The monks who first employed Christian meditation in the Egyptian desert had no concept of stress. They were interested in becoming still and finding Jesus, says Dr. Zeiders. But as it turns out, these monks, known as Desert Fathers, discovered a pretty solid stress buster. Studies show that by getting quiet, disregarding passive thoughts, and repeating a word or phrase, we can actually decrease our heart rates, lower our metabolic rates, and slow our breathing and brain waves. What might we repeat? Dr. Zeiders prefers "Lord Jesus, behold me a sinner" or "Lord Jesus, behold me." Such a manner of prayer triggers the relaxation response, in which tension eases and heart rate and blood pressure drop, the opposite of the stress response, says Dr. Zeiders.

Get out of debt—and stay out. Money in and of itself isn't bad, as the Bible points out (1 Timothy 6:10). It's the love of money and the junk that it buys that hurts us, causes financial hardship, and, you guessed it, brings on stress. "We

How to Settle down When You're Uptight

By Jeanne Hill

"It's not just bad situations that create stress and make you tense," our old friend Vernon, a psychology professor, warned my husband and me as we sat chatting over coffee one Saturday morning. "Moving, changing jobs, getting married, redecorating, making a major purchase, even getting ready to go on a vacation—all of those things can put pressure on you."

Louis and I looked at each other. Not only was he changing jobs, but his new position would make it necessary for us to move from the Sun Belt to the Midwest, from a suburban house to a downtown apartment. Accepting it meant leaving behind friends and our grown-up children—pulling up roots that had been in place for eighteen years. And though the new job was a wonderful promotion for Louis, it also carried more responsibility. "I think our stress circuits are about to be overloaded!" I said.

"Oh, there are plenty of things you can do to counteract stress." Vernon's grin was reassuring. "One of them is to hang on to your sense of humor. I just want you and Louis to realize that when you exchange what's familiar for the relatively unknown, you're in for a certain amount of anxiety. When you know it's there, you can deal with it."

That conversation took place more than three years ago. Thanks to some suggestions Vernon made and some things Louis and I figured out ourselves, we adjusted well to two major changes in our lives that came at the same time. Maybe what we learned can help you take stress in your stride.

1. Put off, when possible, anything likely to produce additional stress at an already stressful time, things like a major decision or expense. In our case, for

example, we decided to lease the family home in Arizona instead of selling it right away.

2. Work off the physical effects of tension by taking up daily exercise if you aren't already someone who puts time into keeping fit. Brisk walking, jogging, biking, handball—they're all good for stretching tense muscles. For Louis and me, it's a half-mile swim every day.

3. Pace yourself so your timetable for accomplishing whatever is on your agenda is as comfortable as possible; don't ask yourself to do too much in too little time. And if there's a perfectionist lurking within you, don't let that side of your nature get the upper hand!

4. Talk about the change instead of just dwelling on it mentally. In other words, don't bottle up your feelings. By bringing the change into conversation before and after it takes place, you will be helping yourself adjust to the difference that change makes in your life. When I told the Bowdens, our new church friends in Akron, about missing my children, the homesick feeling began to go away. (Finding a supportive new church family was one of the first and best things Louis and I did to help ourselves cope after we'd moved.)

5. Pray about your concerns, asking the Lord to help you focus on the positive side of stress and change. Scientists have suggested that these very "upsets" can bring out your God-given assets such as creativity, resourcefulness, and inner strength.

Don't forget to go to the Lord by taking some quiet moments to read the Bible. In the face of change, you will find countless reminders of Christ's constancy and love. I especially like to remember God's Word in Malachi 3:6 (KJV), "I am the Lord, I change not."

can't even enjoy what we bought because we practically have to work ourselves to death to pay for it," says Dr. Zeiders. If we want less-stressed lives, we need to control our desires to spend and pay off the debts that we've already accumulated.

Take a day off. Some may consider it old-fashioned, but the wisdom of carving one day a week—often Sunday—from our overbooked schedules for worship and rest is beginning to look more attractive all the time. Not to mention scientifically sound.

"Look at the biology," says Dr. Worthington. "A Sabbath allows us to relax and focus on entirely different things, to think and feel and act differently. That has to reduce the flow of stress chemicals through our bodies, at least for that day." How do we do it? Cook a roast or casserole on Saturday so that we don't have to fuss making meals. Postpone all but the most basic of chores. Attend church, worship God wholeheartedly, and ponder what the pastor says. And then take a nice, long nap.

Learn when to say no. We never should ignore someone's genuine need, but in our sincere desire to help, sometimes we overdo or overcommit. This not only causes untold physical and emotional stress, but it can also frustrate others who are counting on us. "Jesus speaks directly to people with this kind of problem in Mark 6:31," says Dr. Zeiders. "He and the apostles had been working hard healing a lot of people. But instead of digging deeper and ministering even more to the crowd, He said to His disciples, 'Come with Me by yourselves to a quiet place and get some rest.' He wanted them and us to know that we need to take time to get away with Him by ourselves."

Make prayer a priority. One of the many unmistakable benefits of prayer is reduced stress. "This has been researched a lot," says Dr. Worthington. "Most Christians believe that God is active in intervening in people's lives, and if that is true—and I believe that it is—then prayer can bring a different force to act in a stressful situation. Prayer is a relationship with God, first. But it has calming effects, no question about it."

Meditate on God's Word. Whether reading the Psalms or memorizing passages that highlight God's faithfulness, we can use Bible study not only to help relieve stress but also to lead to a solution to our problems. "Focusing our minds on Christian truths in a situation where danger or threat is all around reminds us of what is really true:

that God loves us and He is never going to leave us or forsake us," says Dr. Zeiders.

Or as Jesus puts it: "I have told you these things, so that in me you may have peace. In this world you will have trouble. But take heart! I have overcome the world" (John 16:33 NIV).

Transcending Pressure

Heavenly King,
The world squeezes me into its own mold.
It's easy for me to let that happen.
I'm attracted to the tangible, seduced by the temporary, and
tempted to journey up dead-end roads.
Give me discernment, strength, and courage,
to live for Your Kingdom,
to conform to Your Kingly rule.
Guide me in Your steps.
Enable me to resist the
pressures of those who are set against You.
Thank You for being my King.
Thank You most of all for loving me.
— NORM NELSON, FROM "*THANK YOU MOST OF*
ALL FOR LOVING ME"

TEMPTATION

The Battle with Temptation

The best way to handle temptation is to avoid it. As soon as you sense the deceiver's enticing you to do something you know is wrong, throw up your defenses.

Sometimes it is possible to do this in advance, by anticipating the tempter's attack. One famous Swedish industrialist never takes a trip without contacting his Christian friends in cities he is to visit. He is an alcoholic. He knows that the temptation to drink is greater when he is away from home, and he defends himself against the weakness by never allowing himself to be out of the company of such carefully selected friends.

Another technique is to plant faith strengtheners where they will be available at need. Scripture passages are excellent weapons against satanic attacks: these were Jesus' only tools in His wilderness experience. Simple scornful laughter is one of the devil's worst enemies. "The best way to drive out the devil, if he will not yield to texts of Scripture," said Martin Luther, "is to jeer and flout him, for he cannot bear scorn."

Far too often, however, despite our best precautions, we find ourselves caught up in the midst of a troubling temptation. When this happens, we can follow this procedure:

1. Acknowledge your weakness. Never make the mistake of thinking you will be able to handle the devil's onslaughts with your own strength. Quickly admit that you are defenseless.
2. Name your adversary and follow Christ's example in telling him to get behind you.
3. Quickly and deliberately draw a mental picture of yourself as you think God wants to see you. As long as you can, hold on to this image.

Then stop. And this is vitally important. Do not continue to struggle against the powers of darkness beyond these first three steps. It is time now to let God Himself battle for you. He will always step in at this point, and provide you with a way out. —GUIDEPOSTS SPIRITUAL WORKSHOP

Taming the Self

MUCH HAS BEEN SAID about the courage of lions. But when hunting, they almost always prey on animals that are weak, weary, sick, or wounded.

Temptation is like that—crouched at the door of our lives, ready to pounce "when we let our guard down or get too tired, too hungry, or too needy," says Dr. David Stoop.

Think of it. We've been running errands all day, and we're hungry from lack of food. But instead of driving home and having a lean, sensible dinner, we answer the call of the drive-up window and chow down on fatty burgers and fries. Or rather than making the rounds at the office Christmas party, we spend time alone with that friendly, attractive, married coworker, whom we like just a little too much.

When we act in these ways, we're giving in to something that appeals to "our lower nature, our physical, glandular, carnal self," says Dr. Stoop.

Obviously, things that look good or taste good or make us feel better about ourselves, even temporarily, are tempting to us all. But there's some evidence that a woman's temptations are slightly different than a man's, says Mary Ellen Ashcroft. "If you asked a number of women, 'Why did you commit that sin?' the answer would have more to do with lack of self-esteem, a lack within that drives them to become compulsive spenders or overeaters or get involved in extramarital affairs." For men, pride is more typically at the root of sin.

HOW IT HARMS US

Male or female, if we indulge, we may gain a measure of satisfaction for a short time. But then comes that sickening feeling, the one that gnaws at us when we realize that what has lured us away was built on a false promise and that it will never fully satisfy. In the words of Jeremiah the prophet, "My people have committed two sins: They have forsaken me, the spring of living water, and have dug their own cisterns, broken cisterns that cannot hold water" (Jeremiah 2:13 NIV).

The trouble doesn't stop there. Repeatedly yielding to temptation can lead to addiction. "Regardless of what the temptation is, if we get a high from it—a temporary emotional lift—it can be very addictive," says Dr. Stoop.

A few words on what temptation is not: for one thing, it's not a sin to be tempted. If it were, Jesus would be in big trouble, since He was tempted at least three times by Satan himself. And temptation isn't going away. Even if we get to the root of something that is tempting us and master it, we will always face another temptation, says Dr. Ashcroft.

The good news is that our temptations can be tremendous points of growth for us. But we need to develop strategies for dealing with them, says Dr. Ashcroft. Here are the thirteen *R*'s for resisting temptation.

Run! While some temptations may legitimately require time to ponder, others should simply make us turn tail and run. "These are the ones that can really do us in, like sexual situations," says Dr. Ashcroft, "or times when we would say something out of rage that we'd later regret."

Resist. Standing our ground against one temptation can prepare us for the next, a spiritual truth best illustrated by the old hymn, "Yield Not to Temptation," said the late Reverend David Wigley, former pastor of the First Congregational Church

How to Deliver Yourself from Temptation

By Barbara Collier*

When I heard the rumors about an apparent affair between two people I knew, I was horrified. I had no patience with people who found themselves in immoral situations. I felt there was no way wrong could happen if you were where you should be, doing what you should be doing. Somehow I felt I was "above that sort of thing." My life centered—happily—on my husband, children, home, and job.

And then a new family moved into our neighborhood. They were our kind of people, and they fit right into our community and church. But over the months it became clear that the husband and I shared more of the same interests than the other family members did. Still, we were merely good neighbors, good friends.

Then something changed. It was nothing tangible, but a light in his eyes seemed to reflect the growing interest and excitement I, too, felt. I knew that our mutual attraction could easily go one step further—then another. And the terrible truth was that I was tempted to go along with it. I plunged from the heights of romantic imaginings to the depths of self-condemnation. What was happening? I was a Sunday school teacher, church leader, devoted wife, and mother. Why couldn't I simply banish these thoughts from my mind?

But in actual practice it was not so easy. Temptation worked like an undertow, and the harder I fought it, the more fiercely it pulled: What was so wrong about what was happening? I rationalized. Who would be hurt? Could this man and I help it if we were "meant for each other"? And didn't other people flirt and fib and cheat all the time—on television, in the news, even in our neighborhood?

With each swell of thoughts I felt myself being swept further and further away from God. It seemed to me I had no right to ask His help in dealing with such shameful matters.

One day as my mind circled in confusion, my teenage daughter sat down beside me. The night before she had dented the family car and even though my husband and I had reassured her that accidents do happen, something else was troubling her. "Mommy, help me," she said—and burst into tears. Instead of my daughter's taking the car to do errands, as we'd thought, a friend had talked her into driving to a boyfriend's home. On the way, feeling uneasy and rushed, she had run off the road. The visit at the boyfriend's was perfectly innocent, but she felt guilty about having lied to us. She was not where she should have been, doing what she should have been doing.

I was touched that my daughter needed me, and wanted to tell me the truth. As I put my arms around her, I could almost feel God's arms slip around me. Just as I loved my erring daughter, so He still loved me.

My daughter knew she could not handle her problem alone. She had faith in my ability—and trusted in my love—to help her. In the days that followed I kept her example in mind.

1. I acknowledged my inadequacies. Like it or not, I did have thoughts that made me uncomfortable—and enticed me to do things I knew were wrong. And my human strengths, which I'd once thought were considerable, weren't enough to dispel these urgings. Neither was any strictly moral standard about right and wrong. I had to face squarely what was happening—and ask for help beyond myself.

2. I accepted God's unbounded love. As shameful as our thoughts seem—when we're tempted to lie or cheat or be unfaithful—they can never separate us from God's love. "I am come to seek and to save that which was lost," Christ said. God cares for me, shortcomings and all—and He would help me just as I would help my child.

3. I embraced—and released—each longing. Increasingly, I knew I could face these desires as being part of me—and put them behind me. Instead of sinking under accumulated guilt, I began each time "at the beginning"; and when I failed, I asked God's forgiveness and began again. Gradually, my inner strength grew; and temptation, instead of gnawing, tickled briefly—and drifted off.

It worked. My thoughts of unfaithfulness slipped away, and the excitement they had generated was redirected toward my husband and our marriage!

Today, I am less arrogant and more patient about others' failings. For I know temptation can attack—or sneak up to undermine—anyone. Temptation never ceases. But God's caring and strength go on.

Name has been changed.

in Kennebunkport, Maine. "The first few lines go like this: 'Yield not to temptation, for yielding is sin. Each victory will help you some other to win,'" he says. "One victory over temptation makes us stronger to face the next. Because then we can say to ourselves, 'I know that I can say no.'"

"Some people look at prayer as kind of a magical incantation," says Dr. Stoop. "But it's the relational aspect of my praying that gives me strength. The fact that I believe that I'm talking to God and that God hears me and cares about me is where that strength is going to come from."

Recollect the ultimate reward. If temptation's pull seems too strong, we need to remind ourselves that a few minutes or hours of pleasure aren't worth sacrificing our marriages, our health, or God's blessing, says Dr. Stoop. "Blessed is the one who perseveres under trial because, having stood the test, that person will receive the crown of life that the Lord has promised to those who love him" (James 1:12 NIV).

Respect escape routes. Has the phone ever rung just when you were about to get into a major fight with your spouse? Or has your child ever called out with a question from another room when your face was buried in the refrigerator? Don't ignore them; the Bible promises that heavenly exit signs will appear as temptation draws

Pray that you will not fall into temptation. —LUKE 22:40 (NIV)

I was meeting a friend for lunch to talk over our new nonprofit ministry. I hadn't seen her for four years, and I got to thinking about all the negative things she didn't know about that had gone on at our church since she left. "Lord, please keep me from gossiping," I prayed. "And help me to actually want this prayer to work!"

As I waited at the restaurant, I was surprised when someone who went to our church walked in. The door opened again. Another church member! Before long three church members were there. Finally, my friend arrived, and I told her about my prayer not to gossip and how church members kept mysteriously coming through the door. Then who walks in, but the choir director!

It's a big, noisy restaurant, I thought as we followed our hostess to a table. *Maybe I can sneak in one or two juicy stories.* You guessed it. The hostess seated us right across from the table full of church members! I looked at my friend, and we both broke out in grins. There was no need to gossip. We'd just been given an answer to prayer well worth repeating.

Jesus, help me to really want this prayer to work. Amen. —KAREN BARBER

near. "And God is faithful; he will not let you be tempted beyond what you can bear. But when you are tempted, he will also provide a way out so that you can endure it" (1 Corinthians 10:13 NIV). "Look at the story of Joseph and his temptation by Potiphar's wife. Often, when a man gets into that type of situation, his glands take over and he doesn't run. And then he gets mad because he was seduced. Well, he didn't use the escape route," says Dr. Stoop.

Reduce stress. Since we're more likely to give in to temptation when we're stressed out, hungry, or at wit's end, we also need to take better care of ourselves, says Dr. Stoop. Regular exercise, eating right, and getting enough sleep should all help keep our physical cravings in check and our spiritual defenses intact.

Reevaluate. If we know that we're liable to go crazy with our credit cards when we go shopping in an attempt to soothe a serious emotional hurt, our best defense may be to leave them at home, says Dr. Stoop. The same approach works for nearly all tempting situations. If we have problems with sexual lust, we need to reevaluate whether it's wise to view or read magazines or books that may inflame us.

Recall the Garden. The next time a smooth-talking someone tries to tempt us, we need to remember Adam and Eve. Sure, they succumbed to fruit that was "...pleasing to the eye, and also desirable for gaining wisdom..." (Genesis 3:6 NIV), something that looked good and promised much, says Dr. Stoop. But they may not have messed up at all if they hadn't listened to that lying reptile in the first place.

Rely on healthy relationships. This is the best guard against temptation, says Dr. Stoop, especially if the healthy relationships are with people to whom we wish to be accountable. "Not because we have been forced to be accountable, but because we have chosen to be mutually accountable," says Dr. Stoop. One way to build these into our lives is to ask a friend to meet with us once a month or more and invite that person to ask some tough questions about how we're spending our time and money and what we're thinking about.

Read the writing on the wall. If we're honest, our temptations can tell us a lot about ourselves. Dr. Ashcroft offers an example: "Anytime I'm doing a talk somewhere, I have this feeling that I need to go out and spend money on a new outfit," she says. "What I've figured out is that sometimes I'm not feeling very confident and somehow this outfit will be a solution to my lack of confidence." Talking to a pastor, counselor, or trusted friend will often help clarify the source of our temptation.

Research new directions. If our temptations are rooted in a lack of self-esteem or fulfillment, we may never gain the upper hand until we get in touch with the true calling that God has for us. How can we possibly figure that out? "Look back at the times when you really felt tremendous satisfaction in your life," says Dr. Ashcroft. "Times when you really felt like you did something good that was meaningful or you felt strongly about. Or that someone said you were really good at. That's probably your calling."

Reconnect. Even if every wish we make is being granted, ultimately, we're not going to be satisfied until we get and stay in touch with our Creator, says Dr. Ashcroft. Three of the best ways to deepen our relationships with God are to attend church regularly, spend time in Bible study, and pray.

Replicate God's love. If we're married and struggling with sexual temptation, we need to love our spouses the way that God loves us, said Pastor Wigley. "God loves each of us as if we're the only one He has to love, and we need to carry that into our own relationships. We're to love them as if they're the only ones among humanity."

Rejoice! That's right, temptation can be good for us. "Consider it pure joy, my brothers and sisters, whenever you face trials of many kinds, because you know that the testing of your faith produces perseverance. Let perseverance finish its work so that you may be mature and complete, not lacking anything" (James 1:2–4 NIV).

"You know that old saying 'No pain, no gain?' There's no growth without having to struggle with something, whether it's temptation or tribulation," says Dr. Stoop.

· HEALING WORDS ·

Praying for Willpower

Lord, give me strength
When every fiber of my body cries out in protest.
When my impulse is to cave in "just this once"
Bolster my willpower.
I am a creature of habit, Lord.
Help me find new, pure ones to replace the old
And until those are second nature
Bear me up when my resolve is tested and tried.
Help me see beyond this moment
To sacrifice this small, fleeting pleasure for my future good
To preserve this temple You have bestowed upon me.
—Susan Scott

· PART 5 ·

Overcoming
Social Challenges

ABUSE

Daily I asked God for the strength to forgive. Early one morning I picked up a legal pad. At the top of the page I wrote "I forgive everybody. I forgive myself. I'm free. I'm free."

Underneath, I wrote my ex-husband's name, and as fast as I could, a list of the many things for which I needed to forgive him. "I forgive you for hurting me. I forgive you for the names you called me. I forgive you for deriding my job. I forgive you for the fear you instilled in me..." In fifteen minutes I filled three pages. Then I set a lit match to them and flung them in the fireplace. As my painful memories flared up and disintegrated into ashes, I felt the stirrings of the relief I so craved. I sat quietly in prayer. Again I recalled that only love is real. Only perfect love exists. And for the first time the meaning of those words was crystal clear: God in his perfect love will exist for all eternity. Anything outside of that—anger, hatred, fear—is impermanent. It cannot survive in the face of God's perfect, abiding love.

My list making became a discipline. Three mornings a week I scribbled on my notepad, then burned the hateful memories, giving up anger and letting love in. Eventually the lists became harder to write. I could no longer remember vividly the terrible acts committed by my ex-husband. Slowly, forgiveness came, like a gentle tide, quenching the flames of my anger, sadness, and hurt. I had confronted each feeling, each memory, then let it go. A different me emerged. A strong, vibrant, happy me. Just like the person my friend Ginna had always believed in and had insisted God wanted me to be.

> I had asked God to change my situation. He had changed me, with His perfect, purifying love. —Joan Gattuso

How to Stop Being a Victim

She was a successful, driven businesswoman. But she also had a terrible secret—one that damaged her relationships and even made her angry at God.

When she was a child, she had been raped by her grandfather while her parents were in the next room.

"To me, there were two kinds of abuse going on in this situation: the grandfather's sexual abuse and the parents' neglect by failing to protect her," says Dr. Charles Zeiders. "She felt used and abandoned."

After several sessions, Dr. Zeiders, who treated the woman, recommended that they pray for her inner healing, a specific prayer where she would ask Jesus to enter into her memory of the incident. The woman agreed. And then, as they prayed, something amazing happened: The woman "experienced Jesus coming in and slipping His hand between her and her grandfather and pushing him off her," says Dr. Zeiders.

"And then, with His right hand, Jesus scooped her up, wrapped part of His clothing around her to clothe her nakedness, and tenderly cradled her," says Dr. Zeiders. After decades of pain and shame, the woman suddenly felt that "God was a protecting God and that she was worth protecting and worth being kept safe."

DEFINING ABUSE

Unfortunately, this concept of having value and significance is tough for most abuse victims to grasp. Whether they've been sexually, physically, or verbally abused, many have such poor self-esteem that they feel they deserve to be treated poorly.

Nothing could be further from the truth, says Dr. Zeiders. "We are all made in the image of God. So if someone is being abused, the very first thing I'm going to think is that someone who is made in the image of God is being sinned against, and that's never okay."

But just what constitutes abuse? The late Daryle R. Woodward, who was a licensed counselor, founder, and clinical director of Colorado MOVES (Men Overcoming Violence Effectively Services), one of the largest state-certified domestic violence treatment programs, suggested that abuse is "any treatment that negatively impacts the self-worth of another person." And that includes verbal assaults.

"They don't have to be obscenities. Even calling someone 'dumb,' 'stupid,' or 'an idiot' or saying, 'I don't know why I stay married to you' can really impact someone," said Woodward. "A lot of people think that constantly hearing things like that is worse than getting slugged."

And it may be more common that we think; roughly one in four families regularly suffers from incidents of abuse.

A VIOLENT STRUGGLE FOR CONTROL

Charming one moment but scary, angry, violent, and sometimes downright dangerous the next—the world of an abuser. But what could possibly turn Mr. or Ms. Wonderful into such a frightening or nasty person? One possible reason is rooted fear of abandonment. Abusers are often scared, dependent people who cling so tightly to their relationships that they often squeeze the life out of them.

As a result, a common trigger among abusive men is the feeling that they're losing power or control. Take a classic issue that causes conflict, such as childrearing. If a couple can't agree how to discipline their child, an abusive husband won't try to negotiate or compromise. Rather, he'll assert his authority by yelling at his wife. If that doesn't work, he'll use threatening gestures, call his wife names, or throw something. Failing that, he may hit her or sexually abuse her—or someone else.

As it turns out, roughly 60 percent of the men who batter their spouses will also sexually assault them. These are angry men who feel like victims, and this is their way of gaining power, by humiliating other people. Sexual abuse isn't about sex; it's about power and control.

There are fewer reports of physical attacks by wives against their husbands, but verbal assaults might even be more common and include attempts to belittle their husbands in the eyes of their children. Another, more subtle way a woman can abuse her spouse is by spending so much money that it threatens the family budget.

After a sexual, physical, or verbal attack takes place, abusers often feel bad about their actions and try to show that they're sorry—something Woodward describes as a hearts-and-flowers routine. "He says all the words that she's been wanting to hear, and he gets really nice. All is forgotten, supposedly," said Woodward. "But the couple hasn't resolved the real issue, which is his choice to be violent, so it's just a matter of time before the tension and stress build again."

Some female victims of abuse respond by changing their behavior, hoping the problem will just go away. "The abused wife says to herself, 'If I'm good enough or do the things that he wants me to and I don't upset him, he won't hurt me,'" said Woodward.

The problem is that the victimized spouse will never be "good enough," since that's not the true source of the difficulty. Often, the abusers are men and women who were abused as children, and they may never have known another kind of relationship.

Christian women are particularly prone to a nonconfrontational approach, since some have the mistaken idea that they are supposed to endure hardship like good soldiers in their marriages. They may believe that if they just get their own spiritual life in order and pray for their husbands, God will change their husbands. But these men are not likely to change without some consequences. It's important for these women to realize that never does God say that He expects the wife to suffer at the hands of her husband.

Remedies
ENDING THE CYCLE

ALL THIS MAY SEEM like a pretty bleak picture. But the Bible offers a much more hopeful scenario for abuse victims—in people from Joseph and David to Jesus. Each was wrongly accused and abused but ultimately restored. Or, in the case of Christ, glorified.

Like the woman abused by her grandfather, such healing is available to us if

we respond to the problem with common sense, prayer, and faith. Here's how.

Leave home. Having an argument is one thing. It happens all the time even in the best homes. But when there's even the suggestion that women and children are in physical danger, they should leave the house to stay with a relative or a friend or at

Invisible Wings

By Anne Culbreath Watkins

The summer of 1992 wasn't easy for me, easy the way those slow, hot months in Alabama should be. I'd just come out of a domestic violence shelter, where I'd taken refuge from an abusive relationship, and was trying to face the fact that I had to start my life over. My father had set me up in an old mobile home a stone's throw from his house, "so you can have some privacy while you get back on your feet," he'd said. Dad had done everything in his power to cheer me up, but it wasn't working. "I know just the thing," he said one day.

On a clothesline outside the trailer, Dad hung three plastic hummingbird feeders that had belonged to my mother before she died. I remembered them well from the summers of my childhood. *Will I ever be that happy again?* I wondered while Dad filled each feeder to the brim with sugar water. "Mother always used to say there's nothing like a hummingbird to take your mind off your troubles," he said. "A tried-and-true remedy." But troubles like what I had didn't go away so easily.

"Thanks, Dad," I said, hugging him before he started home. I forced a smile when he looked back over his shoulder to make sure I was all right. I couldn't quite picture ever being all right again, and part of me wondered if I deserved to be. They'd told me at the shelter that a lot of women who'd been through what I had felt that way.

The next morning I stood in the doorway of the trailer. *Lord,* I asked, *what do I do now?* I moved outside and leaned up against a spot of shade on the aluminum siding. Just then a bright blue-green hummingbird buzzed one of the feeders. He lined up with the flower-shaped feeding port and took a sip through his long needle of a beak. His wings beat so fast they blurred to invisibility. The hummer looked like he was dangling in midair, like a spider dropped from an invisible thread, and hardly much bigger.

For a fleeting second Mother's hummingbird remedy worked: I was distracted from my worries. But how many hummingbirds would it take to truly lift my spirits?

I walked over to Dad's. "One already, huh?" he said when I told him about my first visitor. "That's a good sign."

Back at the trailer that afternoon, I was surprised to see a female hummer at the feeders. She was dressed in more modest colors, but stunning nonetheless. Gracefully she zoomed up for a drink. Then a third hummer jostled for position at the same feeder.

By week's end I'd counted twenty hummingbirds! I took to sitting outside, watching them from a lawn chair just a few feet from the feeders. My presence didn't seem to bother the birds in the least. Every day, rain or shine, they buzzed the feeders. Evenings when Dad sat with me, the tiny creatures flew round his red cap.

One of the females, drab in color but with a beautiful calm air about her, became my steady companion. While I sipped coffee in my lawn chair one morning, she perched on a bit of clothesline above my head and preened her feathers. I should take good care of myself, too, I decided. I relaxed in a cool shower, spent a little extra time on my hair, and arranged a big wildflower bouquet for the kitchenette. By day's end I felt a sense of hopefulness tiptoe into my heart. Maybe, just maybe, I was going to be okay.

When the director of the shelter telephoned to check on me a couple of weeks later, she commented on the change in my voice. "You're finding your wings," she said.

As we talked, a hummingbird zipped inside the door and hovered in front of me. I whispered to my friend, "You aren't going to believe this, but I'm eye-to-eye with a hummingbird." The tiny jewel-toned busybody hung there, turning his head from side to side, as if checking out my trailer. Seeming pleased with the home I had made for myself, he flew off. I felt sort of proud, suddenly. I was safe and secure, and my life was my own again. "I'm going to make it," I told my friend on the phone. "I deserve to be happy again."

As summer passed, my dad and I got to recognize many of the humming-birds individually. When I needed a lift, I had only to glance out my window at the feeders swaying in the breeze and the tiny, feathered bodies darting about on invisible wings. There were just enough of them shimmering outside in the sun-light. Just enough to make all the difference.

a shelter for at least a brief cooling-off peri-od, said Woodward. Danger signs include threats against children, use of objects or weapons or threatened use of them, and threats of suicide, such as "I'll kill myself and it will be your fault."

"Threatening suicide is a way to use power and control over another person and hold them hostage," said Woodward. "The only way women can protect themselves is by leaving because there is no guarantee that they wouldn't get hurt." They should leave, then alert authorities that their spouse has threatened suicide so someone can check on him. Then, if the harassment continues, reporting the violence and getting a restrain-ing order are probably the next steps.

Set some boundaries. It takes cour-age, but setting boundaries will in some cases stop abuse before it spirals out of con-trol. We simply must refuse to allow any-one to abuse us.

"When someone is beating us up ver-bally, we should say, 'That is unacceptable to me. I deserve to be treated with digni-ty and respect. And I refuse to accept that kind of language from you. If you want to be in a relationship with me, that is total-ly unacceptable.' It's not shaming them," said Woodward, "but it's saying that this is unacceptable behavior." It's also a bibli-cally sound concept. "If your brother sins against you, go and tell him his fault..." (Matthew 18:15 ESV).

Consider informing church leadership. Making a pastor or an elder aware of the situation could help address the problem.

"The church could be a powerful instrument to hold abusers responsible and provide safety for victims and children, but church leaders need to be trained," said Woodward.

Insist on change. Since most states have mandatory arrest laws for domestic violence, spending the night or a few days in jail can make most abusers feel sad. But that's not enough, said Woodward. "Anyone would feel bad when arrested, but I think that true repentance is sorrow for our actions, willingness to change, and, in fact, making those changes."

Possible changes include giving up drinking alcohol and refraining from viewing pornography. Alcoholism has been found to increase the risk for abuse because it lowers inhibitions and impairs judgment, while pornography is thought to devalue people in the eyes of the abuser.

Also, a Christian man who is fixated on ruling his home with an iron fist should adopt the attitude of servant leadership that is described in the Bible, where husbands are directed: "...love your wives, just as Christ loved the church..."

(Ephesians 5:25 NIV) and told that they should "...love their wives as their own bodies" (Ephesians 5:28 NIV).

Get them to a group. At first glance, marital counseling seems like the answer to the problem of abuse between a husband and wife. It may not be. It can work against the victim. If she discloses things about him, he may use them against her later. Additionally, many abusers are so manipulative that they can sometimes outsmart counselors.

Some experts suggest that the preferred treatment is group therapy, which provides an environment where other men will hold him accountable. If no group therapy program is offered in a nearby church, call an area domestic violence program and ask.

Don't rush a reunion. "Certainly, the Lord can work very quickly in changing someone, but I would be very leery of fast improvements," said Woodward. The abuser may simply be disguising his feelings so he can rejoin the family.

"Abusers can gain a lot by getting back together with a spouse or family. They're lonely and often paying additional living expenses." Rather than rushing back, however, it's probably best to first meet only when another person is present and then evaluate whether or not it's a good idea to resume the relationship, said Woodward. Research shows that it can take abusers between one and five years to change their ways.

Forgive. The Bible commands us to forgive—in other words, hate the sin and love the sinner, Dr. Zeiders reminds us. "One woman I worked with desired for the man who abused her to die, so we worked on forgiving him and not requiring that a terrible thing happen to him. Eventually, she prayed, 'God, I am willing to have Your Spirit of love come into this wounded place in my heart and be healed of this oppressive hatred that is messing up my body.' That prayer was like removing a barrier that stood between her and the healing power of the Spirit," he says. "When the barrier of unforgiveness was removed, the Holy Spirit rushed in and took away the burden of the hate and the hurt connected with that, and restored her."

Pray for inner healing. As with the woman who was molested by her grandfather, Dr. Zeiders and other counselors say that they've seen extraordinary improvement among those abuse victims who have prayed for inner healing. "Jesus is a healer and He will heal the body, but He will also heal the mind—the memories," says Dr. Zeiders.

Consider counseling. Whether it's guiding us through a prayer for inner healing, helping us establish healthy relationship boundaries, or changing wrong conclusions about ourselves, abuse victims generally benefit from at least a few sessions with a counselor or pastor, says Dr. Zeiders.

Think twice about reconciliation. Although through Christ's strength we can forgive, sometimes trying to reconcile is simply too dangerous. "If the abuser is truly remorseful and willing to make amends, then we certainly encourage reconciliation," said Woodward. But, she adds, if our spouse is violent toward us, we have every right to leave the abusive spouse.

Gathering the Fragments

Gather me, O healing God,
from the four corners of my being.
Draw me in
that I may collect the pieces of my life.
There, within me, gather up the fragments
and with Your healing Spirit
breathe the wholeness I am seeking this day.
May I go forth, then
one with myself and one with You—
to live each moment in holy union
with myself and with You. Amen.

—ANITA M. CONSTANCE

DISASTER

The Paradox of God and Evil

There may be no way to rationalize the paradox of a loving God with the suffering that occurs around us. But speaking from personal experience, the Reverend David Kelsey, Ph.D., professor emeritus of theology at Yale Divinity School, says that that paradox can lead us to a mission. During a few years in the mid 1970s, Kelsey suffered a series of profound personal setbacks and losses as he and his family dealt with serious illnesses. This is what he gleaned from them: "I know that a loving God exists because I have experienced that love. And I know that evil exists, because I have experienced that evil. I cannot explain this seeming contradiction, but I can say this: The reality of the first compels us to minister to the reality of the second. I believe that this is the essence of what it means to live a Christian life."

An Event That Makes Us Question God

In the spring of 1974, a tornado ripped through the town of Louisville, Kentucky, with such quick and devastating force that it ripped the facades off rows of beautiful homes, leaving the structures standing but with damaged, littered, disheveled interiors exposed for all the world to see.

The late Dr. John Boyle, who witnessed the Kentucky tornado while a faculty member at Southern Baptist Theological Seminary in Louisville, never forgot those images. For him, they came to symbolize one of the things that happens to all of us when disaster hits. "Our facades, our assumptions and appearances, and our long-held beliefs are removed, and we're left to deal with one another in disheveled, not always pretty, states of raw emotion," he said. "What's inside us is laid bare."

CAN FAITH SURVIVE?

Be it by the happenstance of nature, the calculation of a crazed gunman, or any of a hundred other scenarios, disaster does this to us: it bares our fears, uproots our beliefs in the orderliness of life, makes us question our sense of safety, and, as the late Charles Gerkin, professor emeritus at Candler School of Theology of Emory University, pointed out in *Crisis Experience in Modern Life,* severely challenges our long-held faith in an all-loving, all-powerful God.

In the face of such turmoil, can our faith still be of any use to us? That depends on our attitudes toward God.

Accepting disasters can be difficult if we think of God as a benevolent fairy godfather who is supposed to lead us through life unscathed, steering us clear of any and all calamities. If that's our view, then "that's a theology that life will take from us," says Kathleen Greider, Ph.D., professor of practical theology, spiritual care, and counseling at Claremont School of Theology in California. "Once we've experienced untold, unjustified, inexplicable disaster, we simply can no longer hold fast to a belief in a God whose will it is to shield the faithful from such things."

Or, as Dr. Boyle said, "We learn what Job learned, that God does not simply reward the saint and punish the sinner. Life is a good deal more random than that."

We can, however, believe in a biblical God Who remained steadfast to the Hebrews through their forty years of wandering and deprivation in the wilderness: "Happy are you, O Israel! Who is like you, a people saved by the Lord...!" (Deuteronomy 33:29 NRSV). To Jesus in His moment of death: "Father, into your hands I commend my spirit" (Luke 23:46 NRSV). And from an imprisoned Paul to the faithful in the city of Colossae: "May you be made strong with all the strength that comes from his glorious power...giving thanks to the Father, Who has enabled you to share in the inheritance of the saints in the light" (Colossians 1:11–12 NRSV). As

Dr. Gerkin says, "God's partnership with the descendants of Israel has always included suffering and tragedy as well as hope and the assurance of His presence."

To many, the incarnation of God as Jesus shows His willingness to share our lot. It is God demonstrating that His love of us does not preclude disasters but instead impels Him to suffer them with us. Jesus crucified is the ultimate enactment of divine love, that is, the guarantee that God's love is such that even in the face of disaster, it does not desert us but, in Paul's words, "remains obedient."

"Nowhere in the Bible does it say that God wills suffering," said Dr. Boyle. "Nor does it say that God insulates the faithful from it. What it does testify to is the fact that God participates in it with us. Faith in God does not mean a life without pain; it means a life without ultimate and total abandonment."

Remedies
COPING WITH DISASTER

A POPULAR POSTER IN OFFICES, classrooms, and church bulletin boards years ago read: "Be prepared; it wasn't raining when Noah built the ark." While no one goes looking for a calamity, let alone anticipates one, it's worth being prepared for the reactions that disaster can bring. Here is some advice that counselors offer.

Don't assume you know the limits of your pain. "There are surprises, hidden faults, and subtle problems that come to the surface when disaster strikes," says the Reverend Ron Mahn, licensed professional counselor, licensed marriage and family therapist, and a pastoral counselor who helped counsel families after the 1995 bombing of the Federal Building in Oklahoma City that left 169 dead. "After the bombing, some families really came together and others really came apart. What we discovered is that by and large, the families that couldn't hold up had deep-seated problems they had been keeping from view. If disaster besets any family where there's even a suggestion of instability, they would do well to commit themselves to seeking outside help, either with their pastors or with professional therapists."

Anticipate the guilt of unexpected blessings. There's often an enormous

And we know that in all things God works for the good of those who love him, who have been called according to his purpose. —ROMANS 8:28 (NIV)

I met Lisa, the newly appointed principal at Creekside Junior High, shortly after our schools reopened following Hurricane Katrina. Creekside is a small school located in the town of Pearl River, Louisiana. Lisa had asked our TV station to cover an event at her school. When we arrived, I asked her how her first year there was going.

She said her biggest concern when she was hired was how she would fit into this small, close-knit community, where everybody knew everybody. "I was an outsider. I'd come from another school district. I wanted to be accepted by this community, whose children would be in my care. But I wasn't sure how to do it."

Days later, Hurricane Katrina hit and sent Lisa scurrying to the shelter down the street from the school. She began making sandwiches, serving meals, and doing whatever was needed to help those who had been forced out of their homes feel comfortable and safe.

"Up until the hurricane hit," she recalled, "I'd been trying to figure out what I could do to be accepted in my new job, in my new town, and with my new students and their parents. The storm took care of that. I just rolled up my sleeves and did whatever I needed to do to help out."

When school reopened a month later, Lisa greeted many of the students and their parents by their first names. "We'd worked side by side, preparing meals together and eating together," she said, smiling. "We're family now."

Dear Lord, thanks for Lisa's reminder that even out of a disaster, something good can come. —MELODY SWANG

sense of guilt that settles into the lives of survivors. We may feel guilt-ridden because we survived and another did not. Or we may feel a sense of guilt simply because

something good inadvertently came to us as a result of a disaster.

For example, says Mahn, "The church that I belong to was severely damaged in the Oklahoma City blast. As a result, we were awarded funds and completed a $6 million renovation we never would have been able to afford otherwise. This is a blessing for us, but as parishioners, we feel so very torn when we recall what made this possible. And as the city rebuilds, there are stories like this all over town."

Dr. Greider says that while such guilty feelings are inevitable, we can cope with them by meditating on the Easter story, in which life emerges from death. "It is the essence of redemption that we weave something positive out of the threads of disaster—that death is not final, but that it yields to life," she says.

Don't minimize the importance of material things. When others die in a disaster that may have inflicted only a loss of property on us, we want to embrace our blessings and dismiss our losses. But we ought to remember that physical things can carry great sentimental attachment. "When the tornado hit Louisville in 1974," Dr. Boyle recalled, "people grieved the loss of the lone family photograph, the great-grandmother's quilt, or the parents' wedding license—irreplaceable things that were links to other times and to people they loved who are long since gone." When we feel pain over the loss of such things, we need to allow ourselves to

experience it rather than trying to dismiss it as frivolous or self-absorbing. How can we express the pain? One way is to talk with friends and family who understand how much meaning those objects held for us.

HEALING AFTER TRAGEDY STRIKES

Just as there are ways we can prepare for disaster, there are steps we can take to heal ourselves and our communities after disaster strikes.

Get angry with God. If you want to, that is. Don't worry, He can take it. "I recall visiting with two of my parishioners, a married couple," says the Reverend Mahan Siler. "They had suffered the loss of two of their young children, at different times and under different circumstances. It was a horrible blow, and at one point, the wife said to me, 'I'm so angry at God that I can't even pray and tell Him how angry I am!' To which I answered, 'You've been praying already. This is what your anger is.' I referred her to the Psalms, and how so many of them, such as Psalm 10 ["Why, Lord, do you stand far off? Why do you hide yourself in times of trouble?" Psalm 10:1 NIV] are prayers of anger. That they are part of our Scripture assures us that this is a valued form of prayer." In addition to reading appropriate Psalms, we can harness our anger at God by actually writing our own psalm, says Siler.

Help one another. To live in the image of God, as the Bible recommends in Genesis, means to help one another in a loving, healing manner. "In the face of disaster," said Dr. Boyle, "church members can do God's work by simply being there for one another and by being able to share with one another their rage, their fears, their puzzlement, and their support. In the case of a disaster visited on a whole community, pastors and lay leaders can gather groups together and facilitate conversation. If it's the kind of calamity that befalls one family, others can go to them quietly and privately, with a dish of food, and simply listen without comment to what the person wants to say."

Create a memorial. While we must get on with our lives after a disaster, it's important to realize that the memory of what happened will continue for future generations. To help them cope, we might want to create some kind of memorial, says Mahn, "a fund, a statue, a park, or whatever is a useful way of securing the event in the community's shared history." However, he also suggests that we consider our choices carefully so the memorial will have meaning for people fifty to a hundred years from now who will have no firsthand knowledge of the event. If our community wants to memorialize an event, he suggests that we visit other cities and towns for ideas.

When disaster strikes, it will disrupt our lives, not just for this day or this month, but forever, said Dr. Boyle. And, he says, we must remember that recovery from disaster is not restoration of the way life was before the disaster hit. Rather, it is a new start in many ways. It requires a new appreciation for the arbitrariness of disaster, a new understanding of the fragility of the world, and a new interpretation of both God's place in it and ours.

But now, O Jacob, listen to the Lord Who created you.

O Israel, the One Who formed you says,

"Do not be afraid, for I have ransomed you.

I have called you by name; you are mine.

When you go through deep waters,

I will be with you.

When you go through rivers of difficulty,

you will not drown.

When you walk through the fire of oppression,

you will not be burned up;

the flames will not consume you.

—Isaiah 43:1–2 NLT

FINANCIAL DIFFICULTIES

Solving Money Worries

Here are eight steps worth trying in the midst of financial struggles:

1. Remind yourself to think creatively. Remember it is impossible to develop creative thoughts in a worried mind. Therefore, ask God to give you a peaceful mind through which He can send an answer to your problem. Start your budget time with prayer.

2. Remind yourself that God will supply all your needs out of His vast abundance.

3. Ask yourself if you are thinking lack. There is a curious law that if you think lack, you tend to create a condition of lack. Shift your thought pattern to one of abundance and believe that God is now in the process of giving it to you.

4. Read and study various methods of money management. There are techniques that others have discovered and proved. Add their knowledge to yours.

5. Plan and pray over your expenditures as a family, and each member will feel pride and cooperation as the budget is controlled.

6. Practice the time-tested principle of thrift and frugality. This requires spiritual power because it involves self-discipline.

7. Take all your bills; lay them on the table. Then ask God what to do about them. Ask Him for a definite plan of financing. Then systematize your

expenses, your debts, and your income on the basis of the insight you receive through prayers.

8. Are you tithing to God's work? A tithe means a tenth. Meditate upon God's promise: "Bring ye all the tithes into the storehouse…and prove me now herewith, saith the Lord of hosts, if I will not open you the windows of heaven, and pour you out a blessing, that there shall not be room enough to receive it" (Malachi 3:10 KJV). —NORMAN VINCENT PEALE

More Money isn't the Cure

THERE'S A STRANGE TRUTH about money. "Whoever loves money never has enough; whoever loves wealth is never satisfied with their income" (Ecclesiastes 5:10 NIV). These thoughts are attributed to wise old King Solomon, the man credited with writing the book of Proverbs.

Even today, how often we say, "If I just had more money" or "If I just had this or that item, then everything would be all right. Then I would be happy."

More money is not the answer, says Mary Hunt, author and founder of the Debt-Proof Living organization. "It doesn't take much contemplation to realize that more money can't be the answer," she says. "Because who among us doesn't make more money than we made ten years ago? Or even one year ago?" Has that increase solved all our problems? Are we now completely satisfied? Are we now debt free? Are we living happily ever after?

The problem, says Hunt, is not a lack of money but what we do with our money, how we view our money, and how we care for our money. The answer is getting out of debt and staying out of debt. The answer is enjoying the money we are blessed with—sharing it, saving it, investing it, and spending it wisely and thoughtfully. There just isn't enough "more money" in this world to make us happy.

Hunt knows. Her family teetered on the brink of financial ruin before she asked God for forgiveness and spent the next thirteen years digging out of their money problems. Now she helps others avoid messes like the one she made or clean them up much more quickly than she did. She has thousands of letters attesting that her advice has turned lives around. "There is always hope," she says.

The Bible offers many lessons about money. We are to recognize that money, even wealth, is a gift from God and we are to honor God with it. We are to be good stewards. We are to enjoy it. We are to invest wisely. We really are not supposed to run up unsecured debt, says Jerry McTaggart, founder of Christian Credit Counselors. Lend to many, but borrow from none, advises Deuteronomy 15:6.

But this is the real world. This is America. This is the land of TV commercials, digital marketing, magazine ads, billboards, and new technology every year. Good people do get into bad debt for many reasons. They need good, sound advice and help.

BREAK THE CREDIT HABIT

The first key to effective money management is to quit using credit cards, unless we truly are going to pay the bills in full each month when they come due, says McTaggart. Give up instant gratification—the buy-now, pay-later syndrome. And give up the pocketful of cards. Most people don't need multiple credit cards, he says. Just keep one for emergencies or for online or phone purchases.

Let's say the problem isn't a bad case of the I-want-it-right-nows. Rather, a job loss or car accident sends our finances flailing, and we see no short-term solution in sight. We should never borrow from credit cards to tide us over when money gets tight, no matter how great the temptation, says McTaggart. This is the quickest way to run up uncontrollable debt.

Remedies
GOD'S PLAN

How SHOULD WE handle money?

"It's an easy formula," says Hunt. "And if you look back in time, you'll see that anybody who has been successful with money has followed this: They were givers, number

one. They were savers, number two. And then, with what was left, they never spent more money than they had."

How can we apply this formula in our lives? Here are some tips.

Give. "I think God blesses us, and it's like exposing your life to God's supernatural intervention if you will just obey Him. What He says is, 'I want the best and the first of whatever you have,'" says Hunt. "That applies to our talents, to our money, and to our time."

The Bible talks of giving 10 percent back to God, to good, holy works, causes, and efforts, but you need not start there if that seems too daunting, says Hunt. "If you can't do 10 percent today, that's fine. Start with 1 percent. And I don't care where you give it. Just give it with no strings attached. Give it out of a heart of gratitude. Say, 'This is what I am doing because I am so thankful for the air that I breathe, for the place that I live, and for the wonderful abundance I am enjoying right now, this is the most wonderful time in all of creation to have lived as far as I am concerned. I'm so grateful for that.'"

If you start with 1 percent, watch what happens, she says. "Then, as God blesses you with more, give more."

Save. "It's very clear in God's Word that He wants us to prepare for the future, and I don't mean in an unbalanced way," says Hunt. "I know that in Matthew, it says not to lay up treasures on earth because they're going to get rusty and they're going to rot out, so you need to lay up treasures

in heaven. But I think that the person who says, 'I'm not going to save money, I'm not going to think about tomorrow in any way' is missing the boat."

"Look at the parable of the talents, where the master gave money to three different servants and then checked to see what they did with it. One servant buried his money in the backyard because he was so fearful of losing it. The master said that was horrible. He said, 'At least you could have earned interest if you'd put it in the bank.' I think that's the principle we need to grasp."

So the second thing is, save 10 percent. It's a pretty good formula. Give away 10, save 10.

Live joyfully. "Live the best life, the most wonderful, fabulous, exotic life you can on 80 percent of what you make," says Hunt. "And I have to tell you, I have drawers full of testimonials that this works. All I have to do is look into my own life and see where I am today as opposed to where I was fifteen years ago, when I fell on my face on that kitchen floor and had to beg God for His forgiveness. Yes, I can tell you that it works."

Spend wisely. Think of it like this: Our money isn't really "our" money. We are simply entrusted with it; we are stewards,

Lost and Found

By Glenda Adair

After my husband's company transferred us to a new town, I gave up working, to help our sons adjust. Money was tight, but we had just enough—until Mike noticed the gas cap had gone missing on our car. "It's not a regular gas cap," Mike explained, "but the more expensive spring-loaded one." An expense we did not need. We'd pumped gas in the car earlier at the convenience store near our house. "I'll go over and see if someone found it there," I said. I decided to walk, hoping to relieve some stress.

"You didn't find a stray gas cap?" I asked the clerk. She smiled, said yes—and pulled out a shoebox full! I searched through the pile. Every lost gas cap in town seemed to be in this box. Every one but ours. I started to wonder if this move was worth it. *God, will we ever really settle in here?* I thanked the clerk and headed back with the bad news. Sometimes the most minor thing can seem to ruin everything.

I turned the corner that led to our house and kicked at a rock. It skipped ahead and landed near a flash of light. I bent down to look closer. Our gas cap!

I ran back home. If God cared enough to help with our tiny troubles, He'd surely be around for the bigger challenges. Sometimes the most minor thing changes everything.

says McTaggart. He suggests that we ask ourselves before we spend money whether, in this situation and under the same circumstances, this is the decision that God would have us make.

BANISH BUDGETS

It's not that you don't have to set aside money for expenses. It's just that the B-word, budget, sounds so intimidating. "I don't like that word," says Hunt. "You know, to me, budget, diet, straitjacket—each is such a mean label. So I call it a spending plan."

So we should give 10 percent and save 10 percent. Then what percentage should we spend on various expenses like housing, food, and clothing?

She recommends that we come up with our own formulas by doing the following:

Gather records. Get together the credit-card statements, online bank statements, checkbook registers, and other receipts going back as far as a year, if possible.

Tally up. Add up typical spending. Divide everything into accounts such as mortgage, car payment, car repairs, gasoline, Christmas gifts, dining out, groceries, utilities, clothing, taxes, prescriptions, doctor visits, savings, life insurance, entertainment, children's schoolbooks and supplies, and so forth. Total your spending in each expense category.

Divide and conquer. We need to divide the total amount for each category by the number of paychecks we receive each year. That's about how much we need to set aside each paycheck in each category to cover our predictable expenses. Nearly all expenses should be predictable, says Hunt. If we create a spending plan like this, a property-tax bill won't be an emergency when it shows up in the mail.

Nearly every conceivable expense will be covered. That's our spending plan.

Keep simple, basic books. Give each account a page in a notebook, and once each week, record deposits into that account and record any expenditures during the previous week.

Plan ahead. We need a second checking account, Hunt says. This one is for expenses not paid on a monthly basis or for unpredictable items. She calls it our freedom account.

Our freedom account gets a notebook of its own, and we create a page for each item. The pages might include auto repair, retirement plan, new bedroom set, life insurance, kids' college, and property taxes, for instance. Figure out how much each of these costs on a yearly basis and divide by twelve to get a monthly figure. Put the pages in order of importance or priority.

Set up an automatic monthly deposit from your regular checking into your freedom account to cover the monthly totals of your irregular expenses. Enter the monthly amount deposited on each separate page.

What if we find that we spend more than we take in? Then we need to run through all the categories and see where we might trim, says Hunt. To get our accounts started, we might wish to have a garage sale and sell some things so we have a little extra money in reserve in each account.

WHAT IF THE WOLF IS AT THE DOOR?

Too late? The phone rings a dozen times a day and we dread answering because it's probably another bill collector hounding us. We can't fund a spending plan. We can't even predict whether we'll be able to buy groceries, pay the rent, and keep the electricity on. What to do?

Credit card companies figure that it's better to help people stay solvent and repay their bills than to hound them, force them into bankruptcy, and lose them as customers, says McTaggart. So they will waive a portion or all of the interest payments and allow a delinquent customer, through the credit counseling service, to pay off the principal. That speeds things up tremendously. To learn more, you can visit Christian Credit Counselors at christian-credit-counselors.org or the National Foundation for Credit Counseling at nfcc.org.

"When you're paying 18 percent interest, it will take you ten years to get out of debt if you pay only the minimum payment," explains McTaggart. "If the companies will waive their interest and we can put all of the payment money toward the principal, we've found that it drops to around twenty-seven months—two to three years versus ten years. What happens otherwise is that people become so frustrated along the period of ten years that they just say, 'You know what? I'm not getting ahead at all. I send in a hundred dollars and I only get twenty dollars knocked off the principal. This is killing me.' So they go and file for Chapter 7 bankruptcy. For biblical reasons, we're not supposed to do that. 'The wicked borrow and do not repay...'" (Psalm 37:21 NIV).

A credit counseling agency will help us determine exactly the minimum amount of money required for our basic needs, including entertainment, and then, hopefully, find enough left over to pay our creditors under new terms the agency negotiates. The agency will collect that amount of money from us each month, usually through direct deposit of a portion of our paychecks, and then pay our bills for us and send us a monthly statement, explains McTaggart.

Stop the outflow of money. A credit counseling agency will insist that we turn in our credit cards until we are out of debt. Occasionally, they will let us keep one credit card with a low limit for true emergencies, says McTaggart. Whether we go to a credit counseling agency or not, if we find ourselves in over our heads, we must stop charging and getting deeper into debt, says Hunt.

Enter a rapid-repayment plan. The nonprofit credit counseling services can set one up for us. Or we can do one on our own, following Hunt's instructions above.

Make room for joy. "I want to help people see that paying back debt—that stopping that frantic I've-got-to-have-more-more-more-me-me-me-I-never-have-enough-stuff—is a great relief," says Hunt. "If we can put the brakes on that sort of thing, that's when the joy starts coming back into our lives."

The Bible tells us that we aren't supposed to love money. It also says, however, that we are supposed to enjoy it—that which we are given. King Solomon speaks to this: "…it is appropriate for a person to eat, to drink and to find satisfaction in their toilsome labor under the sun during the few days of life God has given them—for this is their lot. Moreover, when God gives someone wealth and possessions, and the ability to enjoy them, to accept their lot and be happy in their toil—this is a gift of God" (Ecclesiastes 5:18–19 NIV).

A key, says Hunt, is accepting what we can afford, learning to enjoy it, and not envying others.

Just for Today
Lord, for tomorrow and its needs,
I do not pray;
Keep me, my God, from stain of sin
Just for today.
Let me both diligently work,
And duly pray.
Let me be kind in word and deed,
Just for today.
Let me be slow to do my will,
Prompt to obey;
Help me to sacrifice myself
Just for today.
And if today my tide of life
Should ebb away,
Give me thy Sacraments divine,
Sweet Lord today.
So for tomorrow and its needs
I do not pray,
But keep me, guide me, love me, Lord,
Just for today.
—MORNING PRAYER FROM *"ST. AUGUSTINE'S PRAYER BOOK"*

JOB TROUBLE

The Purpose of Work

At times everyone struggles with work. There's either too much of it, or we can't find it when we need it. Work is an end in itself, and we should not shirk it, suggests this proverb: "Lazy hands make for poverty, but diligent hands bring wealth" (Proverbs 10:4 NIV).

The Bible even offers a formula for success: work, work, work. "Sow your seed in the morning, and at evening let your hands not be idle, for you do not know which will succeed, whether this or that, or whether both will do equally well" (Ecclesiastes 11:6 NIV).

While work is important and valuable, God does not expect us to work all the time or to damage our health through overwork or excessive stress. "Six days do your work, but on the seventh day do not work, so that your ox and your donkey may rest, and so that the slave born in your household and the foreigner living among you may be refreshed" (Exodus 23:12 NIV).

Finding Peace in an Uncertain World

MOST OF US SPEND more of our productive, waking hours on the job than any place else. So naturally, how we get along on the job—with our coworkers, our supervisors, our clients, our customers, and even with the actual work itself—has a lot to do with our moods, our mental outlook, and our health.

It's important that we feel we are producing good work and contributing to the world around us. It's also important that we feel valued and appreciated for the work we do.

Since we do spend so much of our time at work, it is natural that we will at times experience emotional upsets and conflicts through our jobs. And since we are dependent upon our jobs for what they allow us to buy—the lifestyles that they allow us to live—when we lose our jobs or are in danger of losing them for whatever reason, our world turns topsy-turvy. We find ourselves spiritually challenged, notes marriage and family therapist Tim Van Duivendyk, D.Min., M.Div., ordained Baptist minister, association of clinical pastoral education certified supervisor and vice president of chaplaincy and spiritual care at Memorial Hermann Hospital in Houston, Texas, and author of *The Unwanted Gift of Grief.*

Our jobs and our spirituality are tightly intertwined. We need to recognize this and understand that our faith influences every area of our lives, even our jobs and careers. And yes, it is possible to integrate work and faith, work and spirituality, and life purpose and mission from a spiritual perspective. We can even draw on our spiritual centers in handling day-to-day conflicts, bad bosses, job burnout, and even job loss.

Sometimes getting our work, our attitudes about it, and our approaches to it to reflect our spiritual values and our faith is easier said than done. But if our work goes against our spiritual values, our faith suffers.

The Apostle Paul said, "Faith that doesn't show itself by good works is no faith at all—it is dead and useless" (James 2:17 TLB). In the larger context, he suggests we demonstrate our faith by and through our actions. If we don't do that on the job—where we spend as much time as any place else, or more than—where, then, will we live our faith?

WHY AM I HERE?

Sometimes our work environments are so unpleasant that we dread clocking in. Our bosses and coworkers nag and belittle us and seem to unfairly dump the most undesirable and difficult tasks on us, and then gripe and complain about our performance and threaten us. Sometimes we are just so overwhelmed that we think we'll never get caught up—and that leads to mental and nervous exhaustion.

So, yes, when we find our work environments overwhelmingly unpleasant, we are likely to ask, "How did I get here? Why am I here? Why me, Lord?"

This is not to suggest that we should punish ourselves and stay in an untenable work situation. But we shouldn't just throw up our hands and walk away, either, according to the late Reverend Paul F. Everett, who was a Presbyterian minister-at-large with the Peale Center in Pawling, New York. "We have to work things through; we have to deal with challenges and process the experiences," he explains.

"Our growth comes through stress and challenges in one way, shape, or form. What God is allowing in our lives is for our growth and transformation," said Everett. "We may think that it is a big mistake that we are in this job or in this particular position, but isn't God a part of it all? If I have invited God into my life to be my Lord and Savior, then He wants to be a part of every area of my life, and that includes my job.

We need to seek His plan for where we are and what we're doing."

Yes, we may well need to move on to a new job that better uses the talents and skills God gave us and where we are more appreciated and treated more respectfully. But "the way out is through," said Everett. The answer is not to run, but to face the problems and understand what they are teaching us about ourselves, about life, and about others. Pastor Everett suggested, "Ask this question: 'Am I willing to walk with God in the circumstances and situations in which I find myself right now in this job?'"

Sometimes it is when we feel the most pain, the most frustration, and the most stress that God reveals the most helpful life-changing lessons, observed Everett. "He that overcometh," says God in Revelation 21:7 (KJV), "shall inherit all things; and I will be his God, and he shall be my son."

By facing the challenges and discerning the lessons, we clarify our needs and purposes and open the door to satisfying, spiritually fulfilling work.

How to Find Yourself After Losing a Job

By James Masters

Even though I'd seen it coming for a few days, the reality of that December morning was devastating. I was fired after five years as superintendent of a private school near Dallas. I'd thought it was only people who performed poorly that lost jobs. But I was a professional and college-educated; I'd given my all to the school! I'd always had a good job and good pay. Now the letter I held in my hand told me that none of that mattered. A difference in philosophy with a school board had reduced me from an administrator to just another statistic among the unemployed.

At the beginning I was mainly angry and anxious about my family's finances. But then, as I watched my wife, Jeanne, go off to her job and my daughter leave for high school every morning, I became overwhelmed by the aloneness I felt, a prisoner of my own house. I hadn't just lost a job—I had lost my whole identity.

For months I felt that I was hardly a person anymore. But slowly, during that time, I discovered how to deal not only with the loss of a job, but with the loss of me.

1. **Heal the hurt of rejection first.** It was very hard to accept the fact that I'd been fired. I kept wanting to fight for my job. But there was no one to challenge. My job was lost through unfortunate circumstances, not lack of skills or ability on my part. It just happened, and it was happening to many others because of precarious economic times. For weeks I had to remind myself of this constantly, until it finally began to sink in, healing the anger and hurt I felt inside.

2. **Job-hunt, then let God work.** In the weeks after I lost my job, I got my personal file and credentials in order. Then I sent out applications and résumés to everyone I could think of in my field; I visited schools in person, and went on interviews. I heard, "Sorry, we have nothing available," a lot—or I heard nothing. But once I felt satisfied I had done everything possible to search out a job, I felt a new peace, a release from the futility of sitting by the telephone, waiting for it to ring. When I consciously put my future in God's hands, He gave me peace of mind.

3. **Keep busy.** One day the phone did ring, but it wasn't a job offer; it was my father-in-law, asking if I might like to help some around his house. I fixed cabinets, replanted shrubs, and did other odd chores. It made me feel good about myself and put me in motion. I began helping with the church education programs. I worked on my doctoral degree, something I had had little time for. Closets and files that had been ignored for years were cleaned, sorted out, and painted. All that work didn't restore any lost wages, but it showed me that I could still enjoy using my skills to help people and it kept me from dwelling on the injustice of not having a job.

4. **Rely on your friends.** There were days when the job search appeared hopeless, when both Jeanne and I needed a friend to talk with or a shoulder to cry on. By opening up about our feelings and needs to a couple of close friends, we each got warm encouragement.

It was seven months before I found a new job. But during that time, I found myself content in God's will, sure of His leading, confident in His love, and more understanding of others in similar situations.

Living without a job was a terrible burden to bear. Living with myself was a tremendous joy to discover.

Remedies
DEALING WITH A DYSFUNCTIONAL BOSS

"AS ROTTEN AS A boss can be, we have to realize that God didn't promise us that we'd have wonderful bosses and that everything would be lovely and free of work problems," noted Everett. At times, we have to suffer a bad boss, for example, a power and control freak, an antagonist, or a completely self-centered supervisor— one who is more concerned about his own ambitious goals than his people.

In these situations, the best course, if we can manage it, is to escape, says Dr. Paul Meier. Transfer to another department or find a new job, he advises.

Ideally, in the case of sexual harassment, we would report it and it would end. But the fact is, says Dr. Meier, most whistle-blowers face reprisals, suspicion, lies, smears, and humiliation. Before making any report of sexual harassment, Dr. Meier advises, gain the assistance of an attorney experienced in such cases. And even if we do report the abuse, Dr. Meier's best advice is to transfer to another department or find another job. As long as we work for an abuser, we are suffering mental and emotional damage.

If the boss is only mildly dysfunctional, consider these survival tips Dr. Meier suggests.

Keep cool. Stay calm when attacked, when the boss is bellowing, blaring, or berating. Respond briefly, respectfully, and pleasantly. Avoid sarcasm and debating at all costs. It will only invite an escalation of the confrontation.

Don't flinch. People with abusive personalities seek victims. Don't become one. Instead, face the abuser eye-to-eye and respond with self-esteem and courage, politely, carefully, and briefly. If the behavior continues and causes anguish and unhealthy stress, then it's time to look for another job.

AVOIDING OVERWORK

As companies downsize and jobs are eliminated and combined, many of us find ourselves under more and more pressure to work harder, faster, smarter, and longer. Even if our managers aren't pushing us, we feel a need to prove our value so we will survive potential cutbacks or layoffs. Soon, we're in overdrive all the time and our mental and physical health suffers.

We do better work when we are calm and relaxed than when we plow through in a nervous rush, say Dr. Meier and Dr. Van Duivendyk. The most valuable thing we can do to avoid stress damage, illnesses, and burnout is learn to relax, they say. Both cite the work of Herbert Benson, M.D.

The practices involved in meditation help us manage stress so we function more effectively without damaging our health. The steps to eliciting the relaxation response are:

1. Sit in a relaxed, comfortable position.
2. Quiet the mind and breathe slowly and naturally.
3. Gently focus thinking on a single word, phrase, prayer, or sound. Meditators sometimes refer to this object of focus as a mantra. Repeat it during exhalation.
4. Passively disregard other thoughts that intrude, returning the focus to the mantra, statement of affirmation, or prayer.

Dr. Meier points out that the concept of meditation need not be in conflict with anyone's Christian faith. Incorporate faith in the process, he suggests, by using a favorite faith concept or Bible verse as a mantra and praying for the Holy Spirit's guidance.

In fact, Dr. Benson found that a person's religious convictions or life philosophy actually enhanced the effects of the relaxation response.

In addition to daily meditative relaxation, we should remember and respect the biblical teaching about all work and no play. It's not put in those exact terms, but the Old Testament repeatedly admonishes us to respect a day of rest each week. This is the fourth of the Ten Commandments. "Six days you shall labor and do all your work, but the seventh day is a sabbath to the Lord your God. On it you shall not do any work, neither you, nor your son or daughter, nor your male or female servant, nor your animals, nor any foreigner residing in your towns" (Exodus 20:9–10 NIV).

DEALING WITH JOB LOSS

When Houston suffered an economic crash in the mid-1980s, Dr. Van Duivendyk helped the city cope with job loss. The bottom fell out of the oil industry, real estate plunged, and some savings and loans were devastated. A wave of unemployment swept across the city. Even Dr. Van Duivendyk's hospital faced layoffs. To deal with the crisis, he turned to the city churches and helped train many of them to support and set up job counseling networks. He guided congregations in setting up job referral centers at churches all over Houston. He organized job-loss support groups. He often counseled and assessed people who were depressed and needed to be referred to physicians for treatment.

The community of churches made a difference. The support groups, in particular, helped the unemployed realize that they were not alone and that there were creative ways to deal with sudden, seemingly catastrophic change. "People were losing their homes," Dr. Van Duivendyk says. "We're talking pain, frustration, and desperation."

At church seminars, Dr. Van Duivendyk would divide large groups into smaller ones of no more than eight people, and he'd let them tell their stories. After helping them identify and share their problems and pain, he would then ask the same groups to begin talking about resolutions. He'd ask them, "Now, what can we do about that? How do we deal with these problems? How do we face this and go on?" He continues, "This provided a healing dimension for those on the backside of corporate life. For me, this is what prayer, faith, and healing are all about."

The programs in which Dr. Van Duivendyk consulted were later widely recognized, and calls came from churches in other cities asking about Houston's methods.

Let's say our community isn't facing massive job cuts and layoffs, but we ourselves have just been given the pink slip. What do we do now? The following are some principles that Dr. Van Duivendyk used in helping individuals, families, and congregations.

Accept what's happening. "First, understand that the confusion, pain, fear, anger, and sense of impaired self-esteem—these feelings, these emotions—are all normal," says Dr. Van Duivendyk.

Talk it through. Find someone empathic and loving with whom to talk out the feelings, he advises. "Feel your way through the feelings. Identify them, talk about them, and get them out with someone who cares."

When we locate a caring, loving person or community of people, we have found the real church, says Dr. Van Duivendyk. "They are practicing the faith. They are practicing spirituality. They are the loving church community."

We may not always find these people in our churches, he warns. People, including church people, often feel uneasy when around the downtrodden, particularly if the downtrodden are people they have

Job One

BY SETH REAMS

I slouched in front of the computer, my constant companion since I'd lost my job as a concierge. Another morning waking up unemployed! More than three hundred résumés sent, not one response. The service industry was dead. I was feeling completely demoralized, thinking there was something wrong with me.

"You haven't been out of the house in days," my girlfriend, Michelle, said. "Take a break from the job search. Why not volunteer at the Audubon Society?"

"Volunteer? I need to find a job!"

"Just accomplishing something would make you feel better. Think of all the other out-of-work people here in Portland with time and talent to burn."

A lightbulb went on. I wrote a post on Craigslist about pairing up jobless people with volunteer needs. Then we started a blog: wevegottimetohelp.blogspot.com.

The next day I got an e-mail from someone who was out of work: "Saw your post. Great idea! Let me know what I can do." More e-mails flowed in saying the same thing. The organization We've Got Time to Help was born. Then the phone rang: "I have a couch to give a friend who's pregnant and lost her job. Do you have someone who can get it to her?" I e-mailed our new team of volunteers. Delivering the couch wasn't enough. We pooled our resources. The next day we delivered the couch along with furniture, toys, and food. "You've changed my life," the woman said as she watched her apartment transformed.

"No," I said. "You've changed ours."

More than one hundred out-of-work people have signed on to tackle some eighty projects. We've fixed leaky pipes, shingled houses, and painted rooms at an outreach center. Even people with jobs have joined our ranks. I haven't found a job yet, but I've come to see in these times, it's not about being employed. It's about loving your neighbor as yourself. That's what's going to see us through. You know, it might turn out to be the best job-search advice of all.

previously known as peers. Perhaps they fear that the misfortune may be contagious and they don't want to get too close. Also, he says, when times suddenly are economically hard in an area and the first wave of layoffs hits, other people, not grasping the full situation, often are suspicious that those laid off were perhaps somehow in the wrong or not good employees. Those still employed don't want to be associated with perceived failure or possible wrongdoing and may shun the laid-off workers.

We may find this attitude in even our closest circles, he says. If so, we should expand our search for loving, caring, helpful people to find the help we need.

Seek help. Try to find a job-loss support group in the community. "Just realizing that, 'Here I am, a competent person without a job, and I am sitting next to another competent person who doesn't have a job' has tremendous value. It helps us realize that we are not alone," says Dr. Van Duivendyk.

In addition, the group can point us to many resources that can help us quickly organize and implement an effective job search.

Take the anger to God. Accept that we may have a faith crisis. We are likely to question God at times like these. We may express anger because we can't feel God with us.

Go ahead, express it, says Dr. Van Duivendyk. Expressing anger is one form of dialogue with God. "The anger itself, the frustration itself, are expressions of faith in God. You don't express anger toward someone you don't believe exists." God is there, he says. "God doesn't take our jobs away from us, and we don't lose our jobs because God doesn't want to bless us. God is a covenant God Who walks with us in the valleys as well as on the mountaintops of life."

Move into a make-do mode. We need to reframe our thinking, says Dr. Van Duivendyk. A cheaper pair of jeans will get us through if we don't have money for a special name brand. Homemade sandwiches and a picnic in the park can be a fun family get-together when we don't have money for a restaurant and the movies.

Level with the family. "Sitting down with your kids and speaking openly about the pain and fears and asking for help in renegotiating the budget can bring the family together in a new emotional and spiritual way that they might otherwise never experience," says Dr. Van Duivendyk. Families, even kids, can be resourceful with options when parents level openly and honestly with them.

Know that we have a job. Our present job is to find a job. There is a tendency for the unemployed to discount their daily efforts to find work.

Expect to change. The only way we can become new and different is to let go of the old. It's painful to enter the struggle of job loss, but when we do, we begin the journey toward personal growth. "It's true: it is in dying to the old that we rise to the new," Dr. Van Duivendyk says.

Never forget the experience. Once we have new jobs, we should draw on our experiences to help heal others who lose their jobs. We can pass on to others the empathy and care we have learned in this experience.

· HEALING WORDS ·

Challenges at Work

Dearest God,

Bless me this day to remember why I have come to this place of employment.

I see this business as an organization for growth and prosperity for all who enter.

Let me see this work as a gift of healing and my coworkers as people who have come to heal with me.

Fill this workplace with understanding that we may find peaceful cooperation and resolution in all challenges.

Guide us as we work to bring Your love into the world with each task performed. Amen. —CARLA FLACK

· PART 6 ·

*Moving in the
Right Direction*

ATTITUDE

Hum the High Notes

Success is not an accident. We create it out of our expectations, actions, and words, said the late Reverend John Osteen, founding pastor of Lakewood Church in Houston, Texas, and author of numerous books and booklets on adopting a successful attitude spiritually. It is God's will for us, he said.

As Jesus says, "... I am come that they might have life, and that they might have it more abundantly" (John 10:10 KJV). To live life fully, or to have it "more abundantly" as some Bible versions translate Jesus' words, we need to believe that it is what we deserve, said Pastor Osteen. We need to stand on the Bible's promises and "walk by faith, not by sight" (2 Corinthians 5:7).

How do we do that? Get in the habit of expressing spiritually positive desires to ourselves and to others, Pastor Osteen advised in his booklet *What to Do When Nothing Seems to Work*. Additionally, the Bible tells us that "Death and life are in the power of the tongue..." (Proverbs 18:21 KJV).

When things aren't going right, usually "it is because you are not saying what God says about the situation," continued Pastor Osteen. "Instead, you are speculating, surmising, reasoning, and looking at circumstances instead of God's Word." He teaches that we should talk about what God is doing for us and what God promises to do for us, and put our negative thoughts aside.

Yes, contrary thoughts may come to mind, but "as long as you refuse to say those thoughts, they will die. Once you speak them, you give them life. Replace negative thoughts with God's thoughts—the Bible. Say what God says about your situation," wrote Pastor Osteen.

As the late Dr. Norman Vincent Peale said, "You can make your life what you want it to be through belief in God and in yourself."

Besides focusing on the positive and speaking the positive, we need to rub shoulders with the positive, said Dr. Osteen. We need to associate with positive, spiritual people. Besides watching what words leave our mouths, we need to watch what words enter our ears, he wrote.

As Jesus says, "Be careful what you are hearing. The measure of thought and study you give to the truth you hear will be the measure of virtue and knowledge that comes back to you..." —Mark 4:24 AMPC.

It's All a Matter of Choice

THINGS GO WRONG in life. It isn't always easy or exciting. We don't always get what we want. We make mistakes. And we aren't always happy.

That's okay.

Life is a series of experiences, tests, and learning opportunities. Our part in the scheme is not to be perfect, says Dr. Paul Meier. Our job is to remain resilient and maintain hope, despite whatever adversities we face, he says.

That is a healing attitude, said the late Vernon M. Sylvest, M.D., a physician with a prayer-based holistic medical practice in Richmond, Virginia, and author of *The Formula: Who Gets Sick, Who Gets Well*, a book about faith and healing. Our job is to respond to life's challenges in ways that honor the sacred nature of existence.

We do get to make that choice, says Dr. Meier. The process ultimately boils down to attitude, and we do have control over our attitudes.

At any particular moment, we have the ability to choose how we will respond

Learn to Love Your Dandelions

BY SANDRA SMITH

This wonderful old neighbor of mine was retired and spent much of his time in his yard, which was a great source of pride to him. But try as he would, he could not get rid of the dandelions. Despite his using the best grass seed and the most expensive weed killer, they still appeared, bright yellow dots in the midst of his beautiful green lawn.

When he wrote to a gardening expert with his problem, the reply included several suggestions and closed with this statement. "If none of these work, I suggest you learn to love dandelions."

I thought of that advice one morning recently. I stopped by to have coffee with an old friend. For years she and her husband had been saving money to buy a more expensive home.

But she was still at the same address when I called on her. As I walked into her living room and looked around, the words just tumbled out, "Jean, your house just looks beautiful."

It was not an idle compliment. She took me through the rest of the house and every room, every corner, was a gem of imaginative decorating. She had done it, not with a lot of money but with creativity, flair, and hard work.

Over coffee she confided, "I'm sure you remember how much I wanted a bigger house, but after a while I realized it meant making a choice. Either Bob could stay in the lesser-paying job he loved or he could take a position that would enable us to have the finer home but might make him miserable. Once I accepted the situation that was best for Bob, I turned my attention to making this house as attractive as I possibly could. Now I love it."

I guess most of us have our dandelions, of one kind or another. For Jean it was her home. If we can't change outward circumstances, we can change our attitudes toward them.

in any situation, to paraphrase the late Victor Frankl, renowned psychologist.

God wants us to respond to situations morally, lovingly, and constructively. We are human, though, and we won't always be able to accomplish that. That's why Jesus met the cross, says the late Reverend Paul F. Everett. Jesus died so that we might be forgiven our shortcomings, he said.

Remedies
FOCUS ON WHAT'S RIGHT

WE OFTEN FOCUS so much on what is wrong that we don't give ourselves a chance to celebrate that which is right, says Dr. Harold Ivan Smith. Focusing on that which is unsatisfactory is irritating and discouraging. Focusing on that which is right is soothing and encouraging, and it encourages what is right in us and others.

Here are some ways to maintain a positive, constructive focus.

Forgive mistakes. We're humans. We make errors. We shouldn't dwell on them, and we shouldn't inflict self-punishment. God knows our shortcomings and loves us anyway. We should act the same way, says Dr. Meier.

Ignore bad behavior. Some people in the world simply behave badly. This happens even in our churches. Dr. Meier says three out of four people we encounter will somehow disturb us through their words, judgment, rejection, or abuse of some fashion. We need to accept that and not let it bother us too much.

Dr. Smith points out that frequently our efforts at loving, kindness, and fairness will be challenged by unloving, unkind, and unfair behavior, but that doesn't mean

Overcome Your Negative Attitude

By Norman Vincent Peale

One of the basic facts of human experience is that usually you get what your mental attitude indicates. That is, if you believe you can, you can. If you believe you cannot, you cannot. Think negatively, and you will get a negative result, because by your thoughts you create a negative atmosphere, which is hospitable to negative reactions. On the contrary, think positively and you create a positive atmosphere, which makes positive results a natural.

A close-up of one of the most successful men in America, who started with almost less than nothing, reveals that one of his most outstanding characteristics is that he never even so much as entertains the thought of failure in any undertaking.

How does one go about shifting from a negative to a positive thought pattern?

1. For twenty-four hours, deliberately speak hopefully about your job, your children's grades, your health, and your future. Speak hopefully about the prospects for world peace and the business outlook and go out of your way to talk optimistically about everything. This is difficult, but you must restrain yourself from talking pessimistically by an act of will.

2. After speaking hopefully for twenty-four hours, continue the practice for one week. Then you can be permitted to be "realistic" for a day or two. You will discover that what you meant by "realistic" a week ago was actually pessimistic, but what you now mean by "realistic" is something entirely different: it is the dawning of optimism. When most people say they are being "realistic" they are simply being negative.

3. To make your mind healthy, feed it good, nourishing, wholesome thoughts. Begin now to shift your mind to positive thinking. Start at the beginning of the New Testament and underline every sentence that has to do with faith. Continue this until you have marked every such passage in the four Gospels—Matthew, Mark, Luke, and John. But first, turn to Mark 2 and commit to memory verses 22–24. They will serve as samples of the verses you are to underline.

4. Commit the underlined passages to memory, one each day, until you can recite the entire list. This will take time, but remember, you have used time to become a negative thinker and it will take time to unlearn your negative thought patterns.

5. Make a list of your friends and determine who is the most positive thinker among them and deliberately cultivate his or her company. Do not abandon your negative friends, but get closer to those with a positive point of view until you have absorbed their spirit: then go back among your negative friends and give them your newly acquired thought pattern.

6. Be careful to avoid argument, but whenever a negative attitude is expressed, oppose it with a positive and optimistic opinion.

7. Pray a great deal and let your prayer take the form of thanksgiving, on the assumption that God is giving you great and wonderful things. For if you think He is, He surely will. God cannot give you any greater blessing than you can believe in. He wants to give you great things, but even He cannot make you take anything greater than you are equipped to receive.

Make this statement your motto: "If ye have faith as a grain of mustard seed…nothing shall be impossible unto you" (Matthew 17:20 KJV).

that we should quit loving or being kind or helping. It simply means that for us to find satisfaction, happiness, and good emotional health, we do need to recognize and accept that this is the way this world is.

Avoid gossip and rumors. Participating in either can bring us down emotionally and create feelings of fear, doubt, mistrust, and anger—for no real reason. To keep from becoming upset or from judging others unfairly, it's important for us to get accurate information, not hearsay, and to give people a chance to explain themselves.

Believe the Bible's promises. Buy an inexpensive Bible and a highlighting pen, then mark all the inspiring, hopeful, and faith-building verses and read through them during dark and doubtful times, suggests Dr. Smith. Copy some of the verses onto index cards and post them in conspicuous places where they're visible during the day or put them in your phone where you can see them each day.

Memorize the verses in which God promises to walk with us through our difficulties, guide us, never leave us or forsake us, give us peace, and so on. Living these promises and discovering that the Lord is faithful in keeping His promises will deepen our convictions of and trust in his faithfulness, said Pastor Everett. In addition,

we can compile a list of some encouraging experiences, simple and great successes we have had, and some of the positive things the Bible says we are entitled to or positive attitudes that the Bible says we should take, advises Dr. Meier. Then, when a negative thought enters our minds, we can counter it with a positive one from the list. If we counter negatives with true and inspirational positives, he advises, we'll cultivate winning attitudes.

TAKE IN THE BIG PICTURE

Up close, everything seems larger, so standing toe-to-toe with frustrations, pressures, and problems can make them seem overwhelming. Then we begin to feel sorry for ourselves. That is not a holy view, says Dr. Meier. Successful people do not spend a lot of time feeling sorry for themselves. They remember how much God loves them and they stir up their faith and positive attitudes to face their challenges.

Take the long view. How much will anything we're tempted to fret over today matter a hundred years from now, or even one, two, five, or ten years from now? Keeping our lives in perspective helps us avoid reacting based on how something appears through the magnifying lens of the moment, says Dr. Meier.

Think of others first. "Don't be selfish...Be humble, thinking of others as better than yourself. Don't just think about your own affairs, but be interested in others, too, and in what they are doing" (Philippians 2:3–4 TLB).

What better time to do this but when we seemingly can't see beyond our own troubles?

Morning Dance

Even before I opened my eyes this morning, Father, I knew today was going to be good. The sunlight falling through the blinds told me the night had taken the rain away. After days of gray, finally the sky was clear. I rushed through my morning routine and hurried outside to be with You. I have missed our morning walks, Father. I have missed talking to You about my family, my friends, my daily cares. But now the morning seems too perfect to bother You with fretting.

The world has turned from black and white to full color. The trees entice me with the promise of spring, their buds nearly bursting into confetti blossoms. Big white billowy clouds race across the blue sky like sailing ships chasing new horizons. Standing here on the road that runs along the lake, I feel the wind playing with my hair. Last summer's dry leaves sing in the breeze as they hold on to the tall maple by the shore. This will be the last song they ever sing. New leaves are coming to take their place.

Father, I have come here to pray, but Your world is too lovely for words just now. The wind, the sun, the sky stirs something deep inside my heart, and I wonder if...on this lonely road, with no one in sight... You might come and dance with me?

—PAM KIDD

COURAGE

People come and go, civilizations come and go, philosophies come and go, but Jesus Christ is the same yesterday, and today, and forever. And when you live with Him you are not afraid or insecure; you have confidence, come what may.

Drawing Strength from God

THE MORNING AN ESCAPED convict put a handgun in her husband's side and forced his way into their home, Louise DeGrafinried was in the kitchen cooking breakfast.

Lots of cooks would have cowered in fear. Not DeGrafinried. A seventy-year-old grandmother and a faithful member of the Mount Sinai Missionary Baptist Church in Mason, Tennessee, she stood up to the intruder. "I'm a Christian lady and I don't want any violence in my house, so put that gun down," DeGrafinried said. "Now, do you want something to eat?"

The convict complied and sat down for breakfast, and Louise went to work, calmly whipping up another portion of eggs, sausage, bacon, and toast. When she set a plate before him, he got an even clearer sense of who he was dealing with. DeGrafinried wouldn't let him eat without first saying grace, and then went on to explain how a life without Jesus was no life at all.

Eventually, the police arrived and surrounded the house, and DeGrafinried had some words for them as well. "I'll walk him out of here myself," she said.

And that she did, standing by until he was safely ensconced in the back of a patrol car.

"He was ready to give up," said DeGrafinried later. Maybe so. But where did she get the courage to stick around and find out? Or to stay calm during a home invasion? "I wasn't praying all the time, because I was talking to him, but I knew the Lord was surely protecting me."

Remedies
CONFIDENT, COURAGEOUS LIVING

WHEN WE THINK OF courage, we often think of those who are trained to spontaneously do brave things—war heroes, for example, or lifeguards, police, or fire-rescue personnel who are paid to put their lives in jeopardy. But perhaps just as inspiring are the everyday people who face extreme challenges in their lives and, with God's help, overcome them. Especially when those challenges are before them every day.

"I often think the most courageous people I see are single moms and single dads," says Dr. Ray Pritchard. "They get up early every morning, get themselves and the children ready, and drop them off at school or day care. Then they go to work, come home and prepare a meal, spend time with their children, do a million other things, and finally crawl into bed late at night, dead tired. Then they get up the next morning and do it all over again. To me, that takes just as much courage as any soldier on any battlefield in the world."

But whether it's soldiers or single moms, the cornerstone of courage is the same: training—and lots of it. Soldiers undergo basic training, getting in shape, learning to fire and clean weapons, developing teamwork, and building the skills that will help them stand up to adversity.

For single moms and, really, all the rest of us, life is our boot camp. And if we begin to view day-to-day events as mini training sessions, we can build our courage to face hardships, great or small, says Dr. Pritchard.

Admittedly, it's not always easy to do. "We often want to turn away from the difficulties and adversities we face in life, yet clinging to God even in the face of adversity is what makes us become people of

Fear thou not; for I am with thee: be not dismayed; for I am thy God: I will strengthen thee; yea, I will help thee; yea, I will uphold thee with the right hand of my righteousness. —Isaiah 41:10 (KJV)

Sitting across the table from my father, I stare at him. *You have always oozed such confidence,* I think admiringly. When I was a child, my father was always present, always providing, always reaching for the stars. He seemed invincible. I wanted to be just like him. Now this silver-haired, eighty-two-year-old man with a pacemaker and an oxygen compressor as constant companions is still trying new things, like completing educational requirements to become a mediator.

"You never seem afraid," I say to him. "I wish I had your confidence."

"I was afraid sometimes," he replies, and I am startled. This is a side of my father I've never known. I've seen him face down much bigger men, situations that seemed larger than he was. He's never once discussed his fears.

"Like when?"

"When I first went to work at the Pentagon," he says. My mouth drops open. My memories of him going to work are images of a confident man in a suit and tie, reading the newspaper before heading out in the early morning, his ubiquitous cowboy boots clicking down the sidewalk. "The Pentagon was so big," he continues. "There was so much responsibility."

I think of things that have frightened me: raising a daughter and son alone; eventually leaving my own government job and starting a new career. I smile at my father and reach across the table to touch his hand. Though this revelation comes late in life, that he has wrangled with fear, it is a wonderful gift that he has given me.

Lord, thank You for a father who set a fine example of courage in the face of fear. Indeed, You were courageous even unto death. —Sharon Foster courage, people of spiritual faith who can't be shaken," says Ruthanne Garlock, a former missionary and coauthor of *A Woman's Guide to Getting through Tough Times in Life.*

But when we respond to such tasks with courage and faith, amazing things happen. "It's like a stone being thrown into a pond," says Dr. Pritchard. "Our courage and faith ripple out from that moment, that place of difficulty, and it just goes and goes."

Here are some ways we can build our courage, step by step.

Prepare. For challenges big and small, doing some advance work is the best way to nurture courage. So if we're trying to develop the nerve to confront a difficult situation, such as dealing with an alcoholic and abusive spouse, it can help to learn to set proper boundaries, the verbal techniques that can literally shut down abusers. Or, if we're normally afraid of speaking in front of groups and we have to make a presentation, we simply need to study and practice the material until we know it as well as our own names, says Dr. Pritchard.

Find a mentor. Just as a skilled instructor can teach us a musical instrument or a foreign language, we can learn to act more confidently and courageously by watching people who live courageously day by day. And the closer we get to them, the better, says the Reverend Neva Coyle, founder and director of Overeaters Victorious, president of Neva Coyle Ministries, motivational speaker, and author. Look for people who have been where you are now, who have grown through their experiences, and who have the skills to pass on to you what they have learned. "When I see someone exhibiting a virtue such as godly courage, then I get close to that person," she says.

Seek courage from God. People act courageously when challenged in all types of circumstances. But over time, human courage will let us down. "You get to the point where you say, 'I just can't keep doing this; I can't go on,'" says Garlock. "And that's when we have to recognize that God is bigger than our problems and receive our courage from Him." The only way to do that is by crying out to Him. Jeremiah 17:7 says it all: "But blessed is the one who trusts in the Lord, whose confidence is in him" (NIV).

Cultivate Faith. What takes more courage than facing the end of life? In a small study of terminally ill patients at a large Veterans Administration hospital in Long Beach, California, those who attended church more frequently and felt religion was important reported having more courage and less fear of death than those who weren't interested in faith. One reviewer of the study said that these patients exhibited improved coping skills, which not only led to a better quality of life than the less religious but also might lower their healthcare costs. Plus, a good church can go a long way in helping provide encouraging friendships, says Dr. Pritchard.

Look for a purpose. If we knew that one courageous act would have eternal significance, would we rise to the occasion? A single act can and does have significance, and that knowledge should be enough to embolden our efforts, says Dr. Pritchard. "Whether we see it or feel it or understand it, God puts us in situations or allows us to be there for a purpose," he says.

Take the next step. Many Bible characters didn't believe they had the talent, mind, or ambition to complete the assignments God gave them. But when they responded with courage and faith and moved when He said it was time, seas parted, giants fell, and walls tumbled. "Simply taking the next step in front of us and trusting God with the results—that is when the exciting stuff starts to happen," says Dr. Pritchard.

Hang in there. Once we take those courageous first steps, we rest assured we'll be met with opposition. But this, of course, is no time to fold, says Dr. Pritchard. After all, "...the Lord, He *is* the One who goes before you. He will be with you, He will not leave you nor forsake you; do not fear nor be dismayed" (Deuteronomy 31:8 NKJV).

· HEALING WORDS ·

Weathering Storms

A thunderbolt rattles the windowpane, and fear rivets me to the spot. I feel like a small child peering through a crack in the door of my Father's workshop, wincing in frightful fascination as a blue-white arc of chain lightning welds sky to earth. God of all power, give me courage to weather my storms.

—ALMA BARKMAN

DISCIPLINE AND SELF-CONTROL

· FAITH BUILDER ·

Self-control is a benefit, not something we necessarily have to aspire to or even work at, but something that comes as we seek the higher gifts like "faith, hope, and love," virtues Paul enumerates in 1 Corinthians 13.

I like to pray through Galatians 5:22–23 in my head. "Love, joy, peace, patience, kindness, goodness, faithfulness, gentleness and self-control." I thank God for all those gifts, especially that last one, self-control.

Sure, I work at it. But at its best, it comes to me outside of my hard work. It's a gift, fruit of the Spirit. —RICK HAMLIN

The Power in the Heart and Mind

EVERY TWO YEARS, we marvel at Olympic athletes who have dedicated themselves to greatness in their chosen sports. In the quest for Olympic gold, for example, a track star could log more than five thousand miles in training just to run a single hundred-meter event that will be over in less than ten seconds.

But does the track star's five thousand miles of disciplined training start with her first step? Not really, says the Reverend R. Kent Hughes, D.D., D.Min., M.Div., professor of practical theology at Westminster Theological Seminary, senior pastor emeritus of College Church in Wheaton, Illinois, and author of *Disciplines of a Godly Man*.

It begins when she thinks about running and considers the physical and financial costs of her effort, how great the wind feels in her face, and what winning is going to be like.

In other words, it starts in her mind and her heart, the same places where we begin our efforts to develop a sense of discipline and self-control over the challenges in our lives.

The same techniques that help the athlete triumph on the track can help us reach our goals in discipline and self-control, whether we're trying to tame our tongues, keep neater houses, resist lust, bypass all-you-can eat buffets, or master a hundred other troublesome issues in our lives, says Richard L. Ganz, Ph.D., M.Div., senior pastor of the Ottawa Reformed Presbyterian Church, founder and president of Ottawa Theological Hall, where he is also professor of Biblical Psychology and Counseling, and author of *The Secret of Self Control.*

Unfortunately, many people believe developing discipline is impossibly boring. But it doesn't have to be that way, contends Donald S. Whitney in his book *Spiritual Disciplines for the Christian Life.* Sure, there's work involved. But we soon discover that developing control over the important parts of our lives gives us the freedom to achieve our highest goals and aspirations. And what could be a greater source of joy? "Jesus was the most disciplined man who ever lived, yet the most joyful and passionately alive. He is our example of discipline," writes Whitney.

Remedies
DEVELOPING MENTAL DISCIPLINE

SOME PEOPLE THINK OF their brains as a place where thoughts over which they have no control suddenly come and go. They're not. Our thinking is actually the sum of all the information we take in. What we watch, read, hear, and see. Everything from television theme songs and online advertisements to the conversations around the coffee machines at work. Whether we realize it or not, it's all potential subject matter for what's called our thought life—that seemingly secret realm where we ponder, mull, consider, entertain, and fantasize, says Dr. Ganz.

But what we think about doesn't just stay inside our minds. It inspires our actions. We literally become what we think about and value. Proverbs 23:7 puts it this way: "For as he thinks within himself, so he is" (NASB).

To change our behavior, then, we first need to change our thinking. Easier said than done? Maybe not. The Bible says repeatedly that those who follow Jesus are empowered to gain control of their thought lives. This doesn't mean that tempting, slothful, or gluttonous thoughts will simply stop one day. It means that if we control what goes into our minds and replace our bad thoughts with those described in Philippians 4:8 (NIV) as true, noble, right, pure, lovely, admirable, excellent, or praiseworthy, we'll be better able to keep ourselves under control.

Here are some simple suggestions for keeping our thought lives in check.

Create a think list—and use it. Since our thought lives are key to winning the battle for self-control and discipline, every thought that is greedy, gluttonous, or otherwise unrestrained needs to be shut off when it comes to mind and replaced with something truly worthy of our consideration. One of the best ways to discipline our minds is by developing a think list of good thoughts that we can refer to when something inappropriate creeps up on us, Dr. Ganz says.

We might fill our think lists with Scripture verses, for example, but Dr. Ganz says that he also likes to focus his thoughts on family or friends who need a hand, and then devote mental energy to figuring out how to help them.

Turn off the TV, the phone, social media, and the Internet—at least once in a while. In January 2017, the analytics firm Flurry found that Americans spend approximately 5.5 hours per day on mobile electronic devices (www.techcrunch.com), and the average American will spend five years and four months of his or her life on social media, according to a study by Mediakix (www.adweek.com). A 2016 study from Nielson.com indicates that despite the popularity of online interactions and social media, Americans still watch about five hours of television per day. "But if we say no to TV, then we can say yes to undistracted conversation, yes to reading, yes to exercise, yes to cleaning the house, yes to washing the car—all sorts of things," says Dr. Hughes.

Choose good reading materials. Let's face it, it's hard to maintain, let alone develop, discipline and self-control when

I Make Myself Run

BY KAREN S. PHELPS

Maybe it was a childlike idea, but for many years I figured that if you loved God, if you thought of yourself as a Christian, then of course you would read your Bible, you'd pray, you'd do loving things. I thought that God would simply see to it that you had these overwhelming instincts.

Actually, I was bothered by this concept as I was growing up because, even though I was raised in a Christian home and had accepted Christ, I knew that there were always times when I didn't want to pray or read my Bible. And I often found it difficult to be loving to people I loved, much less those people who irritated me.

I now believe that God is not going to insist that we love Him or pray a certain way or do certain things to help others. It's up to every one of us to decide these matters for ourselves. And the best way to get into harmony with Him, I believe, is through Christian discipline. Oddly enough, this realization came to me one day while I was out on a training run.

I'm a distance runner, and I like to compete in races. On this particular day, I didn't feel like running at all, but I made myself because running is a sport you have to practice every day. I wanted to win races, so I had a set plan for training:

- Run daily, even if you don't feel like it.
- Run daily, even if you sometimes have to skip fun and pleasure.
- Run daily, even in bad weather—even if people think you're weird.
- Run daily, even when it gives you aches and pains and you feel like quitting.
- Run daily, even if you don't feel it's doing you any good.

At first, I didn't enjoy daily training —but I did want to run well enough to win. "How fast will you have to run to win a race?" I'd ask myself. And my desire to be fast would push me on. It took a while. I didn't increase my speed in weeks or even months. But I did begin to have a sense of accomplishment after each run. Eventually, I found that running was also an outlet, a way to release nervous energy or frustration. Later, much later, running became a joy—a time of expression, freedom, and power. Through discipline, it became part of me.

One day as I jogged along on my training run, it came to me that daily practice—training—was what my spiritual life needed. I had to have a set plan to follow every day—for praying, reading my Bible, and doing at least one kind thing for someone else.

Since then, I've discovered that daily faith practice, like running, isn't always comfortable or convenient. It's sometimes painful—and occasionally people think I'm weird. As for time, learning about God and living His will isn't a matter of weeks or months. It's an every-day-of-my-life commitment.

But from this daily discipline, I find that my spiritual life is becoming an outlet, a way to unwind, a means of solving problems, and a source of comfort when I'm down. It doesn't help me only when I'm troubled—it gives me confidence that I'm making myself useful. I have a sense of peace and contentment that's new to me.

Do you know what I've learned? Sometimes you may not feel like praying or reading the Bible or going out of your way to help others. But if you're in training—physical or spiritual—you'll do it.

we're watching or reading things that don't support those virtues, says Dr. Hughes.

"Psalm 1 speaks to this idea," says Dr. Hughes. "It says, 'Blessed is the one who does not walk in step with the wicked...but whose delight is in the law of the Lord, and who meditates on his law day and night. That person is like a tree planted by streams of water, which yields its fruit in season and whose leaf does not wither— whatever they do prospers'" (Psalm 1:1–3 NIV).

TAKING ACTION

Once we have our thinking right, we can change our actions, which includes building into our lives habits that strengthen discipline and self-control, such as these:

Find a coach. Aaron had Moses. The disciples had Jesus. Timothy had Paul. And if we need to develop discipline, or any other positive attribute, one of the best ways is by finding a mentor, says Dr. Hughes. "Seek someone you perceive to be a disciplined person and watch them in action. Ask for advice on how they control their desires. Have them hold you accountable for what you say you're going to do. That's going to help a lot."

Start small and stay at it. Trying to change our entire lives in one day is impossible, but we can start on the path toward self-control by taking small steps, such as returning phone calls when we say we will, arriving on time for appointments, or developing the habit of cleaning up around the house and office. Starting with small tasks like these, says Dr. Hughes, makes it easier to succeed, and each success helps us build the resolve and discipline to stick with our goals. That will help when we take on larger challenges.

Avoid petty sins. Stealing pens and paper clips from the office seems like a minor offense compared with cheating on an expense report or embezzling from the company. But giving up petty sins can strengthen our self-control and discipline exponentially, says Dr. Ganz. That's because restraining ourselves in these small ways teaches us the skills we need in other situations, like cutting down on credit card use.

Make a covenant. To maintain financial discipline, we follow budgets. To enforce agreements, we sign contracts. So why not write a covenant to God to ensure that we stay disciplined in challenging areas of our lives? For example, we might write a covenant that we will stop listening to hurtful gossip about the people we know—or contributing to it. Renewed every year and checked regularly, covenants can help us during those moments of frustration when we're tempted to forget everything we believe, says Dr. Ganz.

"I think that when we write things out and read them to ourselves and solemnly commit to keep them, by God's grace we can reflect upon them, and it helps us remember what God really wants us to be," says Dr. Ganz.

May All I Do Be for You

Loving Creator, in Your goodness
You have allowed others
to recognize my work and success.
I sincerely thank You for that.
May I never forget
that all my abilities come from You.
Be with me in the days ahead
so that my decision-making
will be rooted in Your wisdom.
May all I do be praise for Your glory.

—VICKI ZURLAGE

FORGIVENESS

Nothing sets people free in their hearts and minds like practicing forgiveness. Here are ten ways to experience the freedom forgiveness brings:

1. Letting go of deep or long-held resentment is not easy. You may be inclined to abandon the effort because it will seem so hard, but in time you will feel the resentment leave you.

2. Christ recognized the difficulty in learning to forgive, for He said to "forgive seventy times seven" if necessary. To be literal, that means 490 times. Before you have forgiven a person 490 times, you will most likely be free of your resentment.

3. Remember the harm resentment can do, not to the other person, but to you, even to the point of making you ill.

4. Forgive. The fact that unforgiveness hinders spiritual blessings is a basic spiritual law. Goodwill cannot flow *toward* you unless it flows *from* you.

5. Thinking about forgiving is not enough. There must come a moment when you say, "With God's help I now forgive." (Do that now, and be positive.)

6. Repeat the Lord's Prayer, inserting your offender's name. "Forgive me my trespasses as I forgive (name)."

7. Practice praying for the other person, asking specific blessing for him, especially concerning matters that annoy you the most. This will have an amazing curative effect on you and perhaps on the other person. Stop reading and do that now.

8. Speak kindly as often as possible about a person against whom you harbor antagonism.

9. Write a brief letter of goodwill to the individual concerned. Do not be offended if it is not answered. You have cleansed your own heart, and that is what matters.

10. Study the factors that created this situation to correct the "mistake pattern" in yourself. This will reduce the possibility of similar conflicts in the future.

11. Ask Christ now to effect a permanent spiritual change in your nature, a rebirth with all resentment tendencies removed. Sincerely want this, pray for it, believe it is given you, and you will have it. With nothing in your heart against anyone, you will be amazed at the new power and happiness that will be yours. —NORMAN VINCENT PEALE

A Gift That Frees Our Souls

WE HAVE A CHOICE.

- Forever bristle and brood under a burden of rage and hurt that we feel as the result of something someone has done
- Forgive the person who hurt or offended us

Forgiveness is healing, though it may not be easy or quick.

Failing to forgive clearly damages us emotionally and hampers our own growth, progress, and happiness. And, some say, it can make us sick or keep us from getting well. Yet frequently, it seems to be the path that we choose, says Dr. Dale Ryan.

Why?

Often, says Dr. Ryan, we become addicted to our rage. We are so indignant that a certain person violated us that we adopt indignation and the violation as part of our personality, part of our being.

Dr. Ryan says that if we stop at this stage, we don't heal. We don't grow. In fact, we stifle and limit ourselves.

Another reason we often fail to forgive is that we have misconceptions about forgiveness, says Dr. Ryan. Forgiveness is not:

- Sanctioning or condoning abusive behavior
- Conditional ("I'll forgive you if you change")
- Reconciliation (though reconciliation can be a step in forgiveness)
- Denial
- Forgetting
- Saying, "Everything is okay now" or "I'm completely okay now"

Denying, forgetting, or glossing over hurts are ways of burying them. When we bury our hurts or when we nurse them, we hurt ourselves emotionally and perhaps even physically, said Dr. Vernon M. Sylvest. Forgetting is part of forgiveness, but it is not all there is, he adds.

So just what is forgiveness?

Forgiveness is the process of acquitting other people of whatever they've done to us, said Dr. Sylvest. He witnessed cancers go into remission once people processed long-held resentments and forgave.

The process of forgiveness usually means changing a relationship, establishing new expectations and boundaries. It does not mean returning to business as usual, says Dr. Ryan. Forgiveness is discovering what hurt us—exactly how and why we were hurt—healing those hurts as best as is possible, and growing from them and beyond them.

Forgiveness is something that we do for *us*, says Dr. Ryan, to heal *our* lives, not to help the person we feel has wronged us. And it is something that we do because we want to and need to, not because we are told that we must.

Remedies
PRAY FOR OUR "ENEMIES"

How do we forgive people who have inflicted injury upon us?

First, we should speak up and condemn the behavior, says Juanita Ryan, R.N, a licensed mental health clinical nurse specialist with more than thirty years of counseling experience. Then we can and should pray for them, she says.

Be ye kind one to another, tenderhearted, forgiving one another, even as God for Christ's sake hath forgiven you. —Ephesians 4:32 (KJV)

"I don't think I'm very good at forgiving," I told my friend Jim as we were having lunch at our favorite pizzeria. Not that I had anything specific in mind; just a vague feeling that I held on to grudges and kept track too closely of wrongs done to me.

"I can think of one place where you're good at forgiving."

"Where?"

"In your marriage."

"There's nothing much to forgive."

"There you have it." He took a large bite out of his slice of pizza and I chased an olive around my plate, finally stabbing it with my fork.

"Okay," I said. "I can remember a couple weeks ago being really irritated at Carol for not taking out the trash, but then as I was bagging it up, I remembered that she had been annoyed with me for not telling her that I was going to be late one night because of a meeting."

"Did she get angry at you?"

"Not for long."

"Did you get angry at her?"

"Not really... It all sort of evens out."

"That's because you forgive her."

I considered this insight for a moment and cut another slice of pizza. When I got home I'd have to inform Carol of this good news.

Give me a forgiving heart, Lord, as You have forgiven me. —Rick Hamlin

We need to remember that they, too, are fallible humans, just like us; that they, too, are children of God. They may be running from God and from goodness, but we can pray that God will open their hearts so they can remember who they are at the core.

We can pray that they, too, can release the anger, rage, shame, and fear that steer and cripple them, Juanita Ryan says. Maybe they can come to see themselves as God sees them: as loved and loving children.

And, adds Dr. Ryan, maybe they won't. Their response should not be a condition of our forgiveness.

But if we can hope and ask for blessings for someone who has hurt us, we will know that we have forgiven them, or are in the process of forgiving, said Dr. Sylvest. The feeling of forgiveness may not come instantly, but if we persist in our praying, thinking, and acting, it will happen.

How we will respond to the other person who has hurt us is all we have control over, says Dr. Ryan. We can't control how that person will respond to us. "We can forgive an abusive person, and they still may be an abusive person," he says. "We can't recover for other people or from their problems; we can only recover from our own."

FOUR STEPS TO FORGIVING

How do we process the hurt and anger so that we can forgive? Dr. Ryan recommends four steps.

1. Recognize the hurt. This may require therapy if we've long buried a major trauma such as childhood sexual abuse, he says.

2. Own the hurt. We need to accept that we hurt, accept that this is our hurt. We should feel the anger, the shame, and the pain and watch where those feelings take us.

3. Explore the ways our denial has compounded the original offense and subsequent hurts. This one big hurt may have caused dozens of other hurts that cause us to respond negatively in other situations.

4. Work, one at a time, on each hurt and behavior or attitude that handicaps us. "We need to recognize that some of this is not 'our stuff,'" says Dr. Ryan. Instead, it is stuff that we can give back (in our minds and hearts) to the person from whom we got it. We can let go of it. Then we can set about making changes that will be healing in our lives and attitudes.

"Set reasonable expectations about how to move on from here," advises Dr. Ryan. Forgiving does not mean we have to reconcile with the people who hurt us, but we do need to discover how we will prevent that person's past (and perhaps even current) behavior from negatively affecting us and our behavior.

The process is sort of like cancer surgery. "The issue," says Dr. Ryan, "is not speed, but thoroughness. The question is, 'Did we get it all?'"

If we find it difficult to identify and resolve our hurts, we should seek help. If we've suffered severe trauma, we may wish to seek private counseling. Or we can turn to twelve-step groups, which exist for nearly every hurt imaginable and can help us sort through and move beyond our hurt, says Dr. Ryan. (To find an appropriate group, check the Internet or with a doctor, minister, or counseling center.) Even if we only visit a group one or two times, we will benefit from being able to talk about our hurt with people who are constructively working through the same types of issues, he says.

FINDING RELEASE

What if we're the ones who need to be forgiven? The process is much the same, says Dr. Ryan. We need to accept that we have hurt someone and explore the ways our hurtful behavior impacted them. We also need to explore the hurt and shame this causes us. Then we need to do what we can to make restitution or contrition to the person we hurt. It's also important for us to demonstrate in our current lives that we have changed. And then we need to forgive ourselves and move on in a constructive way.

We should not necessarily ask the people we hurt to forgive us, says Dr. Ryan. It's always appropriate to apologize, make amends, and stay in the relationship to help the recovery process. But by simply asking another for forgiveness, we run the risk of being perceived as demanding. We need to make a genuine effort to change our hearts and understand what we've done and then let others forgive us—if they choose to—in their own way and in their own time. That is their choice. Ours is to change and to keep our shame and guilt from forever crippling us.

Generous Hearts

Forgive our excesses, Lord,
and give us generous hearts
with which to share
our many blessings.

—FAY ANGUS

HAPPINESS

Joy Grows from the Inside Out

"WE HOLD THESE TRUTHS to be self-evident, that all men are created equal, that they are endowed by their Creator with certain unalienable rights, that among these are life, liberty, and the pursuit of happiness."

Ever since these immortal words were first published in the Declaration of Independence, the pursuit of happiness has been something of an all-American national obsession. Funny thing is, our pursuits always seem to take us in radically different directions. Some of us look for it through shopping, some look in the woods or mountains, some look on the job, and some look in the grocery store. Some of us look in church.

How many of us actually succeed in the happiness quest depends on who you talk to. Some people are very happy; others wrestle with feelings of sadness or melancholy more often than they are happy or glad. One thing is true: happiness does elude virtually all of us at one time or another. But that's no reason not to aspire to be happy and to continually seek the happiness we long for.

Remedies
CONNECTING WITH GOD

GOD WANTS US TO BE HAPPY, and the people who know God are happy because of it.

Based on their experience, countless Christians agree that happiness stems from a genuine relationship with God. Like any relationship, our connection to God can grow and flourish or it can weaken and die, depending on how actively we cultivate it. Here are some suggestions for ways to keep that holy connection alive and well.

Follow the plan. Being happy is largely a question of eliminating the things that make us unhappy, according to Dr. Meier. That means, above all, avoiding sin. "Sin creates unhappiness in ourselves and in others," he says.

The best way to avoid sin is to follow the fundamentals: Love God, love ourselves, love our neighbors. Pray, worship, serve. That's the standard recipe for contentment, and still the best.

Read Scripture. Another basic ingredient in building our connection to God is reading the Bible. If we're struggling, the Reverend Alison Boden suggests that we meditate on Psalm 63. "O God," it reads, "you are my God, I seek you, my soul thirsts for you...Because your steadfast love is better than life" (Psalm 63:1, 3 NRSV). Leaning on that steadfastness can help us get past our struggles until we're happy again, she says.

Study the Beatitudes. Think of each beatitude (Matthew 5:3–11) as a verb, not a noun, and consider how we can enact blessedness in our own lives, suggests the Reverend Harry Adams of Yale Divinity School. What can we do, for instance, as peacemakers in our own families or among feuding friends? How about organizing a demonstration against illegal sweatshops as a way of demonstrating our hunger for righteousness? Or tearing up a friend's IOU to show our mercifulness?

Love the loveless. Think of the curmudgeon in church or the grouchy neighbor down the block. Drop them a note asking how they're doing. Give them a phone call. Share a joke or a story with them. Be patient, and see if their demeanor begins to soften just a little. If you stick with it, you may find the joy of making an unhappy person happy.

Happiness Is a Decision

BY JOY N. HULME

If it's possible to see red about not seeing red, that is what I was doing. We had misjudged the timing of our autumn trip to see the changing leaves in the Great Lakes states, and I was really upset. No matter how I strained my eyes, I couldn't spot red anywhere. Not even a hint of golden yellow broke through the monotonous greenery.

I recalled an earlier leaf-viewing trip to Vermont in October, and the splendor of the maples, birches, oaks, and sumac that lined the roadway. By contrast this vacation was a complete waste. I sat alone in the backseat of our rented car and fumed as we drove north through the dull, dark green. In the front seat my husband and father chatted merrily, apparently unconcerned.

By the second day I could feel the tension send warning stabs between my shoulder blades. *This is ridiculous,* I thought. I couldn't change what was beyond my control. How could I get out of my funk?

Then an adage came to mind: "Happiness is a decision." It must have been something my mother said. She was always passing on words of advice. When I was a child she gave me a little black book with empty pages. On the flyleaf she had written "Look for a beautiful thing and you will find it." I was supposed to keep a record of the most beautiful thing I saw each day.

I remember spending hours debating what I'd write down. A baby's dimpled smile? A stone glimmering with fool's gold? Pictures in the clouds, or tulips tipping their heads? I found so many things it was impossible to pick just one.

Now, on the road, I played Mother's game again. Grudgingly I took in the all-green landscape. Thick forests lined both sides of the highway. The long conical pines and spruce made dramatic accents among the lighter shades of deciduous trees. Maple leaves danced in the breeze. We passed a small, still pond on which pale birch-tree trunks made zebra stripes. I felt like a girl again—surrounded by beautiful things.

Later in the trip, after we crossed the Upper Peninsula and drove into Canada, I found the bright fall foliage I had been looking for. But by then I'd already seen a million shades of green, the infinite variety and beauty that only our heavenly Father can produce. And that we can always find—if we look closely enough.

Nurture joy. God has instilled in all of us certain ways that we can easily find refuge and access our innate capacity for joy. We should find what those places or practices are and use them. Whether it's in gardening, sailing, painting, having coffee with a friend, or some other hobby or activity, make time for the joy those things bring to you.

A HAPPINESS TOOL KIT

Abraham Lincoln once said that most people are about as happy as they make up their minds to be, says Dr. Meier, and modern psychology basically agrees with him. To a point.

Attitude counts for a lot in our happiness, but it's not everything, says Dr. Meier. We now know that genetics plays a role, for example, and that physical and mental illnesses can keep us from being happy no matter how hard we work at it. That doesn't mean that we can't make up our minds to be happy; it just means that there may be a few extra steps involved in getting there.

Attitude needs to be coupled with knowledge, Dr. Meier says. If we're going to successfully complete the happiness hunt, we need to know where to look, and we need some tools. Here are a few key suggestions for the journey.

Get a checkup. If we're experiencing chronic depression for no observable reason, Dr. Meier says, it's important to see a doctor or psychiatrist who is trained to detect any physical problems that might be responsible.

Keep fit. Reams of scientific research have affirmed what most of us know intuitively: mind, body, and spirit are interconnected. Studies also indicate that if we keep ourselves together physically by eating right, exercising regularly, and getting plenty of sleep, we'll also feel better spiritually and emotionally.

Stifle stress. One of the major blocks to happiness in today's world is stress, according to Dr. Meier. Jesus says, "For my yoke is easy, and my burden is light," he points out (Matthew 11:30 KJV).

If we're burned-out, we need to change, Dr. Meier says. We must make room in our busy schedules for rest and relaxation, time with the family, prayer, and meditation. If we're going to hear the voice of God—the voice of joy—we have to find the time to stop and listen.

Look for the good. Our attitudes are far more within our control than we often acknowledge. We can choose to wallow in negative thoughts, or we can make a conscious decision to focus on what is positive and good about ourselves, about others, and about various aspects of our lives.

Feel the feelings. Although teaching ourselves not to dwell on the negatives is vital, we should be careful that we don't keep ourselves from feeling legitimate pain, says Dr. Meier. Experiencing our emotions honestly is not self-indulgent. To the contrary, covering up grief, anger, or depression can create other, more long-lasting emotional problems, he says. The healthier

way to happiness is to allow ourselves to experience painful emotions honestly, then return to our focus on the positive. One way to turn pain from negative to positive is to ask ourselves what lessons we have learned from our painful experiences and how we can use them to help ourselves and others.

Share what hurts. Where do we take our grief, anger, and other negative feelings when we need to get them out? That's what friends are for. Dr. Meier recommends that we find a prayer partner or prayer group, people with whom we can be totally honest. "We all need to have one or more humans that we can let inside our skin," he says, citing James 5:16: "...confess your sins to one another...so that you may be healed" (NRSV).

If we feel that our problems warrant professional help, we need to seek out a qualified counselor.

Forgive. Dr. Meier calls learning to forgive "the single most important thing we do" in learning to be happy. Nurtured resentments against others and against God can create bitterness, which is the antithesis of happiness. Peace of mind and spirit requires that we let things go, that we learn to forgive and forget. To learn more, see the previous section of this book, entitled "Forgiveness."

Avoid judgment. People almost always have reasons for what they do, reasons even they may not understand and that we don't understand and may be tempted to judge or criticize. Ideally, we should let resentments go by loving people despite their behaviors. That's what Jesus would have us do.

Things That Make Me Happy

I went for a long walk today;
the beauty all around
once again astounded me.
The brightness of the sun
upon the poppies took my breath away.
All was peaceful, the only sound
was that of the chickadee.
The cool breeze scattered the shapely clouds,
and the blue of the sky was brilliant.
Dear Lord, for these things I thank Thee.
No longer did I feel engulfed in a dark shroud,
for Thou hast made me resilient
to withstand daily strife.
I breathed deep the scent of the pine,
standing with majesty,
and I thanked Thee for the gift of life,
and all the many things that make me happy.
—SANDRA ALARCON

Healing

As I drove from Riverside Osteopathic Hospital that beautiful summer morning, I was thinking how fortunate I was. A dedicated and skilled cardiologist, I took satisfaction in knowing I was helping people live longer, healthier lives. One of my proudest achievements had been the founding of an exercise and support group for cardiac patients in our community.

That morning, July 6, 1981, I had read my devotions. A few verses from the Bible helped me start my day connected with God. Now I was heading across town to Detroit Osteopathic Hospital, where I was also on staff.

A stoplight turned to yellow. I put my foot on the brake pedal and glanced at the rearview mirror. The pickup behind me was slowing to a stop. But behind him was a fully loaded gravel truck that I had passed earlier. *That truck's going too fast,* I thought. The screech of skidding tires filled my ears. I watched in horror as the truck plowed into the pickup and the pickup rolled over my car. For an instant, all I could smell was gas. Then my car burst into flames.

A Life Flight helicopter flew me to the University of Michigan's burn center. *I am lucky to be alive,* I kept telling myself. But over 80 percent of my body had been burned. What followed were torturous treatments and devastating setbacks. *A few more weeks of this,* I hoped, *and then I can get back to my patients.* This thought was the only thing that kept me going. But after a month passed, I learned that I had made little progress. I had survived, but what did I have left to live for?

Toward the end of summer my thirty-seventh birthday arrived. The nurses helped me to a chair near an open window. Two hundred people had gathered below to sing "Happy Birthday," accompanied by my hometown's high school band. The crowd waved birthday cards and shouted, "We miss you! Get well soon!" *People want to help me*, I thought. *But can anybody help me be a doctor again?*

After three months in the hospital, I went home. Family members took turns caring for me. I didn't go anywhere except for physical therapy three times a week. I was afraid of people seeing me. My therapist assured me I was healing, but my spirit was still broken. *God*, I prayed, *make me well. Give me back my confidence.*

Then early one morning when the leaves had fallen and the weather had turned bitterly cold, a man appeared at my door. "It's me, Casey Commander," he said. I remembered him well. A year earlier, he couldn't even walk to his mailbox without severe chest pain. I had told him he needed to get exercise every day, no ifs, ands, or buts.

"I took your advice, and I'm up to four miles a day," he said. "I want you to join me."

"I can't," I said.

"You will, though," he said. "I'll be back tomorrow, and we'll start."

Casey returned and bundled me in jacket, mittens, and hat as though I were a child. We walked a quarter of a block. The next day, he came back, and the day after that. Soon we were walking four to five miles a day. I loved our time together, our talks, our silence as we swung our arms in rhythm, our feet bounding over sidewalks, sidestepping patches of ice and snow. As I breathed the sharp, cold Michigan air, I could feel health returning to body and soul. "You're comin' along, Doc," Casey said.

This is how healing happens, I realized. Through doctors who take a little extra time, through friends who lend you their support, through former patients who give you a dose of your own tough medicine. In time, I did return to my practice. Slowly I built up my skills again, and my confidence.

> The key to my healing came from what I had read in my devotions the morning of my accident: "Though our outward man perish, yet the inward man is renewed day by day" (2 Corinthians 4:16 KJV). Day by day. That's how I got better.
> —JOSEPH C. ROGERS

The Remedy Begins in the Mind

WHEN WE'RE FEELING SICK or dealing with a chronic illness, how we think can greatly affect our attitudes and energy levels.

Thinking a beautiful thought and holding on to it may not force remission of every disease or affliction. But certain attitudes and simple behaviors do seem to promote a healthy outlook. And a healthy outlook is helpful and spiritually rewarding, particularly when we must face an unhealthy diagnosis or prognosis.

And there is no reason we should feel guilty or inferior or blame ourselves for being "infirm," as the Bible puts it, if we are unable to heal ourselves.

Statistically, studies suggest that those of us who constructively tend to the spiritual components of our nature tend to live longer, lead healthier lives, and cope better with disease and other setbacks, says Dr. Dale Matthews.

When faced with disease or disability, we have a choice that we can make, notes Dr. Paul Meier. We can choose to become discouraged and invite defeat and depression. Or, as God tells us in the Bible, we can choose life. "...I have set before you life and death, blessings and curses. Choose life..." (Deuteronomy 30:19 NRSV).

Remedies
BRINGING HEALING INTO FOCUS

CHOOSING LIFE IS A matter of choosing a healing state of mind, say counselors. How do we do that?

Focus on God. The worship of God keeps us from falling into the pit of self-pity that is always beckoning when sickness

Friend in Need

By Mary Frank

I was on my way to the hospital to see my grandson Isaac, who suffered second- and third-degree burns when a bonfire on our family farm exploded. He had endured so much and the healing process was only beginning. *Lord, help this child heal,* I prayed as I turned into the hospital parking lot.

Walking down the corridor, I prepared myself for a terrified little boy. As I stepped into his room, though, I did a double take. There was Isaac—his head and hand wrapped in gauze—sitting up and grinning. "Grandma, Willie called!"

Willie is Isaac's friend. Once he heard about the accident, Willie called every day just to talk to his buddy. They giggled like they were on the playground. To heal, Isaac needed the hospital's care, but he also needed to be a little boy.

has its grip on us. If we will focus on God's character and nature, and remember His faithfulness to us through the years, we cannot help thanking Him, praising Him, and worshiping Him.

Focus on purpose. Everyone created has been created for a purpose. As long as we are living, we can do something to fulfill that purpose. Even in times of sickness, if we can do nothing else, we can sow seeds of prayer into the purpose for which God made us.

Focus on sharing peace and joy. The healing mind will think of ways to share happiness, peace, and joy with other people. Especially if we know someone who may be healing physically from illness or surgery or healing emotionally from loss or heartache, doing what we can to encourage and support that person helps us heal as well.

Focus on positive action. Part of healing involves rest and part involves knowing when to get up and become active again. As we are healing, we need to look for positive actions we can take in our homes, families, or communities.

Focus on forgiving. Health-care providers can testify to the healing power of forgiveness. Unforgiveness acts like a poison and can lead to health problems, but forgiveness allows us to release negativity and make room for positive thoughts and attitudes, which can aid in healing. For more on the subject, see the section entitled "Forgiveness."

Focus on acceptance. Perfectionists—those of us who cannot accept our errors, misjudgments, and shortfalls and the somewhat messy nature of our lives—are far too stressed-out, said Dr. Vernon M. Sylvest. And stress clearly has been shown to affect our internal chemistries and interfere with wellness and healing.

People who tend to be the healthiest, in Dr. Sylvest's observation, are those who accept that sometimes we win, sometimes we lose, and that, as long as we live, we always have tomorrow to tackle (or forget) those things that we haven't gotten quite right yet.

Focus on others. Numerous medical and sociological studies show that regular, positive social interaction—the greater number of different types of contacts, the better—tends to enhance our overall well-being and limit depressive episodes in our lives, says Dr. Dean Ornish.

Those of us who have the most diverse types of social contacts and networks are least susceptible to developing colds when exposed to cold viruses, according to Sheldon Cohen, Ph.D., professor of psychology at Carnegie Mellon University. What is important is the range of social contacts, not just the quantity. The wider the range, the healthier, he says. It may simply be that those of us with a wide range of contacts are more distracted from our problems. "Someone whose only social role is as 'worker' will find problems at home more distressing than someone who works, has a family, and belongs to social groups," he says.

Contact with others may contribute to our sense of meaning and sense of purpose, which are fundamental to our spiritual makeup, says Dr. Ornish.

Dr. Cohen agrees. He says that people who have diverse social outlets generally feel better about themselves, have more positive approaches, feel more in control of their lives, and have a higher sense of self-esteem, and that those factors somehow translate into better health.

Focus on fellowship. Studies have shown that people who attend church regularly tend to get sick less often, heal quicker, and live longer, on average, than people who fail to fill the pews most Sabbaths, says Dr. Matthews.

Waiting for Healing

Perhaps the hardest thing for me to do is wait.

Within these walls there's much of that.

I wait for doctors' calls,

for visitors,

for breakfast and my other meals,

for tests to be performed,

results reported.

I wait for news of what the future holds

(yet sometimes fear to hear the news)

and then I wait to see if what's predicted

will take place.

Others wait with me.

Family and friends endure uncertainties,

yet try to hide from me

that they are troubled, too.

Only You, Lord, know for sure

what things must be;

which may be changed.

Help me wait upon You, Lord.

Give me patience,

for Your timing,

for Your continued miracles in my life.

Help me walk in faith with You this day,

and throughout all my life.

—EILEEN M. BERGER

HONESTY

In 1951, when I had been with CBS for only a year, I was given my first big TV assignment—covering the return of General Douglas MacArthur from Korea. We were on the air with cameras grinding when we learned that the general's plane would be delayed in coming down. I realized right then that I hadn't done enough spadework. In the pit of my stomach was the awful fear that I would run out of words and that this broadcast would be embarrassing, perhaps even disastrous, and the end of my career.

Could I ask God to help me here, when I had not done my homework? I could pray that I never make this mistake again, but that was different from asking Him to bail me out now.

MacArthur's plane was delayed fifteen minutes, which seemed like as many years. During that time I recited all of his biography I could remember and ad-libbed wildly to fill the gap. It was not my best broadcast. But to my way of thinking, it would have been a worse loss if I had let panic make me try to cut some corners with God.

At other times, prayer is the honest thing—the only honest thing to do. For instance, when my daughter Nancy came down with a mysterious high fever and lapsed into a semicoma, I prayed hard. Or earlier, when Nancy was an infant and my wife, Betsy, was flying in from Kansas City with her, I went to a rainy, fog-shrouded airport to meet them. I squeezed through the crowd to the airline counter and inquired if the plane from Kansas City was on time. The man looked at me, very concerned.

"Sir," he said, "I'm afraid we've lost contact with that plane!"

A woman screamed. Another fainted. And I prayed as I never had before. Then I rushed to find a phone, to see if I could find out anything about the missing plane—and bumped into Betsy herself. Contact with the plane had been lost simply because it had landed early.

I am not suggesting that my prayers here brought about the story's happy ending, but I do suggest that this was an honest time to ask for God's help.

This is an era when we need honesty in every phase of living as never before, because never before in history have we been so irrevocably members one of another. And while our efforts to be honest can be perplexing—even cost us friendships and material gain—I believe there is a greater compensation: the awareness of being true to something and Someone bigger than we are.
—WALTER CRONKITE

Fabricate It

HONESTY IS SOMETHING THAT we all say we want. But the truth is, it's in short supply. It's hard to find in day-to-day life, in our culture, and sometimes even in our churches. That's sad, and damaging, says Brad Blanton, Ph.D., clinical psychologist, founding president of the Gestalt Institute of Washington, D.C., former director of The Center for Well Being in Washington, D.C., author of *Radical Honesty,* and creator of Radical Honesty.

Without honesty, we live in a world of pretense, unreality, and deception. Neither we nor anyone else is ever truly encouraged to deal forthrightly with our real needs, hurts, and feelings or the actual purposes and consequences of our actions. Everything is a spin on the truth, and we're left spinning and anchorless, says Dr. Blanton.

Being honest in all aspects of our lives does go against the grain. It violates the "law" that says "image is everything." But image—pretense and hiding and glossing over our hurts, shortcomings, and differences—does not free us from these hurts, shortcomings, and differences. Freedom only comes from facing them, viewing them, and dealing with them directly under the bright spotlight of reality, says Dr. Blanton. Jesus says, "...the truth shall make you free" (John 8:32 KJV). With these words, Jesus offers the simplest success formula ever.

Life is oh-so-much easier, healthier, cleaner, more joyful, and more real when we tell the truth, says Dr. Blanton.

The method is almost magical. The Apostle Paul explains it like this: "...lovingly follow the truth at all times—speaking truly, dealing truly, living truly..." (Ephesians 4:16 TLB).

Just how does this make life simpler and easier? Mark Twain explains it well. "Always tell the truth," he writes in *Vice and Virtue*. "That way, you don't have to remember what you said."

SO SIMPLE, YET SO HARD

We aren't taught to tell the truth. "To be perfectly honest," as the phrase goes, we are taught to say that we're telling the truth, observes Dr. Dale Ryan. But the truth is not expected or encouraged in many interactions. From the advertisements we see to our personal appearances and actions, we expect to mislead and be misled; we expect that reality is colored; and we expect that nothing is really exactly the way it seems, says Dr. Ryan.

That is injurious to our health and well-being, says Dr. Blanton. Twenty-five years of practice as a psychotherapist has convinced him that "the primary cause of most anxiety, most depression, and most human stress is lying, and we lie all the time. We're taught systematically by the school systems, by parents, by the church, and everyone else to lie, to play like we are good little boys and girls regardless of how big a lie that is. We are taught to keep secret what is really going on in our lives and taught instead to play the right role."

Remedies
CONFESS AND TESTIFY

How CAN WE MOVE out of our role-playing and into reality?

Old-time religion had the right idea, and the twelve-step recovery programs, such as Alcoholics Anonymous, borrowed it, says Dr. Ryan. What they incorporated are what he calls the traditional Christian spiritual disciplines of confession and testimony.

Traditionally, notes Dr. Ryan, the church would rally around anyone who confessed shortcomings and who testified about their feelings, questions, and experiences with God as they wrestled with everyday problems. Now, he says, the church tends only to encourage "salvation" confessions and "good" testimonies—tales of total turnaround as a result of knowing Christ.

The church, Dr. Ryan says, doesn't encourage people to confess and testify week after week about their sadness, rage, disappointment, setbacks, and ongoing crises of faith. But those kinds of confessions and testimonies "actually help people get some traction in life so that they can grow and move past their problems," he says. And that's how people are helped in twelve-step groups where participants go around a circle and tell—without interruption or comment from others—what's going on in their lives at the moment.

We need to encourage our churches to recover that old-style testimony, says Dr. Ryan. "If the only 'words' that someone has are tears, then tears are a wonderful testimony." We need to allow people to be honest and express their true feelings.

When true confession is encouraged, we learn not only that telling the truth is safe but also that we are supported by the community for doing it, says Dr. Ryan. It allows us to say, "I'm just a fallible human. I belong here because we all recognize our fallibility and all recognize our essential equality. We're all working on the same stuff." Encouraging (and learning to give) "bad," or honest, confessions and testimonies is essential to developing an honest, healing community, he says.

For testimony to be helpful and healing, it must be encouraged and given at each stage of processing any difficult situation that we encounter in life, says Dr. Ryan. The truth—the tears, anger, rage, and confusion—all need to be worked through and processed. Each of us can help by practicing, encouraging, and welcoming honest confession and testimony.

How?

Just start. Tell the truth. We don't have to tell the truth about much, just "what we've done, what we think, and what we feel," says Dr. Blanton.

Make a pact with a friend. We should agree with this person that we will

Therefore confess your sins to each other and pray for each other so that you may be healed.... —JAMES 5:16 (NIV)

As I drove to my exercise class early yesterday morning, my thoughts kept circling around a problem my husband was facing in his retirement, so it felt like my problem, too. As I walked through the parking lot toward the gym, I ran into a friend I hadn't seen in weeks.

"What's going on in your life?" she asked. That was all it took to open the floodgates and let my problem flow out. It was so much more than she asked for, so much more than I needed to say.

By the time I got into class and started stretching, I began a whole new conversation in my head. *Why did I say all that? So unnecessary. So overly vulnerable.* My self-talk continued for most of the class.

When I got home, I called my friend. "I walked away from our conversation feeling bad that I dumped so much on you. I should have said less. I'm sorry."

"I was going to call you," she said. "I walked away from our conversation wishing I had said more. Trusting me with your honesty made me wish *I'd* been more honest and asked you to pray for my husband, who is facing a problem in his job."

She went on to tell me her story, and I felt grateful that she trusted me with her concerns.

Lord, thank You for the privilege of listening to my friend and for the gift of her loving heart. Bless us as we pray for each other's husband.
—CAROL KUYKENDALL

only tell the complete truth and that it's okay and even expected for us to admit what we haven't previously told the truth about. Once we get a little practice at this and notice how good it feels and how great the relationship becomes, we'll want to expand the practice to other relationships, says Dr. Blanton.

Seek support. We need help as we embrace honesty, even if it's from a community of one, such as a counselor. An easy way to get practice with truth-telling in a community setting is to join a twelve-step or other type of support group. Most metropolitan areas have groups for just about every possible struggle. For more information on support-group meetings, check your doctor's office, church, or the Internet.

These groups teach the skills of honesty, says Dr. Ryan. It's good to practice and develop these skills in a supportive environment because if we start practicing total honesty before really learning the skills, we may sound like we're just dumping on people. "It can come out very messy, undifferentiated, and unfiltered, and it can be hurtful. The message here is not to moderate your honesty but to develop the skills."

It takes practice in expressing ourselves honestly and spontaneously, to learn what things we need to sort through and consider in-depth and what things we should just blurt out, Dr. Ryan says. It takes practice to develop a tactful and loving approach. It takes practice to develop humility and realize that we're at least as fallible as the person with whom we are conversing.

Observe one day at a time. We shouldn't expect to replace overnight habits that took a lifetime to build, advises Dr. Ryan. We should consider each day a new opportunity to practice what we're learning.

Avoid secrets. We should put everyone on notice "that we aren't going to keep their secrets for them or indulge in gossip anymore and that, basically, when they tell us something, they can plan on reading it in the paper the next day," says Dr. Blanton. That injects an amazing level of truth and respect into relationships.

Quit aggrandizing others. We realize that we often lie or color the truth to paint what we think is a more impressive picture of ourselves. But do we realize that we do this with others, too? When we put others on pedestals, we create mythical superhumans, and we hurt them and ourselves in the process, says Dr. Blanton. He jokes that Mark Twain had it right when he said, "All I have to know about anyone is that they are a human being. It doesn't get any worse than that." When we see each other simply as humans and not superiors or inferiors, we're making the most room for truthful, loving communication.

The Truth Sets You Free

But whoever lives by the truth comes into the light, so that it may be seen plainly that what they have done has been done in the sight of God.

—JOHN 3:21 NIV

. . . do not swear, either by heaven or by earth or by any other oath, but let your "Yes" be yes and your "No" be no, so that you may not fall under condemnation.

—JAMES 5:12 NRSV

KINDNESS

The Glory of Giving

"The Sea of Galilee and the Dead Sea are made of the same water. It flows down, clear and cool, from the heights of Hermon and the roots of the cedars of Lebanon. The Sea of Galilee makes beauty of it, for the Sea of Galilee has an outlet. It gets to give. It gathers in its riches that it may pour them out again to fertilize the Jordan Plain. But the Dead Sea with the same water makes horror. For the Dead Sea has no outlet. It gets to keep."

—THE LATE REVEREND HARRY EMERSON FOSDICK, FOUNDING MINISTER OF NEW YORK CITY'S RIVERSIDE CHURCH, TALKING ABOUT SERVING OTHERS

Planting the Seed of Compassion

ONE DAY, JESUS ACCEPTED an invitation to have lunch at the home of a Pharisee. As they ate, a prostitute came into the house and approached Jesus, carrying a flask of expensive perfume. She knelt by Him and wept, her tears falling on His feet. Carefully, the woman wiped away the tears with her hair, then kissed His feet and washed them with the perfume.

The Pharisee watched and thought to himself, *This proves that Jesus is no prophet, for if God had really sent Him, He would know what kind of woman this one is!*

But Jesus, Who knew what was in the Pharisee's mind, said that, though the woman's sins were many, with her acts, "she loved me much." And He said to her, "Your sins are forgiven.... Your faith has saved you; go in peace" (Luke 7:47–50 TLB).

We may never be called upon to show the type of kindness this woman showed or receive as immediate a reward for our good deeds, but kindness is still central to our lives. It's what defines us as Christians, as people who care about the others in our world.

"Kindness isn't some benign little gesture; it's something that we're invited to love, to yearn for, to be drawn to, and to desire with ardor," says Melanie Morrison, Ph.D., M.Div., founder and executive director of Allies for Change, and author of *The Grace of Coming Home*. Should we practice kindness? Of course. But more than that, in faith, we are invited to love it. "Loving kindness is what knits us to one another, creates community out of the disparate parts that are our individual humanity."

Put another way, "Kindness is a matter of doing not what life requires us to do but what our souls invite us to do," says Dawna Markova, Ph.D., cofounder and CEO emeritus at Professional Thinking Partners, and coeditor of *Random Acts of Kindness* and author of *No Enemies Within*. "We give to another person not out of a sense of obligation but out of a sense of compassion and connection, of feeling a kinship with that person, such that we can't not do for them."

Remedies
NURTURING COMPASSION

So KINDNESS IS AN important thing, a good thing. We know that. But how do we develop our capacity for kindness, especially if it's not something that comes naturally to us? Here are a few suggestions.

Start small. Small gestures are a great place to begin, says Dr. Markova in *Random Acts of Kindness*. Even something as simple as planting a tree for everyone in the neighborhood to enjoy or letting another driver have an available parking spot are worthy acts.

Help young people. It's easy for children to feel left out or disrespected in an overly adult world, says Dr. Markova. "So sometimes I'll walk down the street in my town and stick comic books in kids' bike baskets or give out balloons to little ones. It doesn't really matter what you do for children; what's important is that you find a gesture that helps you keep them in your daily thoughts. I suspect that it lifts their days a little bit. I know it lifts mine."

Practice at home. In order to avoid taking a spouse for granted, we can spend a few minutes together each night, suggests Dr. Markova, and take turns telling each other at least one reason we are glad we're married.

Listen. Simply listening can be an expression of kindness, particularly if the people to whom we're listening are in distress. We may not always be able to help people solve problems, but we can assure them that they're not facing the problems alone.

Morrison recalls having read a story that clearly illustrates this suggestion. Once in the dead of night, noted Austrian psychologist Victor Frankl received a telephone call from a distraught stranger on the verge of killing herself. "Frankl, being a good clinician, kept the woman on the phone for as long as he could, tried to offer reassuring words, tried probing for the roots of her despair, and finally got her to

agree to see him the next day. He hung up the phone not knowing if she would indeed make it through the night," says Morrison.

To Frankl's delight, she did, and when he asked her what it was he said on the phone that kept her from killing herself, she answered that nothing he said really made much of a difference to her. It was the mere fact that at one o'clock in the morning, he would spend two hours on the phone with her, a complete stranger, that assured her that all was not lost.

LOVING THOSE WHO ARE DIFFICULT TO LOVE

There's another level of kindness: the type that we extend to people who aren't so easy to love. It might be a disagreeable neighbor who never seems to have a pleasant thing to say, a homeless person we see each day on our way to work, or someone at work who has done something cruel. They, too, deserve our kindness. In the Scriptures, there are many examples of people extending kindness to strangers and even enemies. Consider Pharaoh's daughter rescuing Moses, Nehemiah restoring the fortunes of exiled Jews, and Jesus healing the centurion's slave.

How can we follow the example of these biblical figures and extend kindness to

Kindhearted Travelers

By Beatrice Parquet

Mass was just starting with the usual song and prayer as I made my way down the main aisle of St. Ann's Catholic Church. Most weeks I attend the 9:30 a.m. service, but this Sunday I made it just in time for the last Mass at 11:30 a.m. Despite being late, I made my way toward the front. I always felt closer to God when I sat near the altar. This day, I really needed that. I slid in the aisle seat and knelt in prayer. My eyes fixed on the altar, I didn't utter a word. I bowed my head with a heavy heart and prayed. *God, be with me. Just let me make it through. Help me to endure this. . . .*

I had gone through a range of emotions all week after my radiologist informed me during my annual checkup that I might have breast cancer for the second time. He ordered a biopsy. "With your history, we cannot waste any time," he said. I still couldn't believe it. During my first bout with cancer, I had a partial mastectomy and was declared cancer free. After thirteen years of successful checkups, mammograms, and self-exams, this new diagnosis was the last thing I expected. I was sixty-three years old. I had just moved back to Delaware after living in Florida for twelve years. I wanted to be closer to my daughters, and I didn't want to miss watching my granddaughters grow into young ladies. And now this? It wasn't fair. I could barely follow the sermon I was so focused on my own problems. *Why me? Can I make it through another bad diagnosis? Has the cancer already spread?*

I felt a tap on my shoulder. I jumped, and turned around to see a well-dressed couple. I didn't know them at all. Had I dropped something on the floor?

"I don't usually do this," the man said, "but the Lord told me to tell you, you will be healed."

What? Had he really said what I thought he said? There was no way he could've known about my fears. I hadn't uttered my prayers aloud—

"I might have breast cancer," I blurted out. The couple exchanged glances and then, without a word, they each laid a hand atop mine. Their touch was warm and gentle. I felt a comfort. As if a burden was lifted from me. A burden of anger and fear. I wasn't going to worry any longer. I had to leave everything in God's hands. Thanks to this couple, I believed I could do that. I had been healed—healed of my anxiety. I turned back around to listen to the rest of the sermon.

After Mass, I found the couple standing in the vestibule and introduced myself.

"My name is Joe," the man said. "This is my wife, Carol."

"Is this your regular Mass?" I asked.

"Not at all," Joe replied. "We're from New Jersey. We traveled to this church yesterday for a funeral. Afterward, we decided to stay an extra day and come to Sunday Mass."

It was all making sense. There was a reason I had delayed and attended the last Mass. I was there just so I could meet this special couple.

Over the next few weeks I told everyone about my encounter. They all listened with skepticism, but I was certain the message was truly from God. I could feel it. Whatever the results of my test, my health was in God's hands. Thankfully I learned my biopsy was negative. But I had already gotten the good news from two traveling angels.

those whom it's difficult to love, or perhaps even difficult to like? Here are some ideas.

Write a simple note. If someone like the cranky neighbor or mean coworker is more or less unapproachable in person, we can sit down and write him or her a compassionate letter, Dr. Markova recommends, and make it anonymous if we wish. Just let the person know that we're simply thinking of him or her.

Adopt a stranger. Many charitable organizations make it possible for people to help people they have never met. Especially during the holiday seasons, people can

The Kindness Method

From Guideposts Magazine

A man was walking in the countryside with his grandson when they came across a small land turtle. The boy picked up his find, examined it, and tried to pry open the shell with a stick. The turtle promptly pulled in its head.

"That will never get you anywhere," the grandfather remarked. "Let me show you."

They returned to the house, and the man put the turtle on the warm hearth. A few minutes later the turtle stuck out its head and feet and started crawling toward the boy.

"Never try to force a fellow into anything," was the grandfather's observation. "Just warm him up with a little kindness and he'll respond."

adopt and give gifts to children of incarcerated parents, children of soldiers deployed oversees, or elderly men and women who have no family. Some of these organizations and some churches even allow for adopting someone year-round.

Keep it short-term. Don't feel that the kindness we extend to difficult people obligates us to a lifelong friendship, says Dr. Markova. Think of it as a gesture of compassion, not a statement of commitment.

Carry a reminder. If we're stepping into situations where kindness will not come easily, we can feel closer to God's love by carrying something tangible, perhaps a rosary, an amulet, or even a photograph of someone we love as a reminder that God is with us, says Helen Hunt, Ph.D., relationship therapist, leader in global women's movement, and collaborator with her husband, Harry, on *On the Nature of Consciousness*.

Helen Hunt offers an example: "Our daughter had had some rough encounters with a neighborhood bully. We discussed the situation as a family, talking about how, by considering the pain in this bully's life, she could rethink her feelings toward him.

The next day, she went to school with a small religious medal in her pocket, which she would reach for and rub between her fingers for reassurance that God was with her. When she got to school, she steered clear of that bully and did not allow herself to be the brunt of his anger. But more than that, by keeping her distance, she could contemplate the pain in his life and gradually turn her anger into compassion."

DOING WELL BY DOING GOOD

The fruits of kindness are a blessing not only on the people who receive them. We, too, can enjoy our good works. They help us feel connected to others, which helps us feel like part of the family of God, says Dr. Markova, who remembers one particularly meaningful example. "While working with a street gang in Pittsburgh, my group got the gang to agree to do something kind for a stranger," she recalls. "They chose a woman who lived on the street. Every night, the woman would sneak down to an abandoned basement and eat whatever scraps of food that she had collected on the street. One night, the kids sneaked down before she did and laid out a complete banquet, a real feast, candles and all. She was so touched that she wept, and they said that they never felt so connected to another human being in their lives. It was so good for everyone."

As psychiatrist and Rabbi Abraham Twerski, M.D., founder and medical director emeritus of Gateway Rehabilitation Center in Pittsburgh, Pennsylvania says, "When I eat bread, I have but a single pleasure...when I give of my bread to the hungry, my pleasure is doubled. Long after my appetite has been satiated, I can enjoy having provided relief to another person's distress."

· HEALING WORDS ·

A Time to Act

Share with others how important they are to you.

A Time to Pray

Spirit of Love, I ask to wake each day of this year with fresh eyes,
that I may see Your light shining through all my loved ones.

—Sabra Ciancanelli and Marilyn Morgan King

LOVE

True Love

Love delights in giving attention rather than in attracting it.

Love finds the element of good and builds on it.

Love does not magnify defects.

Love is a flame that warms but never burns.

Love knows how to disagree without becoming disagreeable.

Love rejoices at the success of others instead of being envious.

—THE LATE FATHER JAMES KELLER

More Than Emotion, It's an Action

THEY'RE EVERYWHERE—on the Internet, on TV, in advertisements, the movies, the romance novels—couples locked in all manners of passionate embrace.

But who would confuse what these couples on TV are doing with real love?

Romance and attraction are important parts of developing relationships and maintaining loving marriages. But "the tingles" are just that: part of a much larger package that makes marital love last, says Gary Chapman, Ph.D., author of *The Five Love Languages* and *Loving Solutions*.

In fact, whether we're trying to develop or maintain a loving relationship with our spouse, our children, or even a friend, the real key is learning that love is an attitude and a behavior rather than just a feeling whipped by the ever-changing winds of our emotions, says Dr. Chapman.

In other words, love is something that we need to choose to do—even when events may make it difficult to love the other person.

NEWS FROM THE LOVE LAB

Several studies conducted at the "Love Lab" at the University of Washington in Seattle help underscore the power of being loving—especially when we disagree. Researchers found that when couples discussed issues that were clearly sources of conflict, the couples with the strongest love relationships were affectionate, appreciative, and accepting. Not only that, but they joked, shared their joy, and demonstrated concern. And if they said something that hurt, they tried to repair the damage, according to John Gottman, Ph.D., professor emeritus of psychology at the University of Washington and author of more than forty books on marriage, including *Why Marriages Succeed or Fail*. On the other hand, those couples headed for divorce were sarcastic, emotionally uninvolved, and defensive.

Although designed to investigate why some marriages work and others fail, the research seems to confirm what we already know: people are drawn to relationships in which people act lovingly and are poised to leave those where they don't.

But running from our friends, children, or even spouses isn't an option. We're supposed to model what's known as agape love, a selfless love in which we'll go the extra mile or two or three or whatever it takes for the other person. It's Christ-like love, probably best reflected in this passage, often read at weddings as a sort of marching order for both bride and groom: "Love is patient, love is kind. It does not envy, it does not boast, it is not proud. It does not dishonor others, it is not self-seeking, it is not easily angered, it keeps no record of wrongs. Love does not delight in evil but rejoices with the truth. It always protects, always trusts, always hopes, always perseveres. Love never fails" (1 Corinthians 13:4–8 NIV).

Loving people when they treat us well isn't much of a challenge. But loving them always? What about when someone has hurt us or let us down? "To start with, Christ-like love treats small offenses as just that: small," says the Reverend Steven Estes.

"Christ-like love gives people the benefit of the doubt. It says, 'Hmmm, she

The Ingredients of Love

BY ELIZABETH SHERRILL, GUIDEPOSTS CONTRIBUTING EDITOR

In an old notebook I recently found a new way of looking at the familiar list in Galatians 5:22–23. "The fruit of the Spirit is love," Paul writes, and then goes on to set forth what I had always taken to be additional qualities: joy, peace, patience, and so on. But this is how the notebook put it:

Joy—which is love smiling

Peace—love resting

Patience—love waiting

Kindness—love showing itself sensitive to others' feelings

Goodness—love making allowances and sacrifices for others

Faithfulness—love proving constant

Gentleness—love yielding

Self-control—love triumphing over selfish inclination

This clarified for me why Paul could speak of "fruit" in the singular. Since God is love, His Spirit ripening within us will always produce love in all its wondrous varieties.

certainly was curt with me in the elevator this morning, but maybe she has a headache, or got some scary results from a medical test last night, or her marriage isn't going well, so I'll assume the best about her,'" says Estes.

"This is what the Bible means when it says that 'love covers over a multitude of sins' [1 Peter 4:8 NIV]," says Estes. "As we go through life, we jostle each other with our elbows all the time and thus, shouldn't take everything so personally."

What if our spouses or friends are caught in abuse, addiction, or adultery or have abandoned us? Probably the most loving things that we can do are draw some firm boundaries to try to influence their behavior and demand that they seek professional help. But, again, that's just part of the answer.

"When we're in difficult marriages, there is always something that we can do," says Dr. Chapman. "The question is, what can we do for the benefit of our spouses in difficult situations? If we can find what is best for our spouses and do it, it's going to help our marriages. Love always helps. It's the most powerful weapon for good that there is in the world."

Here are some suggestions to help love flow more freely.

Be a vessel for God's love. The biblical answer is simple but profound, says Pastor Estes: "Be kind and compassionate to one another, forgiving each other, just as in Christ God forgave you" (Ephesians 4:32 NIV).

"God loved us enough to bleed on a cross for us, even though our sins were a slap in His face," Estes says. "So how can we hold grudges against anyone?"

Ask God to change us. Often, we want God to change other people and their habits and insensitivities. "But we're better off if we ask God to change us," says Dr. Gottman. "When we come to a problem and we both say, 'I see my part in this

and I own up to it,' we can solve that problem much more easily."

Practice reality living. Reality living means taking responsibility for our own thoughts, feelings, and actions rather than believing that they are somehow dictated by our circumstances, says Dr. Chapman. From Helen Keller to Franklin Delano Roosevelt, people have chosen to overcome their disabilities. And if we have bad marriages or struggling friendships, we need to take responsibility for our share of the problem. Another tenet of reality living, he says, is recognizing that we can't change others, but we can influence them positively.

Go to the other person. "Who is more likely to point out the dandruff on your shoulders, an enemy or a friend?" asks Pastor Estes. "A friend, of course, because he loves you. The Bible says, 'Do not hate your brother in your heart, but rebuke your neighbor frankly...' [Leviticus 19:17 CJB]. If you truly love somebody, you'll do this privately, gently, and humbly, but you will do it."

Tear down the wall. Left untreated, even minor grievances can harden into walls between us and our loved ones, says Dr. Chapman. We begin knocking them down and restoring our relationships when we choose to forgive or ask forgiveness. If we're the ones being asked to do the forgiving, we should recall what Jesus told Peter when Peter asked how many times we're supposed to forgive. Jesus answered, "I do not say to you, up to seven times, but up to seventy times seven." (Matthew 18:22 NKJV).

Ask some questions. Instead of asking, "What have you done for me lately?" we need to ask, "How can I help you?" We have to make the choice to look out for the other person's interests, says Dr. Chapman, no matter how the person may have angered or hurt us.

LEARNING A NEW LANGUAGE

Ever tried ordering food in a restaurant where no one speaks our language? Not only is it frustrating, but it's rare that we get what we want. For some of the same reasons, we need to learn how to speak the "love language" of those we care about. Dr. Chapman says that there are five basic love languages.

1. **Words of affirmation.** Plain and simple, this is praise—for what someone has done, what they're wearing, whatever. "A good solid word of affirmation may carry someone for a week at a time. But others may want and need to hear one every day," Dr. Chapman says.

2. **Quality time.** The trick here, Dr. Chapman says, is making sure we give our undivided attention to the other person. "We can be doing lots of things with the person: playing a game, taking a walk, or sitting down and just talking. The important thing isn't what we're doing, it's that they have our attention."

3. **Giving gifts.** No need to find an expensive or unique gift—even a flower from the garden may do, Dr. Chapman says. "The old saying is: 'It's the thought that counts.' But it's not the thought that is left in your head. It's the gift that came out of the thought," he says.

4. **Acts of service.** From cooking a meal to hanging wallpaper, loving actions can score big points. We just need to make sure that we're doing the right act of service. "We may be expending a lot of time and energy painting the bedroom, but the person is not going to see that as very loving if they wanted us to paint the front door," says Dr. Chapman.

5. **Physical touch.** This means hugs, pats, handholding, kisses, or any number of loving gestures. And it means offering them solely for their own sake, not as a quick buildup to lovemaking. "One of the most common problems is to make

Sundays Are for Love

By Mary Lou Reed

Sundays were quiet and lazy when I was a kid. I came home from church, changed into jeans and a T-shirt, and either went to a movie matinee with my cousins or watched *Flash Gordon* on TV while talking on the phone with my girlfriends. My mum, on the other hand, headed into the kitchen. During the week she worked full-time at a drugstore, so the weekday dinners she made were often quick things like tuna salad or macaroni and cheese. But Sunday was special. Sundays always meant a home-cooked meal whipped up from scratch. I wondered how Mum could do it after such a busy week.

One day Mum was making my favorite, her spinach and cheese ravioli, and I joined her in the kitchen to help out. Mum dragged the pots and pans out from the cupboard and set them on the counter. I followed her to the fridge as she took out the eggs and cheeses, and stayed close by her heels when she pulled the flour and oil from their places in the cabinet.

Mum became so focused while she was working. She cracked the eggs into a small bowl filled with flour, salt, oil, and water. Slowly, she mixed them in. "Why are you doing that?" I asked, seeing her poke a small well in the center of a mound of flour with her fingers.

"You pour the mixture in there and stir it in slowly," she said. She explained that if you just poured it on top, the ingredients wouldn't blend as well. She handed me the small bowl, and carefully I tipped it into the center of the flour. The mixture filled the well and Mum stirred it in. When it was mixed enough, Mum took it out of the bowl and began kneading it with her fingers until it became a thick, rubbery dough. "Make sure you don't forget the secret ingredient," she told me. "What's that?" I said, watching her soft hands twisting and turning the dough. "You have to do it with love," she said. "Make it with love."

I never thought about making dinner that way before. I took my turn pressing my fingers into the dough, massaging it. It was soothing. I could see how after a busy week, even something that took more work, like cooking from scratch, could be relaxing. *So this is how she does it,* I thought. *With love.*

"Now it's time to make the filling," Mum said, wiping her hands. I got the eggs and cracked them over another bowl, though not as expertly as Mum—she had to pluck out a few pieces of shell. Mum mixed in the mozzarella and ricotta cheeses. Together, we threw in some spinach and topped it off with parsley. "There's going to be extra love in this batch," Mum laughed. I giggled along with her, feeling incredibly warm and happy inside.

She showed me how to cut and fold the cool dough around dollops of cheese. Already, I anticipated that heavenly smell. That pungent scent of Italian cheeses and tomato sauce wafting thickly through the air.

Bowls, pots, and pans were everywhere, flour littered the counter, but when that ravioli came out of the pot, the results were definitely worth the mess. My brother, my sister, my father, and I sat down at the table and Mum brought the steaming pasta to us. We all heaped helpings onto our plates. "Tastes great, Mum," my brother said. "Sure does," my father and sister agreed. "What's the secret?" Mum gave me a knowing look and again we burst into giggles.

When I became a working mother myself, I made sure to continue that Sunday tradition. The Bible teaches us to rest on the Sabbath. And I do, by cooking my family an old-fashioned dinner. Even though Mum is ninety-three now and no longer cooks, I still remember the things she taught me. I knead that dough, and all the worries and stresses of the week melt away. Sundays, Mum showed me, are for love.

the mistake that physical touch means sex," say Dr. Chapman. "It may not."

TAKE ACTION

After experimenting with the different love languages and finding the ones that work best, we need to use them often, even if others are resistant. "Not every spouse will respond," says Dr. Chapman, "but we are better for having loved."

In her book *A Gift for God*, the late Mother Teresa of Calcutta, now known as Saint Teresa of Calcutta, explained how people could lead better lives: "Smile at each other; smile at your wife, smile at your husband, smile at your children, smile at each other—it doesn't matter who it is— and that will help you grow up in greater love for each other.... I find it difficult sometimes to smile at Jesus. And it is true, Jesus can be very demanding also, and it is at those times when he is so demanding that to give him a big smile is very beautiful."

· HEALING WORDS ·

Lord, Your harvest is the harvest of love;
love sown in the hearts of people;
love that spreads out
like the branches of a great tree
covering all who seek its shelter;
love that inspires and re-creates;
love that is planted in the weak and the weary,
the sick and the dying.

The harvest of Your love is the life that reaches
through the weeds of sin and death
to the sunlight of resurrection.

Lord, nurture my days with Your love,
water my soul with the dew of forgiveness,
that the harvest of my life might be Your joy.
—FRANK TOPPING

SALVATION

Gateway to Healing—and Eternity

He was an inquisitive eight-year-old, as kids that age usually are. So the house on the big Texas property with the woods and the bushes was the ideal place to explore. There was only one problem: unknown to the boy and his parents, someone had set some steel animal traps in the backyard.

As one pastor tells it, the boy's father was in his study when he heard his son's cry for help. "Daddy, Daddy, Daddy!" the child wailed over and over again. Sure enough, the child had taken a wrong step, and the jaws of a trap had slammed shut on his foot.

When the father heard the crying, he didn't stop and think, *Has my son been good lately? Has he done the dishes? Did he do his chores?* No, the pastor explains. When a father hears that cry, he responds. In an instant, the man rushed out the back door to save his child.

In the same way, the Bible tells us, God will always respond to our cries. And that is where salvation starts—with a cry to God for help.

Many Cries, One Motivation

WE CRY OUT FOR many different reasons. Sometimes we're angry, as after the tragic death of a loved one, after a divorce, or in the midst of a long illness. Other times, disappointment is the trigger, like when we discover that the things that we believed would make us happy—money, power, prestige, success, even family—leave us feeling empty. Also, desperation can lead to cries for help from those who have tried to medicate their emotional pain with alcohol, drugs, sex, or food.

And sometimes it's not tragedy at all that makes us seek God and salvation. We simply feel an emptiness inside and long for the sense of peace and confidence that we see in others who have deep faith.

They're different cries, but they all have the same fundamental motivation: trying to fill an empty space or void inside. "There is a vacuum in all of us that only God can fill, through Jesus Christ," says Dr. Siang-Yang Tan. "We all, deep down inside, long to come home to what we were created for—loving, intimate fellowship and communion with God."

The problem that we all wrestle with is how to develop that closeness and, through it, find salvation.

How We're Saved

THOUGH THE FINER POINTS of salvation are a matter of debate among the major branches of Christianity, there are many things on which they agree.

Belief in the divinity of Christ. "The teaching on the person of Jesus Christ from the Scripture is very clear. He was fully God and at the same time fully man. Any deviation from this position is not only unscriptural, it is also heretical," says international speaker, author, and Christian apologist Josh McDowell.

Belief in the Bible. Although Roman Catholic and Eastern Orthodox churches go beyond the Bible as their source of authority, they agree with Protestant denominations that the Old and New Testaments are divinely inspired.

Belief that true faith involves more than attending church. As the late C. S. Lewis wrote in his classic *Mere Christianity*, "Sitting in a church doesn't make someone a Christian any more than sitting in a garage makes someone an automobile."

Belief in the concept of salvation. "The doctrine of salvation," says McDowell, "is linked with the atoning death of Christ on the cross" as God's perfect sacrifice for the sins of the world.

But just how we "appropriate" salvation is another matter, according to McDowell. Many Catholic Christians, for example, believe that we must work for it. Jesus' life, His death on the cross, and His resurrection planted the seeds of our salvation, and that salvation is a gift.

But that gift is given to us so that we may unwrap it and use it, says Father Kurt Stasiak. "Christians should be living their lives in such a way that the eternal life that we speak of should not come as too much of a shock. There should be a relationship with God already strongly established, and there should be an attitude of forgiveness that is already a habit," he says.

Nearly all Protestant denominations believe that we cannot earn salvation. Good deeds alone will never make us good enough in God's sight to be saved, according to Dr. Tan.

Instead, salvation—the deliverance from sin and from God's punishment for sin—is by grace, a free gift from God to all who believe in Christ. "This view simply says, 'I realize that Jesus died for me. I repent from my sins and I receive Him into my heart as my Savior and Lord,'" says Dr. Tan.

Where Protestant denominations seem to differ with regard to salvation is their level of commitment to Christ. Evangelical Christian churches believe that it is not enough to simply know that Jesus died on the cross for our sins; we need to make a personal commitment to accept Jesus into our hearts and make Him Lord of our lives. In other words, that commitment must guide how we live from that point forward.

"Saving faith begins with the truth about Who God is, who we are, and Who Jesus is, but it doesn't end there," says Dr. Ray Pritchard. "True saving faith is complete trust in the person of Jesus Christ."

Remedies
COMMON GROUND

HOW WE ULTIMATELY DECIDE to take the final steps toward salvation will depend largely on the teachings of our own individual churches and our own personal beliefs. But regardless, there are several things that we ourselves can do to get

An Odd Little Man

By Diana J. Jeansonne

Mr. Morgan was sad and frail-looking, with eyes that appeared to hold a painful secret. To my junior-high scrutiny he seemed an odd little man, pale and sickly. He was our new Sunday school teacher, and during that first class I thought, *I am never coming back here.* He wasn't fun or entertaining, and his teaching style was not peppy enough for my taste.

To add to the boredom, Mr. Morgan wanted to close the lesson not in prayer, like we always did, but in song. I couldn't wait to get out of there as we started to sing the first stanza of "The Old Rugged Cross."

On a hill far away, stood an old rugged cross,

the emblem of suffering and shame...

Suddenly a noise made me look up. It was a sniffle. A tear trickled down Mr. Morgan's cheek.

And I love that old cross,

where the dearest and best

for a world of lost sinners was slain.

There was another tear, and another. *What is this poor man so upset about?* I wondered.

So I'll cherish the old rugged cross...

He seemed to be trying to hold back his tears, but they continued despite his best efforts. At first, the boys looked embarrassed. Then they began snickering, elbow-jabbing, and pointing. The girls found it too painful even to look up; their eyes remained glued to the pages in front of them.

But I had never seen a man cry. I couldn't take my eyes off the teacher.

I will cling to the old rugged cross and exchange it some day for a crown.

The song ended, and Mr. Morgan blew his nose on a handkerchief, "I'm sorry," he said. "I just can't sing that hymn without thinking of what Jesus did for me. He hung there, almost naked, on a rough wooden cross. A spear was stuck in His side and He spilled His blood. For what? For me! For my sins."

All the sniggers had stopped. There was complete silence in the classroom now. Everyone was still as Mr. Morgan paused and looked around at us.

"And for your sins, too," he said. "Because of Him, we have a home in heaven forever."

I was overwhelmed and in awe. I had never heard a man make such a personal, down-to-earth statement about salvation before. Even to the mind of a seventh grader, the meaning was apparent: Mr. Morgan made it clear that Christ was his reason for living. The tears he shed were tears of gratitude. And through them, for the first time, I saw a personal God. Until that moment, Jesus had been merely a character in a book. I had never before been grateful for Christ.

I haven't forgotten that day thirty years ago, or Mr. Morgan's gift. He taught me that there is no greater joy than throwing your pride and a few shed tears to the wind, if hearts are implanted with the seeds that open eternity.

closer to God and to the salvation that He offers.

Ask God for direction. Who would we rather get directions from, someone who studied a map, or the guy who built the road? If we're having doubts about our faith, salvation, or God, we should simply talk to God, says Dr. Tan. "Pray a simple prayer like this: 'Dear God, if You're really there and You can show me what life is all about, and if Jesus is really the answer, please make this clearer to me. I really want to know. I am really seeking after You. Help me to find You.' This is opening our hearts up to the God Who is there, Who will then reveal Himself eventually. It's a real, heartfelt, sincere cry for God to reveal Himself. And God always answers that prayer."

Study God's Word. Between its covers, the Bible contains literally thousands of promises and truths on everything from eternal life to taming our tongues to managing our time and money to having better marriages. If we're faithful in our studies, God will show us these and other insights that will help us grow in our faith and find salvation.

Read the Gospel of Mark. Lots of folks say that they've tried to read the Bible but stopped in frustration when they encountered Old Testament names they couldn't pronounce or ancient battles that seemed irrelevant. Instead of trying to read from beginning to end, says Dr. Tan, it may be more helpful for seekers to explore the New Testament Gospels, especially Mark. "For the modern mind, Mark may be the best. It's the shortest of the Gospels and provides fast-paced snapshots of Jesus' life and words," he says. For doubters, Dr. Tan suggests praying before reading: "If this is really Your Word, God, please speak to me through it."

Seek an inspiring service or small group. We have a flavorless meal at a restaurant. Or the waitress is surly. Does that mean we'll never eat out again? Of course not. In the same way, if we have a bad taste in our mouths from boring or irrelevant sermons or unfriendly church members, we simply need to find another church or group. "Some churches have what are called seeker-sensitive services that are offered on Saturday night or Sunday morning with bands or music and a relevant message that isn't preachy," says Dr. Tan. Small-group Bible studies are often informal and surprisingly fun ways to explore the big questions such as salvation, he adds.

Accept God's grace—and share it. "In her book *Stripping Down*, Donna Schaper says that God spreads grace around like five-year-olds spread peanut butter. He gets it everywhere. And if I had to tell you my theology in a nutshell, that is it," says Dr. Harold Ivan Smith. "There has been great emphasis on salvation from sin, but to me, it's salvation into inclusion in the Kingdom and the family of God. It's an invitation to participate in the great purposes of God for humankind."

The Work of God

But I can imagine someone say, "If that is to have a new birth, what am I to do? I can't create life. I certainly can't save myself." You certainly can't, and we don't preach that you can. We tell you it is utterly impossible to make a man better without Christ, and that is what men are trying to do. They are trying to patch up this old Adam's nature. There must be new creation. Regeneration is a new creation, and if it is a new creation it must be the work of God.

—D. L. Moody, nineteenth-century evangelist

THANKFULNESS

An Attitude for Good Times and Bad

Remember how easy it was to thank your mom and dad for the shiny new bike you got for your tenth birthday, but how hard it was to say thank you when Aunt Martha gave you that ill-fitting, unattractive sweater?

Thankfulness comes naturally as a response to something that brings us obvious pleasure, but is difficult when we have to struggle to find out what, exactly, there is to be thankful for. Yet it is possible to maintain a sense of thankfulness, as the Bible describes it, even when things aren't perfect, even when the world seems bleak.

Think of Jesus, Who on the night when He was to be given over to the Roman authorities, still managed to give thanks for the food and drink He received. Think of Daniel, who offered thanks and praise to God even though the Jews were locked in pitched struggle against pagan intruders. Think of the Psalmist who gave thanks to God despite suffering unjust accusations. Their secret? Thankfulness for them, this true biblical sense of thanksgiving, was not tied to the offering of earthly rewards. It was rooted in Who God is, in His nature of unfailing goodness, infinite wisdom, and unconditional love. This is why Paul could encourage us to "…give thanks in all circumstances; for this is God's will for you in Christ Jesus" (1 Thessalonians 5:18 NIV).

Getting by the Barriers

ONE OBSTACLE TO DEVELOPING and maintaining an attitude of thanksgiving is that the stress and busyness of everyday life, in addition to the trials and challenges we face, can cause us to be worried or anxious, and that anxiety drowns out our thanksgiving. The difficulties of life sometimes can be so overwhelming and difficult that we lose sight of God.

Another obstacle to thanksgiving is our "compulsive need to treat gifts as things that are traded rather than given," says Brian H. Childs, Ph.D., community professor of bioethics at Mercer University School of Medicine in Savannah, Georgia, and author of several books on pastoral theology and pastoral care.

"It's hard to receive a gift and not want to repay it, whether that gift comes from God or from your uncle Louie," Dr. Childs says. "Recently, when a friend invited me over for dinner, I asked what I could bring. A bottle of wine? A salad? Some flowers? But I was told only to bring myself, nothing more. It was an odd feeling, to receive the gift of this person's meal and not somehow compensate them for it. Initially, I felt indebted."

In addition, our own egos can interfere with our ability to be thankful, says Dr. Childs. "I remember counseling a family in which the father had abused the son. We reached a point where the boy was extending forgiveness to his dad, but in order to receive this extraordinary gift, the man had to completely humble himself, accept it despite his unworthiness, know he couldn't repay it, and admit his need for it. But the hardest part was, as it often is, accepting one's acceptability, that God embraces us no matter how heinous our sins might be. This acceptance required of the man a posture of utter thanksgiving," he says.

"As a counselor, I realized that the worst thing I could do at that moment was to get in the way, so I sat back and let the two of them play it out themselves," says Dr. Childs. "The boy was wonderfully relentless—very much like Jesus—in his willingness to forgive. And the dad was terrified. But the boy just stood at the 'door' and knocked. And knocked and knocked. And finally, in a heap of tears, the father answered. In subsequent sessions, we spent long hours helping the father come to

Dinner at the McClendons'

By Cynthia Ros McClendon

How was I going to feed our family the next four nights? A peek in the cupboard revealed a box of macaroni and cheese and a jar of peanut butter. I looked in the fridge. Some leftover chicken, three eggs, a carton of milk, and a few slices of American cheese looked back. Half a loaf of bread sat in the pantry, with a lone potato and two onions. With car repairs and the closing of the electronics store where my husband, Barry, worked, we were left with exactly three dollars till I got paid.

Lord, I'm in a fix. Not even a five-star chef could pull together a meal out of this stuff. For weeks I'd been holding out hope that Barry would find a new job and we'd get back on our feet. I made do without the extras; I'd been raised with a healthy sense of frugality. Now I was worried. Dad used to say Mom could make a banquet out of thin air, but things were different back then. What would she do now, in modern-day hard times?

"There's nothing here," I muttered, finding a bag of limp carrots in the vegetable bin. Mom was fond of telling me to be thankful for what I had. "Even now?" I wanted to ask her. Mom's voice came back to me like a whisper from an angel. I knew good and well what she'd say. Even now.

Staring into my near-barren refrigerator, I gave in. *Thank you, Lord, for my family. Thank you for my job (even if payday is still four dinners away).*

Just then Barry walked in with the kids. "Hey, Mom, what's for dinner?" Heather asked.

"Well, let's see," I said, stalling. *Thank you, Lord, for milk . . . eggs . . . bread . . . And what's that hiding behind the milk? Syrup!* "How about French toast?"

"For dinner?" Heather asked. "Sure. Why not?"

"Cool," said Ryan.

"You really know how to keep dinner interesting," Barry said, and smiled.

The next evening I thanked the Lord that Ryan had been invited to a friend's, so there were only three of us to feed. With the leftover chicken, half a box of biscuit mix I discovered in a drawer, and the carrots, I fixed a darn good chicken potpie. The night after that—grilled cheese sandwiches and home fries made with that single potato.

Only one more meal to go. All we had left was the macaroni and cheese and the peanut butter. *Thank you, Lord, for—*

Barry interrupted to tell me about his job-hunting. No luck so far. "Payday's tomorrow," I said, "but we're going to be awful hungry by then unless you can think of a recipe that combines macaroni and cheese and peanut butter."

"If we had some ground meat and a can of chili, I could make my famous chili-mac," Barry said.

"That's wishful thinking." Then I remembered the three dollars! "Feel like a trip to the grocery?"

"I'll be right back," Barry said. "You take a break. Chili-mac's coming up!"

After dinner, Ryan asked, "Anything for dessert?"

I almost exclaimed that he should be thankful we'd had a decent meal, but something stopped me. *Thank you, Lord, for Ryan's healthy appetite.* And then I thought, *Well, we do have peanut butter, flour, and sugar . . .*

"Who wants peanut butter cookies?" Not only had we made it till payday, but God had even allowed for dessert. Maybe I wasn't a five-star chef, but you never met a more inspired cook.

terms with two striking realities of pain and promise: first, that like all of us, he was a sinner who had to take account of his sins, and second, that like all of us, he had this enormous capacity to beg and receive forgiveness, and that being able to do so is something for which we must all be profoundly thankful."

Remedies
CULTIVATING A GRATEFUL ATTITUDE

IF WE LOOK CAREFULLY at our lives, we'll see that they are rich with things we can be thankful for, things both significant and seemingly small. They are rich, too, with opportunities to build the sense of thankfulness that Dr. Childs suggests "we feel in the face of the limitless outpouring of God's love for us." Here are some suggestions.

Give thanks for everyday things. We can thank God for the simple things we normally take for granted, such as health, housing, utilities, family and friends, a blue sky, or a sunny afternoon. We should choose one such item each day and give thanks for the ways it brings some sliver of happiness to our lives.

Thank God for small surprises. We can thank God in prayer for the old friends we ran into or for the dollar bills we found in the pocket of last year's winter coat, for example. In Dr. Childs's view, things like this are small symbols of the serendipity of God's love.

Study the Psalms. The Psalms are the Bible's book of praise and thanksgiving. If we take time to read them, we see that the Psalmists were thankful for all kinds of blessings—from the beauty they saw in nature to victories in battle. The Psalms will help us develop thankful hearts toward God, and when we are thankful to Him, we are also inclined to be thankful to and for other people and things.

Do without. When the power goes out in our homes or our cars break down, we become very thankful once these things are working again. Spending some time without something we need or even something we enjoy will help us realize that we should be thankful for it.

Accept the thanks of others. If a friend or relative wants to offer us a meal or a gift, we need to quell any feelings of indebtedness. "Thankfulness is a dance that requires two partners," says Dr. Childs, "one giving and the other receiving freely. It is the same with God. He offers us His grace, His mercy, and His love, but if we refuse to receive it, it falls dead at our feet."

SHOWING LOVE

When we are feeling thankful for our lives, for God's love, or for the world in which

Count on It

BY LORA CLARK

The phone rang. It was my friend Annette. She had been going through a rough time. "I feel so alone," she said. "I've even lost God and don't know how to find Him."

I'd felt the same way once, and told Annette how making a gratitude list had helped.

"Write the numbers one through fifty down the side of a piece of paper," I explained. "Then go back and count the things you're thankful for. And remember, it's not the things you're supposed to be thankful for, but the things you really are thankful for."

"Okay, then, I'll give it a try," Annette said, hanging up.

Not long after, the phone rang again. It was Annette. "I found Him!" she exclaimed joyfully.

we live, we can do specific things to sustain that feeling.

Make a thankful gesture anonymously. We can try doing a few good deeds for others, with no expectation of compensation. Smile and compliment others. Cut a neighbor's lawn. Offer to carry someone's luggage to a bus stop.

Appreciate a public servant. Countless people we never see work to make our lives easier—from postal employees to those who stock grocery stores to city workers who drive snow plows to people who keep us safe. We can leave a thank-you note or gift card for them or make a point to thank them verbally when we see them, letting them know how much we appreciate what they do.

Thank a family member. We can write an unsolicited letter of thanks to any members of our family for one act of kindness they showed us at one time in our lives. If it's an obscure memory, we can remind them of the details of the event.

Collect food for the church or neighborhood pantry. We could organize a food drive at a local grocery store, invite shoppers to purchase one food item, collect them, and donate them to the local pantry. It's a tangible way of giving thanks to God for our ability to feed our families, says Dr. Childs.

In a world for which we give constant thanks, no gesture is too small, nothing is meaningless, and everything is sacred.

This morning I drive through mountains half an eon old.
The highway winds upward
in long, dark arcs—
its asphalt silhouette looking like the black snakes
I used to catch in September cornfields.

Pine trees grow in profusion,
peaks stretching toward the distant blue of hazy skies.
At the base of the mountains,
daisies bloom—
their lithe bodies
swaying in the swoosh of
watermelon-laden semis.

As I drink in passing scenery
peace settles on me,
assuring me that
God indeed cares about
even the littlest
things in my life—
for He Who sculpted the
mighty mountains
took time to create the
daisies, too.
—MARY LOU CARNEY

TOLERANCE

Yours Truly

On September 11, 2001, I was with my college friend Denise visiting a cathedral on a hill in Kilkenny, Ireland's medieval capital—thousands of miles from New York, the city I call home—when I heard the terrible news. Hijacked jets had hit the World Trade Center, church workers said. Denise and I hurried to find a television. In a pub near the foot of the hill, we saw what our minds had refused to believe. The Twin Towers—and the lives of so many—were no more.

For a long moment, neither of us could speak. Then Denise whispered, "Church. We need to go."

The first place of worship we came across was the Black Abbey, founded by the Dominican friars in 1225. Denise sat in front of the altar and began to pray the rosary. Unsure what to do myself, not being Catholic, I looked around the sanctuary.

My gaze was drawn to a statue bathed in the soft glow of candles, a figure of a dark-skinned man in the robes of the Dominican order. He was St. Martin de Porres, a plaque explained, known for his work to heal not merely physical ailments but also the deeper wounds of prejudice and hate. I lit a candle and set it before the statue. "God, let us hear Martin's message," I asked. "Let your love prevail."

Everywhere Denise and I went after that, Irish men, women, and children showed us their hearts were with the people of the U.S. That evening, our bed-and-breakfast's owner comforted us with tea and biscuits in her cozy library. In seaside Greystones the following night, two schoolgirls overheard me phoning New York. When I hung up, they came to tell me, "We want you to know we love Americans." On Friday, declared a national day of mourning in Ireland, I went to a secluded park in Dublin hoping to find some peace. An older gentleman walking his dog paused at my bench. Tipping his cap, he said, "God be with you and yours."

I realized then that God was in all the strangers who drew close to two Americans abroad to share our sorrow, reminding us of what Martin de Porres knew—we are strongest when we stand together. —AMY WONG

Seeing Past Our Differences

IN THE EARLY 1990S, once every quarter, a reconciliation Sunday was held at the Rock, an evangelical free church on the West Side of Chicago. First, in what they called the "chocolate" meeting, founder and pastor emeritus Raleigh Washington met with African-American members of the congregation to discuss issues from the black perspective. Then, in the "vanilla" meeting, he met with the white membership, and their views were aired.

Immediately afterward, there was "fudge ripple" meeting. Fudge ripple ice cream was served, as were Oreo cookies. But the main course was exposed feelings. As Pastor Washington puts it, "My job was to go in there and rat on both groups." According to the church website in 2017, those meetings "are no longer needed."

Airing issues before they turn into resentments is what Pastor Washington calls acting in a preventive mode. The idea is to promote tolerance by short-circuiting misunderstanding. "If you deal with an issue before it becomes a problem and talk about it," he says, "you can reach common ground. If you don't, never the twain shall meet."

Fudge Ripple Sundays were an example of a very basic fact about achieving true tolerance: it takes work. This applies to tolerance between spouses and between drivers racing along the highway as much as it does to tolerance between racial, religious, or political groups. "In any human relationship, there's one thing I can guarantee you," Pastor Washington says. "Conflict will come. That's inevitable. The question is, what are you going to do about it?"

IT'S MORE THAN JUST ACCEPTANCE

Many spiritual leaders aren't particularly fond of the word *tolerance*. They feel that it doesn't adequately convey the degree of love and commitment that the Bible requires. Pastor Washington shares that view. "The Bible says we have to do more than tolerate one another," he says. "We have to actively love one another."

This is not to say that conflicts are to be ignored. To the contrary, the Bible states clearly that differences are to be actively confronted: "If another member of the church sins against you, go and point out the fault when the two of you are alone. If the member listens to you, you have regained that one. But if you are not listened to, take one or two others along with you, so that every word may be confirmed by the evidence of two or three witnesses" (Matthew 18:15–16 NRSV).

This passage demonstrates that tolerance is not a synonym for acquiescence. "Tolerance often has a very superficial meaning of simply putting up with people you don't like, pretending that your most important differences don't really make any difference," said the late Father Richard John Neuhaus, cofounder of Institute on Religion and Public Life, an interreligious, nonpartisan research and education organization. "It's not tolerance that you want to cultivate so much as respectful engagement and Christian love." The appropriate stance, he says, is to stand up for what we believe in but to do so without coercion or deception. Referring to the Apostle Paul's advice to the Ephesians (4:15), Father Neuhaus also said, "We 'speak the truth in love' and hope to persuade."

Often, the respectful part of engagement is what we have trouble with, and this is a large part of the reason tolerance is such hard work, says Richard Mouw, Ph.D., Ph.M., professor of faith and public life at Fuller Theological Seminary. Remaining civil in the company of people whose views we find repugnant requires a degree of patience that may be hard to muster.

Dr. Mouw believes Christians are often guilty of intolerance—a weakness with which they are frequently charged—because they tend to focus more on declaring their own moral convictions than on listening carefully to the convictions of others. "I don't want to make tolerance the ultimate virtue," he says. "Faithfulness to God is what we're ultimately all about. But I think that we Christians often rush to judgment without thinking of how we relate to other people." He explains that preachers often quote the first part of 1 Peter 3:15–16 (NRSV)—"Always be ready to make your defense to anyone who demands from you an accounting for the hope that is in you…"—but forget the second part—"…yet do it with gentleness and reverence."

It is a Christian duty, Dr. Mouw says, to strive for compassionate understanding, both for the sake of tolerance and for constructive dialogue. "If the goal is really to bring the truth to people, then listening, patience, empathy, and civility can be an important part of that. It's not our job to make everything go right and to correct all the mistakes in the world. Every human being has to stand someday before God. That's when things will really be straightened out."

Remedies
STEPS IN THE RIGHT DIRECTION

GIVEN THAT THE TASK of Christian love can be difficult, showing tolerance can be a big step in the right direction. Here are some steps that can help bring it closer.

Make a commitment. Pastor Washington remembers one of his African-American parishioners saying, "My mother never taught me to hate white folks," to which he replied, "Yes, but did your mother teach you to go out of your way to actively love white folks?" The answer to that was no, Pastor Washington says. It should be yes, for all of us. We must actively dedicate ourselves to increasing tolerance in the world and in our own hearts.

Take the initiative. The best way to work on actively loving our neighbors, Pastor Washington says, is to actively seek them out. "We must establish committed relationships with people of different races

Lasting Impressions

By Walter J. Hintz

Born in Cleveland, Ohio, I was raised in a small town close by, a predominantly white Anglo-Saxon Protestant community. I attended the Methodist church, and my knowledge of people of different religions and races was confined to the stereotypes I found in books and in the media. My parents and grandparents never taught me to hate, but I knew they wanted me to keep my distance from those who were different.

Our Methodist youth group met at the chapel on Sunday evenings. Most of us attended because it was something to do rather than to make serious study of the Scripture we read. When I was sixteen, that changed.

A new adviser took over the youth group. He made the Scripture come alive for us. We visited other churches. We attended a Catholic Mass. We went to a synagogue. We sat through a black Pentecostal service, where the congregation stood and shouted amen (a practice alien to our staid Methodist environment). Exploring other religions deepened my own faith.

The adviser worked as a salesman of spices and an amazing new product called Frisk. It was one of the first commercial dish detergents sold exclusively door-to-door. I was proud the summer he asked me if I wanted to help him with his sales. Bright and early in the morning this man knocked on doors, offering to wash the breakfast dishes. No one ever refused him, and we usually sold at least one bottle per household and signed on the housewife as a regular customer.

The adviser met my family and the family of my girlfriend (now my wife of forty-five years). My mother, who was very protective, let me go with him without question. He had more charisma than anyone I'd ever met. He taught me about

> having a work ethic. He taught me respect for others, and tolerance for their be-
> liefs. He taught me about equality and morality. He taught me to be the teacher
> I am today.

or colors," he says. "Virtually none of us lives in a vacuum where we don't come into proximity with people who are racially different from ourselves. Wherever we have that proximity, then we must capitalize on it by initiating a relationship."

The direct approach is often best, Pastor Washington says. He offers as an example a white person who might have a Hispanic mailman. "You can go up to that person and say, 'You know what? You're my mailman. I don't know you, and you don't know me, but this world would be a better place if we could learn more about each other. Could we get together and have lunch? I'll buy!'"

Another way to develop relationships with people of different ethnic groups, Pastor Washington says, is to regularly attend a church with a different racial makeup than the one we usually attend. Similarly, there are community service organizations, such as Habitat for Humanity, that do volunteer work in neighborhoods we might not ordinarily frequent. We should choose one that will bring us into regular, loving contact with people who are different from us.

Keep practicing. True tolerance takes practice, just as golfing or playing the piano takes practice. It's not a onetime event, but a continual attitude, a mind-set of inclusiveness. To practice, we may make deliberate efforts to expand our horizons and build relationships with people who bring diversity to our lives.

Tell the truth. Sitting down with people whose opinions may differ from our own is only half the task. The next step is telling them the truth about ourselves, especially about our perceptions and differences. "Sincerity is when you're willing to be vulnerable," says Pastor Washington. "If you're not willing to do that, you'll never establish an atmosphere of trust."

Listen. Few things are less tolerant than refusing to listen. If we need help understanding someone, there's no better way to get it than by asking. "Three of the most critical words you can use in any situation are 'help me understand,'" says Pastor Washington. "When you say that in a loving fashion, people are glad to oblige."

Watch our reactions. Our culture or upbringing may have ingrained intolerance in us, so it's important to watch for it in ourselves. We need to pay attention to our thoughts, words, and actions when we encounter people or situations that are new to us or different than what we are accustomed to.

Avoid generalizations. Stereotypes take on a different dimension when we get to know individuals who supposedly fit them. We will often find the stereotypes do not apply at all. In fact, we may often make new friends when we avoid generalizing them.

HEALING WORDS

Bearing Fruit That Will Last

This is my commandment, that you love one another as I have loved you.

No one has greater love than this, to lay down one's life for one's friends.

You are my friends if you do what I command you.

I do not call you servants any longer, because the servant does not know what the master is doing; but I have called you friends, because I have made known to you everything that I have heard from my Father.

You did not choose me but I chose you. And I appointed you to go and bear fruit, fruit that will last, so that the Father will give you whatever you ask him in my name.

I am giving you these commands so that you may love one another.

—Jesus addressing the apostles (John 15:12–17 NRSV)

TRUST

At a Crossroads

Restless and looking for a change, I had recently moved to Asheville, North Carolina, from Chicago, leaving friends and a secure job behind to start a new life. I loved my new town, but weeks went by and despite numerous interviews, I couldn't find a job. I began to wonder if I was doing the right thing. After all, I had prayed about it. Maybe I had misunderstood the Lord's direction.

I started writing in my journal. One morning, inexplicably, I wrote the word *trust* at the top of the page. I wrote it a second time, then a third. I kept writing the word until the whole page was full.

Still feeling uncertain, I decided to go for a drive. As I drove aimlessly on winding country roads, a three-way intersection came into view. On one corner stood a log-cabin restaurant. Across from that was a huge wooden cross sticking out from a rock. On the other corner was a small chapel. Curious, I entered and read about its builder: a woman who miraculously recovered from a terminal illness. When all else had failed she kept her trust in prayer. I sat down on one of the wooden benches. "Lord, I could use a faith like hers," I prayed.

My stomach began to growl. *I'll get a bite to eat at the restaurant.* Right by the entrance I noticed a metal sculpture spelling out TRUST. I ran inside and asked

Reasons to Believe

WE LIVE TODAY IN a culture filled with lack of trust and suspicion.

Conspiracy, betrayal, dishonor, and deceit are staples of our daily news reports and sometimes themes of the movies or videos we watch for entertainment. We habitually joke about the dishonesty of politicians and lawyers. We assume that used car salesmen and advertising pitchmen will cheat us if they can. Doctors, bosses, even ministers also receive their share of derision. And sometimes we think twice about our spouses and our children. Ultimately, not even God is safe from the skepticism of this cynical age.

"Study upon study shows that people have low confidence in their leaders, the government, and the press, in addition to a lack of trust for one another," says Amitai Etzioni, Ph.D., author of *The Spirit of Community*. "It's not a sound foundation for a system of government or for anything else."

What's even more painful is the way mistrust isolates us personally. After all, if we can't trust the people around us, we're all alone. "Trust connects us to the world," says John Townsend, Ph.D., founder of the Townsend Institute for Leadership and Counseling and the Townsend Leadership program, and coauthor of *Safe People* and *Boundaries*. "It's the link that brings us into a relationship—any kind of relationship. Without trust, we're lost in our own orbit."

Often, people who have trouble trusting learned to be that way in early childhood. "Psalm 22:9 tells how God teaches us to trust at the mother's breast," Dr. Townsend says. "That's backed up by a lot of clinical evidence and research. We don't come into the world trusting. We emerge from the womb in a state of alienation, and one of the first tests of the parenting process is to teach the child that reaching out into a relationship is a good thing."

Failing to learn that most basic of childhood lessons can lead to problems sustaining almost any type of relationship later in life. Mistrustful people tend to withdraw at the first sign of difficulty. Since difficulties are inevitable in every relationship, that makes it hard for them to develop long-lasting connections. "That's why you see people having serial relationships, serial jobs, serial churches," Dr. Townsend says. "When they get let down, they tend to regress to the point of original injury; they become that terrified infant again. They feel that a relationship is a bad place to be, so they go into what the Bible calls darkness."

Dark as our hiding places are, venturing out of them into the light isn't always easy, but it's far from impossible. There's a lot we can do to strengthen our own ability to trust others and a lot that we can do to become more trustworthy ourselves.

Remedies
IT STARTS WITH SMALL STEPS

DEVELOPING OUR ABILITY TO trust is a lot like developing our muscles in a gym, Dr. Townsend says. We must practice, building up gradually from trusting a little to trusting a lot. Here's where to start.

Have faith. We will find it easier to trust ourselves and others if we first trust God. One step toward developing trust in God, says Dr. Townsend, is realizing that God will stand by us through thick and thin. Knowing that His love for us is secure—unshakable, in fact—allows us to relax, trusting Him. Jesus states explicitly that God will open the door if we knock on it (Matthew 7:8), and in the Beatitudes (Matthew 5:1–11), Jesus makes it clear that God's love extends especially to the weak. "He doesn't expect us to stand alone," Dr. Townsend says.

Risk honesty. An essential step in learning to trust is to open up and talk honestly about ourselves, our problems, and our needs even when doing so feels uncomfortable. "It's a very difficult but very important task to bring our needy, broken parts into the light," says Dr. Townsend.

When we take that risk, the people around us will tend to be more open and honest with us, and trust begins to build. "We need to have the experience of seeing

Perfect Trust

By Edith A. Miles

I never knew how well Mother could keep a confidence until I was going through her things after she died. I discovered something I had long forgotten, something that happened to me as a child.

One night, as I lay in bed after my sisters and I had said our prayers, I recalled the events of the day and how badly I had behaved toward Mother. *I must make things right before going to sleep,* I thought.

Quietly I slipped out of bed and picked up pencil and paper from the dresser, then tiptoed into the hall. The light from the living room shone dimly through the banister railing and across the wooden floor. I knew Mother was downstairs mending socks.

I quickly wrote a note asking Mother to forgive me for being so naughty. I didn't want my siblings to know our business so I added a postscript: "Please don't let anyone see this." Then I crept into my parents' bedroom and tucked the letter under Mother's pillow.

The next morning, when I made my bed after breakfast, I found a return note under my pillow. Mother wrote that she loved me and forgave me.

This became my way of apologizing whenever I talked back or was stubborn or disobeyed. Mother always left a return note, but she never spoke about our under-the-pillow messages in front of the family. Even when we were grown, she never mentioned them when my sisters, brother, and I reminisced about our childhood.

When Mother passed away, I had to go through her personal belongings. In her bureau was a bundle of notes tied with a faded ribbon. On top was a message in her handwriting. It read "In the event of my death, please destroy these."

> I turned the packet over and glanced at the handwriting on the bottom. To my surprise I recognized my childish scrawl, "P.S. Please don't let anyone see this. Love, Edie."
>
> I gently placed the unopened bundle in the wastebasket along with other scraps for the trash burner. "Lord," I prayed, "make me like my mother."

that people can be warm, accepting, tender, encouraging, open, and honest," Dr. Townsend says. "Eventually, we learn to say to ourselves, 'The world is a better place than I thought.'"

Be generous. We can encourage people to behave in a trustworthy fashion by trusting them, says Maxie Dunnam, president emeritus of Asbury Theological Seminary. "The key is to give people the benefit of the doubt," says Dr. Dunnam. "It's very easy for us to jump to judgment. We need to resist that temptation."

Protect ourselves. Despite the need to extend trust to others, we also need to accept the fact that some people aren't trustworthy. Identifying who fits that description and who doesn't is essential, says Dr. Townsend. Yet many people put their trust in untrustworthy people and situations over and over again.

To end this destructive pattern, we need to examine our reasons for choosing such relationships. Dr. Townsend suggests asking ourselves the following questions:

- Are we choosing to be involved with this person for purely emotional reasons, despite what an objective look at his or her character might tell us?
- Are we choosing to be involved with this person because we're afraid of being alone?
- Are we choosing to be involved with this person as a means of avoiding our own issues?
- Are we choosing to be involved with this person because we think that being associated with him or her will make us look good to others?
- Are we choosing to be involved with this person because we think he or she will take care of us?
- Are we afraid of confronting this person?
- Are we trying to rescue this person?
- Do we enjoy playing the victim?
- Are we simply afraid to change?

"Yes" answers to most or all of these questions suggest that we're choosing a relationship for the wrong reasons, Dr. Townsend says. Untrustworthy relationships will likely result.

Look for friends in the right places. Once we've committed to avoid untrustworthy people, we need to find alternatives. Dr. Townsend advises looking in places where people with whom we might have deeper relationships are most likely to gather, where sharing honest feelings is the specific goal. Where might we look? To Bible study groups or support groups sponsored by a church.

In the Methodist tradition of Dr. Dunnam, sharing with fellow believers is called Christian conferencing. The idea is for each person to testify to what God has done in his or her life, thereby strengthening the faith of the others in the group that God will move in their lives as well. "When one person is down, another is up," Dr. Dunnam says. "I think that's the whole meaning of Christian community."

Practice acceptance. Recognizing that someone can't be trusted in certain ways doesn't mean we should automatically discard the entire relationship with that person. "We need to acknowledge that there's only so far that some people are able to go," Dr. Townsend says. The task then is to work on forgiving and accepting while searching for other relationships that can provide the emotional support we need.

TO BE WORTHY

FINDING ROLE MODELS OF trustworthiness in this day and age isn't all that easy. But we really need look no further than the New Testament. Who was more trustworthy than Christ?

The challenge is how best to follow His example. Here are some suggestions.

Be reliable. This is perhaps the most basic and simplest of all the rules of trustworthiness, according to Wilford Wooten. "Trust is doing what we say we will do, whether or not it's convenient," he says. That means coming through on small as well as large commitments: calling when we say we will, arriving at appointments on time, or bringing what we say we'll bring to a picnic. Such details may not be as momentous as honoring our wedding vows or meeting our responsibilities to care for our children, but they count.

Be a steward of relationships. Trustworthy people are those who can successfully nurture and preserve relationships with others, says David Schroeder, Ed.D., S.T.M., M.A., president of Pillar College in Middlesex, New Jersey, and founder of MasterWorks. That takes commitment and effort. "Relationships are among the most important assets we have," he says, "and we shouldn't be quick to compromise them or place other things above them."

For example, it's easy to place our careers above our relationships, Dr. Schroeder says. Being a steward of relationships means leaving work early to show up for our children's ball games or school functions, doing our share of the housework to lighten the load on our spouses, and taking the time to check in with our friends periodically on the phone.

Take the lead. Trustworthy people set an example by living lives of integrity and Christian purpose, says the Reverend Leo J. O'Donovan, Th.D., interim executive director for Jesuit Refugee Service/USA, and president emeritus of Georgetown University, in Washington, D.C., and professor of theology. "We cannot alleviate the mistrust around us and inspire the caring and trusting leaders of the future if we wilt beneath challenges," he says. This might mean, for example, speaking out clearly on a difficult issue of public importance and working to solve the problem,

rather than quietly wishing it would go away or letting others take care of it. Or it might mean being honest about the limits of what we can do in a certain situation. Opportunities for demonstrating what Father O'Donovan calls "trust in action" appear daily in each of our lives.

Pause to reflect. Spiritual leadership is easier, Father O'Donovan says, if we know where we're going. Taking the time to pause and reflect on our sense of mission and direction can help solidify our sense of purpose.

For Father O'Donovan, reflecting on his mission means each morning repeating the Latin vows that he took when he was ordained as a priest decades ago. "Sometimes I need to hear the words so I can translate their meaning in new ways," he says. "At other times, I am simply invigorated by knowing that they have become a part of me."

Trust to get trust. Beyond the example He set with His actions, Jesus spells out a simple maxim for trustworthy behavior, says Wooten. "We call it the Golden Rule [Matthew 7:12]. If we begin to treat other people as we'd like to be treated," he says, "more often than not, that will be mirrored back to us."

Taking the First Step

Ask, and it will be given you; search, and you will find; knock,
and the door will be opened for you.
For everyone who asks receives, and everyone who searches finds,
and for everyone who knocks, the door will be opened.
Is there anyone among you who, if your child asks for bread, will give a stone?
Or if the child asks for a fish, will give a snake? If you then, who are evil,
know how to give good gifts to your children, how much more will your Father in
heaven give good things to those who ask him!
In everything do to others as you would have them do to you;
for this is the law and the prophets.
—MATTHEW 7:7–12 NRSV

CONTRIBUTORS

Jacqueline Abbott, Dr.P.H., R.D., L.D., nutritionist and medical educator at Northwest Primary Care in the Portland, Oregon, area

The Reverend Harry B. Adams, Horace Bushnell professor emeritus of Christian Nurture at Yale Divinity School

Mary Ellen Ashcroft, Ph.D., vicar of the Spirit of the Wilderness Episcopal Church, Grand Marais, Minnesota; owner and retreat facilitator at WindCradle Retreat in Grand Marais, Minnesota; and author

William Backus, Ph.D., S.T.M., M.Div. (deceased), founder of the Center for Christian Psychological Services; staff member of North Heights Lutheran Church, Roseville, Minnesota; and author

Dwight Bain, L.M.H.C., founder of The LifeWorks Group, Inc., in Orlando, Florida; national trainer in community crisis management through the International Critical Incident Stress Foundation; and author

Frank Baker, Ph.D., consultant at Connecticut Department of Correction; former director of research at the Connecticut Department of Mental Health and Addiction Services; and research professor at the University of Connecticut School of Social Work

Herbert Benson, M.D., founder and director emeritus of the Benson-Henry Institute and mind body medicine professor of medicine at Harvard Medical School

Brad Blanton, Ph.D., clinical psychologist; founding president of the Gestalt Institute of Washington, D.C.; and former director of The Center for Well Being in Washington, D.C.

The Reverend Alison L. Boden, Ph.D., M.Div., dean of religious life and of the chapel at Princeton University in Princeton, New Jersey; ordained minister in the United Church of Christ; and author

Carole Bohn, Ed.D., M.Ed., M.T.S., associate professor of counseling psychology and religion at Boston University School of Theology; training director for the Ph.D. program in counseling psychology and religions; and supervisor and seminar leader at the Danielsen Institute

The Reverend John Boyle, Ph.D. (deceased), founding director of the Lorene Replogle Counseling Center at Chicago's Fourth Presbyterian Church; associate pastor; counselor; and parish associate

The Reverend Steve Carr, senior pastor of Calvary Chapel in Arroyo Grande, California, and author

Margaret Caudill, M.D., Ph.D., M.P.H., instructor of anesthesiology at Dartmouth-Hitchcock Medical Center's Pain Management Center, Lebanon, New Hampshire; clinical associate professor of Community and Family Medicine at Dartmouth Medical School and The Dartmouth Institute; and author

Gary Chapman, Ph.D., senior associate pastor at Calvary Baptist Church in Winston-Salem, North Carolina; speaker; counselor; director of Marriage and Family Life Consultants, Inc.; and author

The Reverend Brian H. Childs, Ph.D., community professor of bioethics at Mercer University School of Medicine in Savannah, Georgia; diplomate in supervision and a diplomate in psychotherapy with the College of Pastoral Supervision and Psychotherapy; clinical fellow of the American Association of Marriage and Family Therapists; and author

Sheldon Cohen, Ph.D., professor at Carnegie Mellon University in Pittsburgh, Pennsylvania

Grant Correll, M.D., board certified in family practice; fellow in the American Academy of Family Practice; and global health outreach team leader with the Christian Medical and Dental Associations

The Reverend Neva Coyle, founder and director of Overeaters Victorious; president of Neva Coyle Ministries; motivational speaker; and author

The Reverend Rowland Croucher, D.Min., founding director of John Mark Ministries, serving pastors, ex-pastors, church leaders, and their spouses throughout Australia and elsewhere; counselor; and author

Cheryl Cutrona, J.D., executive director of the Good Shepherd Mediation Program; mediator; facilitator; conflict coach; trainer; arbitrator; editor; attorney; and adjunct faculty at Temple University Beasley School of Law

Maxie Dunnam, D.D., president emeritus of Asbury Theological Seminary in Wilmore, Kentucky; director of the board of global ministries of the United Methodist Church; member of the executive committee of the Association of Theological Schools; evangelist; pioneer of small-group ministries; and author

The Reverend Steven Estes, senior pastor at Community Evangelical Free Church in Elverson, Pennsylvania; board member of the Christian Counseling & Educational Foundation; and teacher of preaching at Westminster Seminary

Amitai Etzioni, Ph.D., professor of International Affairs; director, Institute for Communitarian Policy Studies at the Elliott School of International Affairs at The George Washington University in Washington, D.C.; and author

The Reverend Paul F. Everett (deceased), minister of evangelism of the Wayne Presbyterian church in Pennsylvania; radio moderator; national conference and small group leader; associate and executive director of the Pittsburgh Experiment; minister at large with the Peale Center in Pawling, New York; and author

Anne Bachle Fifer, J.D., attorney; Christian mediator; arbitrator; and mediation trainer in Grand Rapids, Michigan

Sharon Fish, M.S.N., R.N., poet; teacher of nursing research, gerontology, and parish nursing and spirituality; public speaker; and author

The Reverend Richard L. Ganz, Ph.D., M.Div., senior pastor of the Ottawa Reformed Presbyterian Church; founder and president of Ottawa Theological Hall, where he is also professor of Biblical Psychology and Counseling; and author

Ruthanne Garlock, missionary; teacher; ordained minister; and author

James G. Garrick, M.D., orthopedic surgeon; founder and director of the Center for Sports Medicine in San Francisco; founder of sports medicine division at the University of Washington; founding and board member of the American Orthopedic Society for Sports Medicine; clinical professor in the department of pediatrics at the University of California, San Francisco School of Medicine; member of the editorial board of several journals; and author

Mark E. Ginter, Ph.D., theologian; consulting ethicist; Catholic education administrator; evangelization coach; parish missionary; motivational speaker; researcher; and author

Sister Elaine Goodell, chaplain in Austin, TX; director of pastoral care at

(Avera) St. Luke's Hospital in Aberdeen, South Dakota; and staff chaplain at the Healthcare Chaplaincy, Inc., and Memorial Sloan-Kettering Cancer Center in New York, New York

John Gottman, Ph.D., professor emeritus of psychology at the University of Washington in Seattle; cofounder of the Gottman Institute in Seattle; editor; and author

Kathleen Greider, Ph.D., professor of practical theology, spiritual care, and counseling at Claremont School of Theology in the Claremont Lincoln University Consortium in Claremont, California; professor of religion at Claremont Graduate University; and author

Stephen Halpern, Ph.D., composer; recording artist; researcher; public speaker; seminar leader; pioneer sound healer; and author

The Reverend George Handzo, M.Div., B.C.C., vice president of health services research and quality at HealthCare Chaplaincy Network in New York, New York; president of Handzo Consulting; lecturer; and author

The Reverend R. Kent Hughes, D.D., D.Min., M.Div., professor of practical theology at Westminster Theological Seminary; senior pastor emeritus of College Church in Wheaton, Illinois; founder of the Charles Simeon Trust; preacher and speaker at churches, pastor's retreats, mission conferences, men's events, and workshops on biblical exposition; editor; and author

Helen Hunt, Ph.D., relationship therapist; leader in global women's movement; and author

Mary Hunt, motivational speaker; syndicated columnist; and author

John W. James, founder and president of Grief Recovery Institute in California, with affiliates in Canada, England, Sweden, and Mexico; visiting faculty member at UCLA, Chapman University, University of Southern California; guest lecturer at Kings College in London; and author

Joan Kavanaugh, D.Min., psychotherapist in private practice in New York City; ordained minister in the United Church of Christ, who served as clergy and the founding director of the Pastoral Counseling Center at The Riverside Church in New York City; and author

The Reverend David Kelsey, Ph.D., theologian; Luther A. Weigle professor emeritus of Theology at Yale Divinity School; and author

Dana E. King, M.D., vice chair of the department of family medicine and professor of research division, Medical University of South Carolina in Charleston; cochair and founder of Spirituality and Health Interest Group; public speaker; faculty mentor; and editor

Mark Laaser, Ph.D., M.Div., founder of Faithful & True, a Christian-based counseling center in Minneapolis, Minnesota, specializing in treatment of sexual addiction; founder of The Laaser Center for the Family, public speaker; workshop facilitator; seminar leader; and author

Kenneth A. Larsen, Ph.D., D.Min., A.B.M.P, clinical psychologist in the department of medicine and director of clinical pastoral education and counseling at New England Baptist Hospital in Boston, Massachusetts; clinical instructor in Medicine at Harvard Medical School, adjunct professor of psychopharmacology at Massachusetts School of Professional Psychology; member of the American Psychological Association; member of the Board of Directors of the Massachusetts Psychological Association; Diplomate-Fellow in the American Association of Pastoral Counseling; researcher; and author

David B. Larson, M.D. (deceased), psychiatrist; founder and director of the National Institute for Healthcare Research; and leader in the field of religion and health research

The Reverend Mel Lawrenz, Ph.D., minister-at-large at Elmbrook Church in Brookfield, Wisconsin, teaching in North America, Asia, Africa, and Latin America; adjunct faculty member at University of Wisconsin, Milwaukee, and Trinity International University; and author

The Reverend Ron Mahn, L.M.F.T., L.P.C., pastor of Lifecare Ministry at Crossings Community Church in Oklahoma City, Oklahoma

Dawna Markova, Ph.D., cofounder and CEO emeritus at Professional Thinking Partners; public speaker; and author

Dale A. Matthews, M.D., board-certified specialist in general internal medicine caring for adult patients with Executive Healthcare Services in Reston, Virginia; staff physician in the Primary Care Division of the Virginia Hospital Center Physician Group in Arlington, Virginia; researcher and lecturer on the doctor-patient relationship and the psychological and spiritual dimensions of medicine; and author

Michael J. McManus, cofounder, president, and cochair of Marriage Savers, based in Potomac, Maryland, whose goal is to cut the divorce rate and raise the marriage rate; syndicated columnist of "Ethics & Religion"; public speaker; and author

Jerry McTaggart, philanthropist and founder of Catherine's Kids, whose vision is to change the way the world cares for abandoned special needs and medically fragile children worldwide; Catherine's Children's Home in Rosarito, Mexico; Christian Student Loan Relief Inc.; Credit Counselors of America Inc.; and Christian Credit Counselors

Paul Meier, M.D., psychiatrist; ordained minister; founder of Meier Clinics; cofounder of the board of physicians, called Physicians Resource Council, to advise the Focus on the Family on medical issues; author; and lecturer

The Reverend James E. Miller, D.Min., president of Willowgreen Inc., Fort Wayne, Indiana; clergyman; grief counselor; retreat and workshop facilitator; photographer; public speaker; and author

Melanie Morrison, Ph.D., M.Div., founder and executive director of Allies for Change; anti-oppression educator, activist, and author; adjunct faculty at Chicago Theological Seminary; cofounder of Doing Our Own Work; facilitator; public speaker; trainer; and author

Richard J. Mouw, Ph.D., Ph.M., professor of faith and public life, school of theology at Fuller Theological Seminary in Pasadena, California; philosopher; scholar; Beliefnet.com columnist; and author

The Reverend Richard John Neuhaus (deceased), cofounder of Institute on Religion and Public Life, an interreligious, nonpartisan research and education organization; Lutheran pastor; Catholic priest; public speaker; political theologian; editor; and author

Michele Novotni, Ph.D., assistant professor of counseling at Eastern College in St. Davids, Pennsylvania; licensed psychologist; certified school psychologist; certified elementary and secondary school counselor; public speaker; and author

The Reverend Leo J. O'Donovan, Th.D., interim executive director for Jesuit Refugee Service/USA; president emeritus of Georgetown University, in Washington, D.C., and professor of theology; Trustee of The College of New Rochelle; theologian; and author

The Reverend Gary J. Oliver, Ph.D., C.F.L.E., executive director of the Center for Healthy Relationships; psychologist; member of the executive board of the American Association of Christian Counselors; professor of psychology and practical theology at John Brown University in Siloam Springs, Arkansas; editor; and author

Dean Ornish, M.D., clinical professor of medicine at the University of

California, San Francisco; founder and president of the nonprofit Preventive Medicine Research Institute (PMRI); columnist; advisor; and author

The Reverend John H. Osteen, D.D. (deceased), founder and first pastor of Lakewood Church, in Houston, Texas; evangelist; teacher; and author

Les Parrott, Ph.D. and **Leslie Parrott, Ph.D.,** cofounders of the Center for Relationship Development at Seattle Pacific University in Washington, a program dedicated to teaching the basics of good relationships; public speakers; and authors

Rob Parsons, founder of Care for the Family, a charitable organization, based in Cardiff, Wales, that offers parenting, relationship, and bereavement support; ambassador for Tearfund, a Christian relief organization; and author

Ray Pritchard, D.Min., M.Th., president of Keep Believing Ministries in Dallas; public speaker; and author

William Richardson, Ph.D., professor of marriage and family therapy and clinical director of the Center for Marriage and Family Therapy at Reformed Theological Seminary in Jackson, Mississippi, and author

The Reverend Kent D. Richmond, S.T.D., chaplain, Coronary Intensive Care, Lutheran General Hospital, Park Ridge, Illinois; speaker at clergy retreats and pastor schools; and author

The Reverend Herman Riffel (deceased), pastor; and lecturer and seminar leader about the voice of God and dreams in nearly fifty countries

Pastor David Roper, M.Th., cofounding director of Idaho Mountain Ministries, a ministry of support and encouragement of pastoral couples, based in Boise, Idaho; contributor to the daily devotional Our Daily Bread; and author

Dale S. Ryan, Ph.D., M.Div., director of the Fuller Institute for Recovery Ministry and associate professor of Recovery Ministry at Fuller Theological Seminary in Pasadena, California; CEO of Christian Recovery International, an organization helping the Christian community become a safer and more accommodating place for people recovering from addiction, abuse, or trauma; lecturer; consultant; and author

Juanita Ryan, M.S.N., R.N., clinical nurse specialist in psychiatric mental health nursing; therapist in private practice at Brea Family Counseling Center in Brea, California; and author

David E. Schroeder, Ed.D., S.T.M., M.A., president of Pillar College in Middlesex, New Jersey; founder of MasterWorks; public speaker; missionary; and author

Sharon Scott, L.M.F.T., L.P.C., founder of LifeSkills for Positive Living, based in McKinney, Texas; columnist for *Families On-line Magazine*; counselor; public speaker; workshop facilitator; trainer; and author

Bernie Siegel, M.D., pediatric surgeon; clinical professor of surgery at Yale University, New Haven, Connecticut; founder of Exceptional Cancer Patients, a specific form of individual and group therapy for patients with chronic illnesses; public speaker; workshop facilitator; author

The Reverend Mahan Siler, S.T.D., M.Div., pastor and congregational consultant, with an interest in clergy support and accountability, and author

Harold Ivan Smith, D.Min., Ed.S., counselor; grief educator; public speaker; workshop facilitator; trainer; faculty member at St. Luke's Hospital in Kansas City, Missouri, and Carondolet Medical Institute in Eau Clare, Wisconsin; and author

Scott Stanley, Ph.D., research professor in psychology and codirector of the Center for Marital and Family Studies at the University of Denver, Colorado, and author

The Reverend Kurt Stasiak, S.T.D., S.T.L., M.Div., professor emeritus of sacramental-liturgical theology at Saint Meinrad Seminary & School of Theology in Meinrad, Indiana, and author

David Stoop, Ph.D., clinical psychologist; family counselor; ordained minister; founder and director of the Center for Family Therapy in Newport Beach, California; adjunct professor at

Fuller Theological Seminary in Pasadena, California; member of the executive board of the American Association of Christian Counselors; and author

Vernon M. Sylvest, M.D. (deceased), founder of the Healing Waters Lodge to address the holistic approach to health maintenance and health in the Mountains of Highland County, Virginia, and author

The Reverend Slag-Yang Tan, Ph.D., professor of psychology, at Fuller Theological Seminary in Pasadena, California; senior pastor of First Evangelical Church Glendale in Glendale, California; editor; member of the National Advisory Board of the American Association of Christian Counselors; and author

Elizabeth Tener, M.S.W., L.I.C.S.W., C.A.R.T., psychotherapist; pastoral counselor; and addiction counselor at CAB Health and Recovery in Salem, Massachusetts

John Townsend, Ph.D., psychologist; founder of the Townsend Institute for Leadership and Counseling and the Townsend Leadership program; public speaker; consultant; leadership coach; syndicated talk show host; and author

The Reverend Justin Tull, D.Min., M.Th., S.T.M., ordained United Methodist minister; seminar leader; clergy coach for the Healthy Church Initiative of the United Methodist Church; teacher; mentor; active participant in the Habitat for Humanity program; and author

Rabbi Abraham J. Twerski, M.D., ordained rabbi; founder and medical director emeritus of Gateway Rehabilitation Center, an alcohol and drug dependency treatment center in Pittsburgh, Pennsylvania; lecturer; and author

The Reverend Tim P. Van Duivendyk, D.Min., M.Div., ordained Baptist minister; association of clinical pastoral education certified supervisor and vice president of chaplaincy and spiritual care at Memorial Hermann Hospital in Houston, Texas; board-certified chaplain with Association of Profession Chaplains; licensed profession counselor; licensed marriage and family therapist; and author

Elizabeth Lee Vliet, M.D., diplomat of the American Board of Psychiatry and Neurology; founder of Hormone Health Strategies medical practices in Tucson, Arizona, and Dallas, Texas; founder and medical director of HER Place: Health Enhancement and Renewal for Women, Inc.; public speaker; member of the Board of Directors of the Association of American Physicians and Surgeons; researcher; and author

Catherine Wallace, Ph.D., cultural historian; literary critic; faculty member at Northwestern University Feinberg School of Medicine in Chicago, Illinois; and author

Raleigh Washington, M.Div., president and chief executive officer, and the vice chairman of the Board of Directors of Promise Keepers; founder and pastor emeritus of Rock of Our Salvation Evangelical Free Church in Chicago, Illinois; third recipient of the Doctor of Peacemaking by Westminster College, (the first went to Mother Theresa and the second went to Bishop Desmond Tutu); and author

The Reverend David E. Wigley, Sr., M.Div. (deceased), minister for 59 years in such Maine communities as Belfast, Benton Falls, Biddeford, Fort Fairfield, Kennebunkport, Scarborough, and Winslow

Redford B. Williams, M.D., professor of psychiatry and behavioral sciences; professor, department of psychology and neuroscience; professor of medicine; and chief, division of behavioral medicine, department of psychiatry and behavioral sciences at Duke University School of Medicine in Durham, North Carolina; researcher; and author

The Reverend Terry S. Wise, Ph.D., J.D., D.Min., professor; senior executive; minister; consultant; and conference speaker with extensive leadership experience in ministry and higher education; and author

Daryle R. Woodward (deceased), cofounder Colorado Moves Counseling Center with wife, who is now the administrative director

Wilford Wooten, L.M.F.T., L.C.S.W., therapist; counselor; and author

Everett L. Worthington, Ph.D., professor of the department of psychology at Virginia Commonwealth University in Richmond; founding editor of *Marriage and Family: A Christian Journal*; founding executive director and treasurer of A Campaign for Forgiveness Research, a not-for-profit organization devoted to supporting research into forgiveness; leader in the field of forgiveness research, teaching, publishing dissemination; editor; and author

Iris M. Yob, Ed.D., professor emerita and contributing faculty member at the Richard W. Riley College of Education and Leadership at Walden University in Minneapolis, Minnesota, and author

Charles Zeiders, Psy.D., psychotherapist; adjunct instructor at East University in St. David's, Pennsylvania; lecturer; public speaker; seminar leader; peer supervisor; author; and poet

SCRIPTURE REFERENCE INDEX

TOPICAL INDEX

Note: **Bolded** main headings refer to boxed material content

C

car accidents, 163, 284–286
caregivers, of loved ones with
     Alzheimer's, 16–23
Carney, Mary Lou, 98, 326
Carr, Rev. Steve, 105–106, 108,
     109
Carter, Jimmy, 171, 190
Caudill, Margaret, 53
challenges
     courage and, 259–263
     emotional. *see* emotional
          challenges
     of illness. *see* illness, challenges
          of
     physical, coping with, 7–67
     social. *see* social challenges
Chapman, Gary, 304, 305,
     307–308, 311
cheating, 203–205
children, 79–84, 115
Childs, Brian H., 320, 323, 325
Christian discipline, 267–268
chronic pain, coping with,
     39–42, 143–144
church community, 14, 91,
     140–141
Ciancanelli, Sabra, 303
clarity, 148
Clark, Lora, 324
cognitive therapy, 141
Cohen, Jo Ann, 43–44
Cohen, Sheldon, 288
Collier, Barbara, 203–205
comfort
     in death, 54, 156–157
     from God, 37
     from prayer/praying, 23,
          44–45
     words of, 160
commandments, 171, 172
commitment, to marriage,
     103–105
communication, 21–22, 28, 30,
     104, 105–109, 107–109, 117,
     328–329

communion, 92
community, strength from, 5–6,
     14, 224, 246, 327–328
compassion, 297–303
confession, 4–5, 106, 292–295
confidence, 207, 259–263
conflict
     damage caused by, 86
     ways to resolve, 72–77, 82, 87,
          88–92, 105–110, 115, 187
Conflict Scenarios (Wise), 72
Constance, Anita M, 220
coping
     with chronic pain, 39–42,
          143–144
     with depression, 136–137
     with disasters, 221–227
     with end of life, 55–57
     with grief, 156–166
     with illness and physical
          challenges, 7–67
     with loneliness, 175–183
     with pain, 32–42, 284–286
     with tragedies, 223–227,
          284–286
Correll, Grant, 195
counseling, 12, 106–107, 138,
     141, 152, 154, 219
courage, 259–263
Coyle, Rev. Neva, 262
Crabb, Larry, 173
Crisis Experience in Modern Life
     (Gerkin), 222
Cronkite, Walter, 290–291
Croucher, Rev. Rowland, 101, 108
crying, freely, 56, 161
Culbreath Watkins, Anne,
     215–217
Cutrona, Cheryl, 73, 75, 77

D

death
     healthy ways to face, 55–57
     of loved ones, 54, 156–166
debts, ways to get out of, 230,
     234–235

depression, 133–142
Diaz, Pablo, 113
dignity, 55
disasters, coping with, 221–227
discipline, self, 264–270
Discipline of a Godly Man
     (Hughes), 264
discouragement, 143–149
divorce, 102, 104
domestic abuse, 211–220,
     215–217
Duewel, Wesley, 30
Dunnam, Maxie, 338, 339

E

eating disorder(s), 24–31
     anorexia nervosa, 25–27
     bulimia, 26–27
     causes and signs of, 26–27
     compulsive, 24
     emotional eating and, 61–62,
          63
     solutions for, 28, 30
     symptoms of, 29
Edison, Thomas, 144
emotional challenges, 111–208
     caused by stress, 192–199
     combating anger issues,
          113–121
     coping with grief, 156–166
     coping with loneliness,
          175–183
     dealing with heartache,
          150–155
     overcoming anxiety and fear,
          112–132
     overcoming jealousy and envy,
          167–174
     pride and, 184–191
     support for depression,
          133–142
     support for hopelessness,
          143–149
     temptation and, 200–208
employer, dysfunctional, 87,
     242

A Note from the Editors

We hope you find *Spiritual Remedies*, published by the Books and Inspirational Media Division of Guideposts, helpful and inspirational. Guideposts is a nonprofit organization that touches millions of lives every day through products and services that inspire, encourage, help you grow in your faith, and celebrate God's love.

Thank you for making a difference with your purchase of this book, which helps fund our many outreach programs to military personnel, prisons, hospitals, nursing homes, and educational institutions.

We also create many useful and uplifting online resources. Visit Guideposts.org to read true stories of hope and inspiration, access OurPrayer network, sign up for free newsletters, download free e-books, join our Facebook community, and follow our stimulating blogs.

To learn about other Guideposts publications, including the best-selling devotional *Daily Guideposts*, go to Guideposts.org/Shop, call (800) 932-2145, or write to Guideposts, PO Box 5815, Harlan, Iowa 51593.

NOTES

NOTES

NOTES

NOTES

NOTES

NOTES

NOTES